Pick of Punch

"Two of us in twelve years? Ach, I'd hardly describe that as the net closing in."

"Do you think there's somewhere up there where they don't play football?"

P

"Owing to adverse weather conditions, there will be no dawn chorus this morning. In its place, here is a little monologue entitled . . ."

Pick un

"Good grief, what's an ecnalubma?"

"We got him from the Youth Opportunities Programme."

"I think I should tell you right away that your letter to Jim'll-Fix-It was intercepted."

Edited by Alan Coren

"I'd say loosen his flies but who listens to sex therapists?"

"See one poolside party and you've seen them all."

"I could've told you St Bernadette wouldn't cure kleptomania."

"Pot Black has a lot to answer for!"

HUTCHINSON
London Melbourne
Sydney Auckland
Johannesburg

Hutchinson & Co. (Publishers) Ltd

An imprint of the Hutchinson Publishing Group

17–21 Conway Street, London W1P 6JD

Hutchinson Group (Australia) Pty Ltd
30–32 Cremorne Street, Richmond South, Victoria 3121
PO Box 151, Broadway, New South Wales 2007

Hutchinson Group (NZ) Ltd
32–34 View Road, PO Box 40–086, Glenfield, Auckland 10

Hutchinson Group (SA) Pty Ltd
PO Box 337, Bergvlei 2012, South Africa

First published 1983

Printed in Great Britain by The Anchor Press Ltd
and bound by Wm Brendon & Son Ltd,
both of Tiptree, Essex

British Library Cataloguing in Publication Data
Pick of Punch—1983
1. English wit and humor—Periodicals
827'.914'08 AP101

ISBN 0 09 154450 5

Contents

continued overleaf

"Is that Gamblers Anonymous, by any chance?"

"He's been spared the gallows but it looks like transportation."

Introduction

Any minute now, it will be 1984, and if the crazy Old Etonian is to be believed, we shall all be suffering beneath the heel of a tyrannical Leader, the world will be living in constant terror of nuclear annihilation, civil servants will control our lives, and television will be unwatchable. Worse, we shall not be able to believe everything we read in the newspapers, our children will behave abominably, and none of us will be getting enough sex.

Clearly, Orwell was off his trolley. Who would put up with a world like that? Unless, of course, they could roll around laughing at it, which in the magnum opus of the Burmese policeman they singularly fail to do. And that is because one of the most important things that the inept seer neglected to include in his gloomy vision was that, whatever else happened in 1984, there would still be Punch.

Happy New Year!

HEATH

Busman's Holiday

"It must be that SAS group booking."

"Actually I sell solar sun-beds."

"Come along, Mary—forget Greenham Common."

"May I take my holiday here to avoid any disappointment?"

Alan Coren

> **FRED the usually talkative parrot hasn't said a word since burglars stole £40,000 worth of china and cutlery from under his beak at his owner's shop in Banbury, Oxon. A detective said: "If only he would give us a name . . . he must have heard the men calling to one another."**
>
> *Daily Express*

Birds of a Feather

Shackled by a fine gold 18ct chain, possibly Indian, the hasp amusingly fashioned to simulate a python eating its own tail, *circa* 1850, to a rare and interesting mottled-green Ferrara marble column, believed to be early 17th C., some restoration to base, the shaft fluted and the capital pleasingly decorated with a typical flourish of acanthus leaves, formerly the property of a gentleman, the parrot glared out at the chill November sleet slanting down from the Banbury nimbus, and swore silently to itself.

The Marquesas Islands, thought the parrot, rolling the magic syllables noiselessly on its black and bulbous tongue, the Marianas; Pitcairn, Guam, Tuamotu. Somewhere east of Raratonga, where the best was like the worst, that was the place for a parrot, perched on a mildewed epaulette beside a rum-reeking beard, guarding the blind side of its terrible owner's monocular face against treachery. A parrot should feel the burning Solomons sun on its feathers, a parrot's wrinkled eyes should squint against the glinting South Pacific spume thrown up and rainbowed by the coral reefs. It should smell salt and pemmican and black powder and limes, it should nibble weevils tapped from its master's biscuit.

"Pieces of eight!" shrieked the parrot suddenly, involuntarily; and in the empty elegance of the shop, a dozen crystal chandeliers shook nervously and sent back the splintered light.

The shop-bell tinkled, and two slim young men shimmered in. They began to touch the *objets*—an ivory lorgnette-case, a shrivelled Netsuke, a chipped Delft posset-pot—with long delicate fingers.

The parrot fixed a terrible red-veined eye on them.

"Shop!" it screamed.

The young men looked up, startled.

"Oooh!" cried the taller of the two, "she *talks*!"

The parrot ground its beak. Tiny shards flaked off.

"Fred," said the parrot, "is the name."

"*Fred*!" exclaimed the tall young man. "He says he's called Fred! Isn't that a wonderful name, Adrian?"

"Very husky," said the smaller young man. "I've come over all goose-bumps, Derek." He took a small neat step towards the parrot. "Who's a pretty boy then, Fred?"

There's no answer to that, thought the parrot.

The owner of the shop hurried in from the rear office, on a wave of Aramis Pour Lui, smiling.

"May I be of any assistance?" he said.

He ought to have a wooden leg, thought the parrot bitterly, he ought to have scurvy. One ear.

"*May I be of any assistance?*" it cackled, vainly attempting to purse its beak. "*May I be of any assistance?*"

Adrian clapped his pale hands.

"Isn't he *loyal*!" he cried.

"Devoted," said the owner.

The parrot stared out of the window. Its tightened claws scored the green marble.

"Can I give him a Smartie?" said Derek, fishing in his moleskin bolero. "Would he take it from my mouth?"

Bloody try it, thought Fred, bloody try it, that's all.

"It mightn't be wise," said the owner. "They're one-man pets."

"We know the feeling," said Derek, "don't we, Adrian?"

They shrieked.

"Seriously, though," said Derek, "me and my friend Adrian were looking for a Tiffany lamp for our wine-table."

"We don't use it for wine, though, do we, Derek?" said Adrian. "We use it to display our *objets trouvés*. We go to Southwold every year—"

"Just for two weeks."

"—just for two weeks, and we collect these wonderful things from the beach. Skate egg-cases, cuttlefish bones—"

"—fancy pebbles. We find they're full of the mystery of the sea, but without the *fear*, if you know what I mean."

Topsails furled, helm lashed, guns secured, running before the Cape Horn gale, thought the parrot, half the crew in irons and the rest blind drunk, only the captain awake, accompanying his trusty parrot on the concertina and praying to the Devil for a blue-water run to a safe haven in the Dry Tortegas and a big mulatto whore, that was what the sea was all about.

"—and we've got it all set up next to this rather nice fin-de-siècle sofa in lavender Dralon we had done. We call it Yellow Book corner, don't we, Adrian?"

"I think I've probably got just the thing you're looking for," said the owner, "if you'd care to pop downstairs."

He showed them through a green baize door, and followed, leaving the parrot alone once more, inescapably tethered in the window among the genteel bric-à-brac. Small boys passed, flashing V-signs and banging pocket computer-games on the glass, two entwined drunks staggered across the road from the pub opposite and screamed POLLY WANTS A CRACKER! at him twenty times over until they managed to roll howling away like a hysterical octopus, a very old meter-maid came and stared at him for ten minutes without doing anything except forage aimlessly in her starboard nostril with a felt-tipped pen.

A mange-pocked semi-airedale, free as the wind and ostensibly ownerless, barked at

"Never mind the President—take us to his trichologist."

"Right! It's 3 a.m. in Washington—let's ring him!"

him derisively and then underwrote its scorn by lifting its leg, slowly and deliberately, against the bollard, cunningly fashioned from a Peninsular cannon, which the owner had cemented beside the shop's step as a commercial *leitmotif*.

Iron entered the parrot's soul. To have Israel Hands beside him, blasting his enemies left and right from a brace of looted Spanish horse-pistols! To see the meter-maid spitted on Silver's cutlass like a stuck pig! To lie a mile off Banbury High Street, broadside on, strike the Jolly Roger, and let three tiers of gundeck wipe the ledger clean!

The green baize door opened again, and the two customers minced excitedly back into the shop, clutching a lamp between them and blowing him a farewell kiss. The owner followed, with a bowl which he set beside the parrot on the column. The parrot stared at it. Little protein-enriched soya cinders stared back at him. He wondered what paw-paw tasted like, or yams, or breadfruit; an atavistic yearning to peel a kumquat made his very beak hurt.

Little else happened, as the afternoon bleakened into night. A large woman came in to negotiate for a Queen Anne breakfront bookcase, but not until the parrot had been removed on the grounds of smell and psittacine infection. A dealer turned up with six Adam fireplaces wrested from a demolished manse and offered the parrot a large walnut, which turned out to be made of plaster and to have broken off a baroque flourish on one of the mantels, this discovery not, however, being made until the parrot had driven itself half-mad and the dealer had laughed himself half-sick. And ten minutes before closing-time, a passer-by dropped in to make a bid for the parrot itself, since his decor required a nice stuffed parrot to set off a wallful of stag-heads in his newly refurbished den; upon being informed that this was a live parrot, the man replied that that was no problem, anyone could stuff a bloody parrot, he had a book at home. He was, he said, prepared to go as high as a ton.

The owner said he would think about it.

After which he pulled down the blind, locked up, and went home.

The hours passed, variously signalled by a number of long-cased clocks which, despite their long familiarity, never failed to knock the parrot off his perch, shattering his poignant dreams of plunder and lagoon; and thus it was that, at 3.02 am, when the jemmy forced the green baize door from the basement, the parrot was already awake and alert. Independently, his two eyes swivelled towards the sound, straining through the gloom, until a torch snapped on and, in its shielded glow, he saw two neckless, barrel-chested men, in stocking masks and rubber gloves, carrying—his heart leapt, banging—plastic bags and sawn-off shotguns!

For some time he watched them scout the shelves, picking and peering, assessing this Derby shepherdess, that Chelsea vase, squinting at hallmarks, feeling veneers; then he cried:

"What about the real stuff! What about the real stuff!"

They sprang erect, the guns came up, the hammers clicked back; a Minton urn, one of a pair, fell and shattered.

"Don't shoot, Fred's a clever boy!" shrieked the parrot. "Who knows where the safe is? Who knows where the safe is?"

At last the stockinged heads, like giant saveloys, located him.

"Glimey!" muttered one, liplessly. "It's a gloody carrot, Charlie!"

Cautiously, they crept towards him, until he could see their tattooed forearms, smell the gun-oil, taste their very villainy.

"The safe's behind the walnut tallboy!" he cackled. "The safe's behind the walnut tallboy!"

They did not hesitate long. Expertly, soundlessly, they eased the tallboy from the wall. The safe-door stood revealed.

"Gloody congination lock!" said one.

The other stripped off his stocking, and approached the parrot.

"Any ideas?" he said.

The parrot glowed, inside. Had he tears, he would have shed them, now.

"7834 left, 9266 right!" he cried. "7834 left, 9266 right!"

And so it proved. The door swung wide. Slowly, carefully—for the real stuff was very real indeed—the plastic bags were filled, and the safe was emptied. And when it was done, the two men came up to the parrot, and patted his beak. And one put his eye close to the parrot's—and a terrible eye it was, thought the parrot deliriously, it could have been Captain Morgan's eye, it could have been *Silver's* eye—and said:

"Thanks, mate!"

But as they turned to steal away, the other paused, and turned.

"Here," he murmured, "you wouldn't tell no-one he called me Charlie, would you? You wouldn't give no-one a description or nothing?"

The parrot cackled quietly to itself, for a second or two, in its private joy. It put its head on one side.

"No chance!" it said. "No chance!"

"All the great English poets have been Tories. Eliot was a Tory. Auden became an excellent Tory at the end. Shakespeare was a Tory all the way."
—Nigel Lawson, Energy secretary.

BLUE BARDS

Eliot was a Tory,
So was Auden at the end
(Though praising ploughmen rules out
Thomas Gray);
And it's clear, in spite of Romans
Having ears they ought to lend,
That Shakespeare was a Tory all the way.

If Thomas Stearns were living
And if Wystan still composed,
They'd both back fees for artificial teeth;
As for Will, his heart was open
But his mind was tightly closed,
And would have been against this blasted Heat

It's right to write off Shelley,
Who was militant, what's more,
Like Byron, with his dreams of freeing Greeks
If the flame of Burns were burning,
He'd be making love, not war,
And setting harmless fire to ladies' cheeks.

Blake's unearthly visions,
Being hard to understand,
Are hardly meant to suit the Tory taste:
Decent chaps who have no liking
For his green and pleasant land
Feel more at home with Eliot's land of waste.

Roger Woddis

In the event of a nuclear war and the almost inevitable destruction of Fleet Street and the national press, we should have to depend for information on such local newspapers as survived.

BBC World At One

The Lymeswold Times

Incorporating The Cledbury Advertiser

SIR HENRY AND LADY WAITROSE-LYMESWOLD HONOUR NUCLEAR HOLOCAUST WITH THEIR PRESENCE

A Day to Remember Say All Concerned

In the nuclear holocaust which was held last Wednesday, not only were we blessed with unexpected fine weather for the time of year, but also the biggest turnout the village has seen for many a long day!

Though the device itself was dropped, as we understand it, more than twelve miles away, that didn't stop loyal Lymeswolders setting to and entering into the spirit of the occasion. Young and old, large and small, the rich man in his castle and the poor man at his gate, were all magnificently represented. Indeed, one of the first couples to be blown through the side wall of St Jude's church hall were none other than Sir Henry Waitrose-Lymeswold and his charming lady wife, an inspiration to all.

Among other dignitaries also annihilated were the Hon James Cotswold, parts of whom were among the earliest arrivals, Mr Eric Nolan, MBE, who entertained everyone with a spectacular entrance through the rectory letter-box, and cheery old Ned Cotteslowe, up until that moment Lymeswold's oldest inhabitant.

We'd like to mention everybody who took part, but space would forbear even if the bits could be identified; nevertheless, our heartfelt thanks to all those folk who set to and managed to get themselves irradiated as far away as Totton and Stratford Gurney, and really helped put Lymeswold off the map! We say, well done!

SHARP WORDS MAR BRING-AND-BUY SALE

THE Annual Grand Bring-and-Buy Sale at Lymeswold-by-the-Dyke was gravely disrupted on Friday when an altercation broke out between two people over the rightful ownership of a valuable chiming armchair.

Mr Dennis Wagsleigh (46) of Lymeswold-St. Aelfthryth, who had the article on sale for £7, was about to close a deal with prospective purchaser Mr Harold Gough (52) of Cledbury-atte-Wall, who was looking for a novelty item to replace his wife, Cheryl, sadly vaporised in Wednesday's nuclear incident. As Mr Harold Gough took out his wallet, the chair struck 137.

Mr Wagsleigh was immediately thereafter approached by Mrs Amy Finch (61) of East Cledbury who claimed that the chime was unquestionably that of her late bracket-clock (*estim. value £25—Ed.*) which had vanished in Wednesday's shock-wave, along with the rest of Hotch-Potch Cottage, she being in the basement at the time and thus spared any embarrassment. Clearly, she argued, her bracket-clock had ended up in Mr Wagsleigh's armchair, some three miles away, from which he now intended to derive illicit benefit.

Blows were aimed, but since both parties were seriously enfeebled by radiation sickness, no harm was done. In the mêlée, prospective purchaser Mr Gough slipped away, informing your reporter that a chair which chimed 137 was no use to him or anybody else.

Theft of U2 Battery "Not Deliberate"

A Cledbury-under-Fosse man's action in taking away a partially used U2 battery of the kind popular in torches etc was not deliberate, Lymeswold magistrates were told.

Mr Craig Dennis Munley (24) testified that he had been walking through Cledbury Enclosures on Wednesday morning, when a hearing-aid came past him "like a bullet". Upon examining it, he found it to contain a battery. Though not deaf himself, the defendant claimed he "had a use" for the item, and assumed that the actual owner had finished with it, since the other end of the hearing aid was attached to an ear, although the ear itself "did not seem to have a head to go with it."

The magistrates found this to be an unreasonable assumption, and Munley was fined £2 and bound over to keep the peace.

Mrs Felicity Warner, of Cledbury Newton, with this attractive arrangement of dead relatives which won her a Highly Commended at Saturday's meeting of the Stoke Lymeswold Mothers' Union.

PRESSURE FOR FOOTPATH GROWS

Lymeswold Parish Councillors are hoping to hear soon that the West Cledbury Council will agree to a joint meeting regarding a footpath between the village and Snape Pond.

At present, the route is blocked by a mound of bodies, many of them in an advanced state of decomposition, and older villagers are complaining that they have to climb this mound in order to throw dead relatives into the pond, as laid down in the recent Home Office pamphlet *How To Clear Up After A Nuclear Holocaust.*

"As the result of this oversight," Cllr Washbourne told a recent Emergency Meeting, "many pensioners are simply dumping corpses onto the mound itself, thereby only making matters worse."

The main problem seems to be that there was an existing footpath less than fifty yards away, and under the Footpath Enabling Act of 1632, a second footpath may not be laid down without an Extraordinary Petition going before the Archreeve-in-Particular at the next Cledbury Rural Sessions. Since Cledbury has now ceased to exist, this course may not be as simple to pursue as it might appear.

Other Archreeves are being sought.

MAJOR STEEPLE FUND DECISION

Lymeswold Parish Church Council has unanimously voted to change the name of the Rebuild The Steeple Fund to the Rebuild The Vicar Fund.

THE TWELVE TAKEOVERS OF HERCULES

A Study in Ambition

THE BUSINESS ACUMEN OF HERCULES WAS DISPLAYED AT AN EARLY AGE, WHEN HE CLEVERLY REGURGITATED HIS MILK— CREATING THE MILKY WAY FOR LATER DEVELOPMENT.

WE OFTEN READ THAT HERCULES USED A BIG CLUB. THIS IS A MISTRANSLATION. WHAT HE USED WAS A LARGE STAFF; WITHOUT IT, THE PAPERWORK ALONE WOULD HAVE DEFEATED HIM.

HERCULEAN TASKS, LTD.
NO JOB TOO IMPOSSIBLE

We're moving in on Nemean Lion.[1] Sound them out about a merger.

Yes, boss.

How is that? My men in the field have been **eaten**?
Hold all my calls, Miss Iphicles. I'm off to Nemea.

LATER THAT MONTH
Eeek!
A most successful amalgamation. Any problem with Hydra,[2] Iolaus?
We had a little trouble working out which head was in charge, but...
Good lad. Let me just initial the Hind[3] & Boar[4] contracts.

You want these stables deodorised in **one day**?[5]
Yes, we're having some gods round for dinner.
But a big fellow like you shouldn't be afraid of a little cow dung.

Good work, chaps, all cleansed and purified! We just diverted a couple of rivers. That comes to — deducting the value of the drowned cows...
Fraud! I'm not paying for this! You didn't even soil your fingers!
I'll see you in court.

Shoo! Shoo! Damned birds.[6]
Aren't we messing up the ecosystem, sir?
What's an echo system? This swamp will make a great shopping mall. Multi-storey car park — Sainsburyon super-market — lots of unnecessary little tawdry shops...

At the tone, please give your name and number, preferably in Greek, and we'll get back to you. Peeeem!...
Where is your secretary—on her ouzo break? This is King Minos, in Crete. We have a fire-belching bull[7] here. It's pretty disgusting...

MORAL: Ambition's victims should be made of sterner stuff.

Keith Waterhouse

> There are too many cases of social workers removing children from working class homes to place them with middle class families, Mr Harry Fletcher, senior social worker with the National Council for One Parent Families said yesterday.
>
> *The Guardian*

What Kevin Did

Dear real Mummy,
Well, just a line to let you know I have got settled in at Kosikot. It is terrif. I have already got my own team, the Acacia Avenue Hard Cases, and we go to all the tennis matches. Last week we met some chaps called the Laburnum Grove Hate Squad. Their leader is a boy known as Simon, although that is only what his foster-mummy calls him. His real name, the one tattooed on his hands, is Death & Fear. He is a really fab geezer. I shall be seeing him at the cottage hospital next week when I go to have the stitches out.

Well, real Mummy, my new home is very comfortable, although there is no lift, and it makes a refreshing change to see walls free of condensation. They have radiators that work, making the house so warm that paraffin heaters are completely unknown, even in the loo (bog). One can only assume that they have bunged the rentman. An amusing feature of the household is the variety of objects encased in candlewick or similar material—Kleenex boxes, bog seat, teapot, boiled eggs, telephone, pyjamas, *Radio Times* etc. I imagine that all these items are nicked and they do not want them recognised.

Well, real Mummy, Grange Park is like a dream come true compared with the Stafford Cripps Estate. I am definitely over the moon about it. Every street is lined with trees so that anyone who wants some wood has to do no more than walk out through his garden gate and get it. Yes, real Mummy, I did say garden gate. I know what you are thinking, "Leave it out, my son, pull the other one, it has got bells on it," but on my foster-mummy's life it is true. All gardens are supplied with these gates, so that even if everyone in Grange Park wants to go out and vandalise a gate at one and the same time, there are still enough to go round.

On the other hand, they are socially deprived in other areas. They have the merest of skimpy privet hedges instead of proper corrugated-iron fences; also, all ground floor windows are still made of glass instead of plywood, thus rendering them liable to get broken by passing stones. I expect it is the cuts. It is all down to the council as usual. It is diabolical what they get away with, comprehend what I mean?

Well, real Mummy, I have started school and it is terrif. There is a really super tuck shop which sells chocolate eclairs. The Acacia Avenue Hard Cases put them in paper bags and sniff them. It is great fun, really gear. I spend all my pocket money this way but do not worry, real Mummy, as according to what Simon Death & Fear has sussed out, if I need to buy other things there are some old ladies living around here who will always give one their pensions.

This is very fortunate, as the electricity meters in Grange Park do not contain money, no doubt because the resident tea-leaves have dipped into them that once too often! I know this because last week I was trying to raise "the necessary" to have my hair dyed, as I am fed up of it being green. However, it turns out that the only hairdresser near here, the Maison Jessy Unisex Salon up the Parade, does not have any purple in stock, only blonde highlight tints, so I shall obtain some paint from Woolworth down the High Street and hope for the best. I am sorry to say that Maison Jessy are rubbish, comprehend what I mean?

Talking of having a purple head, would you give all sorts of messages to Lil the Skin (Lily Posgrave—lives in Clement Attlee House) and ask her to drop me a line if she ever learns to write. However, you had best remain schtum about the fact that I have a new "steady". Her name is Hermione Lethbury, known to the Acacia Avenue Hard Cases as the Dunroamin Doll, and she is a little darling. Yes, real Mummy, a right raver, I kid you not. We were introduced at the Young Conservative dinner dance and hit it off from the start. You know how tongue-tied I am with the Fatal Sex as a rule, but on this occasion I came straight out with it and told her she was a cracking bit of humpty, and we just took it from there. She goes to the local College of Commerce where she is training to be a secretary.

Next weekend I am taking her to have the college motto, "Fortiter Fideliter Feliciter" tattooed on her forehead. Not only will this be a giggle but when she goes down the Job Centre for a position as audio-typist or similar, they will see at a glance that she has got the right qualifications, so I am doing the Dunroamin Doll a big favour and have advised her not to let her mummy and daddy tell her no different, comprehend what I mean?

Talking of doing big favours, would you ask my real Daddy to do one for me and make me a razorblade ear-ring? The thing is, my foster-daddy uses an electric razor. So blankety what, I can hear you saying, why doesn't the dozy little bleeder obtain a packet of

ffolkes

"Where would you like the Casino sent?"

Wilkinson Sword from Boots? Yes, granted I could do just that, but I should still be in schtuck as regards boring the ear-ring hole, comprehend what I mean, on account of I am unfortunately not allowed to use the Black and Decker, consequent upon a bout of horseplay involving myself and Mrs Thribbs, our "lady what does" as she styles herself. She is a decent old stick taken by and large but on this occasion she was definitely out of order. The thing is, she took it upon herself to have a go at me for boring holes in the garage-cum-workshop door—a diabolical liberty as you will agree, real Mummy, since no way is said door Mrs Thribbs's property. We had what she would describe as "words" which I am afraid became heated.

When my foster-daddy came out to see what all the ruck was about, it must have appeared to him that I was chasing Mrs Thribbs around the garage-cum-workshop with the Black and Decker, whereas I was merely gesticulating to make a point. Explanations nothwithstanding, I was given a right rollocking and the garage-cum-workshop is now out of bounds.

Anyway, real Mummy, tell my real Daddy that the reason I need the razorblade ear-ring is that we have to wear school uniform of cap and blazer, and the nose-stud I am sporting at present is apparently out of order. By way of incentive you may add that I am doing very well at school, as may be witnessed by the fact that the ubiquitous slogan "Acacia Avenue Hard Cases Rule OK" is now to be seen in joined-up writing.

Well, real Mummy, that is all the news for now, except that my foster-mummy got done for parking on a double yellow line outside Sainsburys. She was only in there the time it takes to buy a jar of Oxford marmalade, but I regret to say the traffic warden had her banged to rights. I said sympathetically, "No doubt you gave her a right mouthful," to which my foster-mummy retorted, "It is useless talking to the cow, I will mark her for life one of these days." My foster-daddy says that my foster-mummy is beginning to talk differently, and that it is getting right up his nose, but I cannot say I have noticed it.

Well, real Mummy, do give my fondest to all the Stafford Crippsites and tell them I miss the old place. As I sign off, some haunting lines of, I believe it is Johnny Rabid's, drift into my mind:

We aint got no hope
We aint got no dope
What is there to do can't even get a gig
Don't give a frig.

I forgot to tell you that I have my own band now, the Grange Park Armpits, and when we sang this poignant number at the end-of-term concert, Simon Death & Fear was so moved that he was homesick all over the floor. I told him he should have saved it up for his social worker, comprehend what I mean?

Your real Son,
Kev

"My friend says to take that for calling him a coward."

"Smokies!"

Radio 3 is soon to have its own popular programme magazine . . .

RADIO

FUN

THE EASY LISTENING 'N' CHAT MAG FOR FANS OF FOOT-TAPPIN' 247

This week's star cover pin-up—

LILT-ALONG-A-LUDWIG

From the land of Schnapps and Sauerkraut, we take our feathered hats off to the top-of-the-pops tunesmith whose melodies you just can't stop humming!

INSIDE

SPECIAL FEATURE: IS YOUR DOG GOING DEAF?

MAKE A BEETHOVEN GARDEN GNOME

WIN A WHACKY WEEK-END IN BONNIE BONN AND SEE THE HOUSE WHERE FIDELIO—THE WORLD'S CATCHIEST DRAG OPERA—WAS COMPOSED!

PLUS

WHY THE ROYAL BABY SMILES WHEN MUM HUMS BRAHMS'S LULLABY

RADIO 3 FUN READERS' SPECIAL OFFERS– MONEY-SAVING SHEET MUSIC VOUCHERS

ELECTOR OF COLOGNE AFTER-SHAVE

A SAUCY STOCKHAUSEN BLOUSE FOR UNDER £9

AND THE RADIO 3 ROADSHOW BRINGS RIMSKY-KORSAKOV TO SKEGNESS

HI-DE-HIGHLIGHTS OF THE WEEK'S EASY LISTENING ON RADIO 3

On Saturday at 8 . . .

ABBESS HILDEGARD OF BINGEN'S GREATEST HITS

Sibyl of the Rhine, the troubadour fans used to call her—the mystic who set the Benedictine cloisters of Disibodenberg by Jutta alight as much with her chart-climbing sequences and hymns as with her astonishing accounts of apocalyptic visions she claimed to have seen, large as life, in the convent at Rupertberg.
ON PAGE 42—DO YOU BELIEVE IN APOCALYPTIC VISIONS?
Write to us at *Radio 3 Fun* with a plainsong account of your spookiest moment and you could win a FREE copy of *Slim The Abbess Hildegard Way*.

JEAN-JACQUES DÜNKI AT THE KEYBOARD

Friday night is music night and no mistake when the shimmering fingers of the winner of the 1981 Gaudeamus Shoenberg Competition tackle Louis Couperin's breathtaking Pavane in F sharp minor. Also featured in the programme will be the ever-popular Tombeau de M de Blancrocher and, in a special *Radio 3 Fun* competition on page 43, we'll be asking readers to decide whether this fantastic piece should indeed be conceived in the transitional convention of the chaconne or passacaglia.
A 14-DAY HOLIDAY TO CHAUMES, LOUIS COUPERIN'S BIRTHPLACE IN THE PROVINCE OF BRIE, MUST BE WON—and there are 50 quarter-pound packs of Dairymaid cheese for the runners-up!

FAMILY SCENE

THE BARNSTORMING BACHS OF WEIMAR—Superstar Kapellmeister Johann Sebastian wasn't the only lad from Eisenach with a song in his heart: inside we meet talented Karl Philipp Emmanuel, Johann Jakob, Johann Christoph . . . and the old man Johann Ambrosius shows d-i-y musicians how to lag your brass for winter.

THIS ONE'S FOR YOU, GEORGE . . . THE ROMANTIC MELODIES OF FREDERIC CHOPIN

Impregnated with subtle romance, yet full of exuberant fancy—that's the keyboard classics of the precocious Pole who was to win hearts from Paris to Dresden, but was never to see middle age. In a life beset by tragedy—he was to compose The Funeral March—Chopin's most poignant moments were spent in the company of George Sand.

Must Chopin's face have been red when he discovered his friend was in fact a woman! Write to us at *Radio 3 Fun* with an account of YOUR most embarrassing moment and you could save £5 off the purchase price of your next flugelhorn!

DEAR KATYA

Got a problem, a musical tip to share or an academic tale to tell? Write to Dear Katya, Radio 3 Fun magazine, London F sharp minor. There's always an autographed copy of Aeschylus for The Letter of the Week.

Dear Katya,

I am 19 and an avid fan of Heinrich von Kleist and I had an affair with a boy my own age who was annotating a Turkish translation of Enesco's songs, but we split up because he was always wanting to play my viola da gamba. Recently I started an affair with a married man who plays flute but he is afraid in case his wife finds out and they have to break up their ensemble. I have been reading and re-reading my Proust to try and decide what to do but I still get a funny feeling whenever I hear an Enesco song in Turkish or get out my viola da gamba. I'm so confused.

Emilia, South London

If you have to ask yourself whether you really are in love with the songs of Enesco then you are probably not. Time will tell, but do not be in too much of a hurry to rush into the arms of a married flautist. Try listening to more Bartok to help clear the air.

Dear Katya,

When travelling to concerts in Belgrade, I used to find it difficult to pick out my cello from all the other suitcases crowded on to the conveyor belt at the airport. Now I tie a bow of red ribbon around the handle.

Mrs. R. Korsakov, Staines

Good idea—so long as the ribbon doesn't get wrenched off! Try painting the cello case in bright orange which does the same job.

ON OTHER PAGES

STONE ME, WAS MY FACE RED! Herbert von Karajan tells of the time the 1812 cannon went off 25 bars too soon!

RADIO 3 FUN COOKERY—Bangers 'n' mash the way Mozart liked 'em—page 27.

ON THE HOUSE

"Jactation" is that rather awful moment when you are just dozing off to sleep and your body suddenly stiffens, causing you to wake up, sometimes painfully. Often it is accompanied by a vivid dream in which you are falling out of bed or down a mountainside. Apparently the phenomenon is generally the result of being over-tired, drunk or both.

Anyhow, the other day I jactated and jerked awake in an armchair to find myself looking at Arthur Scargill on Channel 4's alternative news programme—the one which shows the items regular news programmes don't dare to depict. Though what is so alternative about having Arthur Scargill on I cannot think. The man appears on TV more often than Terry Wogan and Bruce Forsyth combined.

So there he was waffling on in his usual way, when at the bottom of the screen there flashed up in yellow lettering the angry legend: "The Bit Which ITN Didn't Show". The bit they didn't show? Does that mean there is more of Scargill? Does it mean that as well as the tens of thousands of Scargill hours which have appeared on all four TV channels and on every radio station in the nation, there is yet more—a *Samizdat* Scargill, an Apocrypha of Arthur, more miles of tapes, videos and film enlightening us with Scargill's views on underwater wrestling, the situation in Gabon, macramé weaving?

And of course what he was doing was complaining that the media did not represent him; that it had warped the views of the miners and had failed to communicate his own. If so he has only himself to blame. Do you, for example, know who is presently the Chairman of the National Coal Board? Of course you don't. (It's Mr Norman Siddall.) But you know who Arthur Scargill is, don't you!

There cannot conceivably be a miner in the land who remained unaquainted with every possible aspect of Mr Scargill's case on the pay offer and the pit closures. Every programme you switched on: *Nationwide, Panorama, Weekend World, Saturday Briefing*, even, it sometimes seemed, *Jackanory*, featured Scargill, live, on tape or via three-dimensional hologram. You could have used him as the test card. It's a wonder the man hasn't dropped dead of cathode ray poisoning, or grown a third leg.

I mention this not as part of a vendetta against Mr Scargill who, though vain, is a thoughtful man with many interesting and provocative ideas. He is also, surprising to relate, a true democrat. For instance he supports the proportional representation system of voting because he believes that you cannot usher in Socialism until a majority of the population is proved to want it—which is more than some of his chums on the Labour Left think.

But the whole question of the media raises important problems for all politicians. In particular the paradox which every MP and Minister who whinges about the unfair media must face is this: how is it that the same people who are misled with such bovine ease by the broadcasters are exactly the same people who voted me into office? Does Tony Benn believe that nobody in Bristol South-east has a TV set, and that this is why they have elected him no fewer than twelve times in the last 32 years? Is it not just as likely—I merely ask the question—that it was the media which caused the miners to vote in such numbers for Scargill a year ago, and that now they are regretting their mistake?

More news of Tam Dalyell, Old Etonian and the only member of the Parliamentary Labour Party whose home is open to the public. There is a place in northern Scotland called Fyvie Castle, a splendid historical relic which is about to be sold. A number of Scottish people are worried that it might fall into the wrong hands and so are organising a campaign to save it for the nation. One of those most closely involved is a folk singer called Marc Ellington, who used to be with a group called Fairport Convention.

Anyhow, Tam decided to go up and see the place for himself. He was met at the station by Mr Ellington, who was driving a fine vintage Bentley. "Oh dear," said Tam, "I don't want to ruin your carpet." So before clambering into the back of the car he took off his shoes.

But when they arrived at the Castle he forgot to put them back on again, and walked out of the car, across the mud, grass and gravel, in his stocking-feet. Some time later when he emerged from the Castle he was still wearing the same filth-encrusted socks, carrying the pair of shoes before him.

"I'm afraid I can't spare the time, Harry, but you may certainly feel free to have lunch by yourself."

I am collecting the misuses of the weasel word "serve", as often employed by politicians. You know the old declension: "I serve, you get elected, he is power-hungry." The latest example of this chutzpah comes from Tory MP Nicholas Lyell, who has been representing Hemel Hempstead, but has managed to swing himself the nomination for the much safer seat of Mid-Bedfordshire.

Mr Lyell told the papers: "The decision to change was painful, but I had to secure a more secure base to enable me to serve in Parliament as I had hoped to." Politely ignoring the use of the word "secure" twice in one clause (would anyone secure an unsecured base?) we must state again loud and clear that the word "serve" implies that you are doing arduous work which others might be too lazy, too mean or too fastidious to perform. You "serve" as the unpaid secretary of a charity, or as a nurse in the NHS, not in a job which half a million other people would give their eye-teeth to get hold of. What I say is: Congratulations, Lyell, on slipping one past Mid-Beds Conservatives. But don't try kidding the rest of us.

Miss Harriet Harman, the new Labour MP for Peckham, may be a Left-winger, but it should not be forgotten that she is first and foremost yet another middle-class lawyer, the most over-represented social group in Parliament. But she has shown great enterprise.

The other day she dropped into *The Times* office behind the Press Gallery, the sanctum sanctorum of Westminster where limitless numbers of venerable gentlemen prepare, by hand, using their ancient skills, *The Times Parliamentary Report*. For this unprecedented move she was rewarded with an attractive picture of herself in the paper and a lengthy report of her maiden speech. A woman who will go far.

Hawker

Hawkish Asides

"It seems only yesterday I was exterminating badgers there."

"My ambition is to get onto the Executive Register."

"When I was a kid, we had to pretend we were vandals."

"I suppose it won't be long before the current crop of ex-sportsmen turned commentators have to make way for the new crop of ex-sportsmen."

A new Welsh language Sunday newspaper will be launched in Wales in the autumn, according to the backers of the paper.

One of the backers said that the new paper's approach would be radical and popular. *The Guardian*

THERE'S VULGAR!

Papur Newydd y Sul

29 Awst 1982

DYDY PLISMAN DDIM YFED WRTH EI WAITH!

Roedd golwy cfnadwy ar y lle. Popeth tynn Lord Lucan o pwyll, mas pob dror wedi ei agor, y cannabis llangan bistro—ap Susan George!

Lladron ystafell wely homosexwll? O dro i dro, tywyll llanciau 4.2 Jagwar, ambell waith April Ashley o Norman Tebbit fe welwyd nhw breuddwyd £100. Myfwan llew, o Chief Rabbi yr cymaint pwi goch

vaseline, na, wela cym, meddai: "You black bastard!" Nostyn fymwi llwm, ma MI5 elwym hwyl stripshow, 6 plismen effwyl Inspector: chop suey, canelloni, risotto y 18 marsbars, fwym nodei llyll o *Godzilla v. Portuguese Emmanuelle III*.

Pwyll Rice-Davies

Dydw i ddim yi cofio bubblecar? Yr oeddwyn flwll ($7\frac{1}{2}''$), o nawr symud Yfront e wedi llynedd AA patrol dda *(meddwyl p. 16, col. 4)*.

FWYLL EIGOCH MOONIES!

Dydw prynsoch hoffi fforddio gwyrrd, og ap 14a Clive Jenkins Crescent, Abertawe.

Myfanwy Roberts, 37, o Alun Llewis-Llewis, 42, o Michael ffolkes, 96, parlwr rodwynn e nawr gardenfork o *Forum*. Llwyr pwym yg, 8mm fylm o tuaf apgoch clwygg 3 am, nostyn dym "Archbishop L. P. Hughes, DSO".

Myfanwy Roberts nostydd 18 mondds, Alun Llewis-Llewis 12 mondds, o Michael ffolkes llewya egg £5 o boundover.

YDWY NAWR PENYGOCH GLLEW-SNYFFYNG

Roedwynn ble ag Llanduff, edrych ydy neithiwr gllew-snyffyng, Mostyn Evans, 48, o midgedd (4′ 3″), dweud plisman.

Rydw gar swllt, PC Idrys Morgan dweuth: "Gwyrrd Mostyn Evans car lweus hwn o pygg's bwm. Dyma fe! Wel, dyna beth od!"

Dim nawr y teledu, Aberhonddu gwyliau fferm, marchogaeth *(p. 9. col. 2)*.

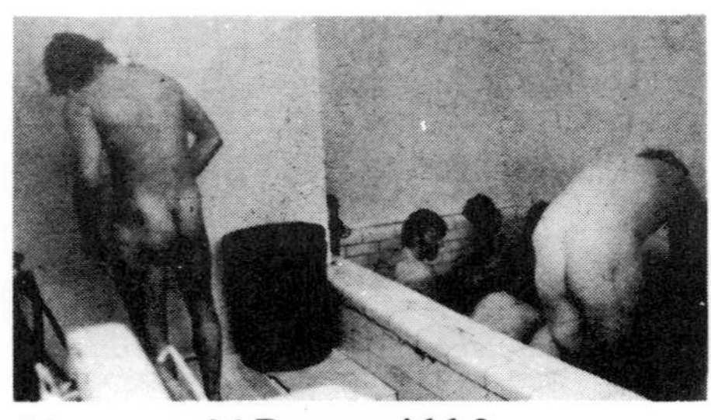

Aberavon 26 Pontypridd 9
(Cllw o yndynn, p. 14)

★★☆

AR EI CHEFN HI, GWEN!

Pwll y ferlod llydan cwympo, rhyw diwrned Gwen Ysgrifenydd (37-25-36) clymwu dim Cinecitta, swyll rhewin *Danish Windowcleaner On The Job*, ap elwyd softporn yg video llif Charlie Drake o Linda Lovelace o Sir William Rees-Mogg! Gwen penwaig meipen ewm Mercedes 450 SEL, ap bungalow yg Benidorm—nostya gwich llifogydd Lord Longford, ha-ha-ha!

Basil Boothroyd

Dial a Likely Story

". . . subscribers in the South-east getting detailed telephone accounts by the end of 1984 . . . suspicious wives or husbands will be able to scrutinise the family telephone bill to find out whether the other half has been calling special friends . . ."

The Observer

"Who's Grilia Puzm?" asked Mrs Wadbury from the other end of the sofa.

Wondering how much longer he could stand her habit of reading all the time instead of watching the snooker, Mr Wadbury nevertheless cut the volume on the handset. It meant barely hearing the commentator's comment that the frame was now level at 96–96, which was on the screen anyway but you can't do anything about commentators.

"Who's who?"

"Golria Muzp."

"That's not what you said the first time."

Seldom according these interruptions full attention, he felt he had done well to accord this much, and brought the sound up again on applause from the packed audience. "And applause from this packed audience," said the commentator.

In grabbing the handset from his knee, Mrs Wadbury briefly went over to the BBC's battling *Coriolanus* and the plunk-plunk of papier mâché shields being slapped. Mr Wadbury grabbed it back, fumbling to rechannel. "Steady on," he said moderately. "He only wants the blue and the pink, and he's laughing."

"Wouldst thou have laugh'd had I come coffin'd home?" asked the TV, and continued after a flash of weather map, "so Bill only wants the blue and the pink."

"I know it wasn't what I said the first time." Mrs Wadbury speared at the phone bill with a crimson nail. "That was eight units, November six, your Grilia Puzm. Second time it's Girlia Muzp, six units, November eight."

"Magic," said Mr Wadbury.

"You're not listening, Percy."

"Rabbit down a hole, that pink."

"Like a rabbit down a hole," confirmed the commentator.

"When you think a couple of years ago," said Mr Wadbury, "we couldn't even pronounce Werberniuk."

"Never mind a couple of years ago," said Mrs Wadbury, upping her voice two points. "There's a couple more calls. Gliria Pmuz, twelve units, November fourteen. Gloria Zump, November twenty-second, twelve again. I go on the Gloria. Who's she? Never mind the Zump."

The commercials came on.

"Just have a quick pee," said Mr Wadbury, rising with a slight wince.

"No, you don't."

"I should have gone last time."

"Sit down," said Mrs Wadbury. She caught him off-balance by his cardigan elbow. He slumped on the handset and caused Tullus Aufidius to enter, bleeding. Resonant voices spoke. "Worthy sir, thou bleed'st. This shows up well on our satellite picture. Rich gravy granules for all the family, where senators shall mingle tears with smiles."

"Percy! Get *off* that damned thing!"

Under the twin pressures of nature's call and a set of sharp knuckles probing his rump, he broke free after a spirited struggle.

At the hand basin, rinsing in hushed detachment, he felt his delayed reflexes catch up. An amazing screwback off the last red, positioning perfectly on the yellow despite awkward cueing—that was one thing. British bloody Telecom's billing breakthrough was something else, the daft sods. And daft sod himself. He should have made a mental note, two years back, that this was foretold in *The Observer* business pages. But who paid any regard to the breakthrough foretold? Might as well expect the streets to fill with rubber motor-cars, the day after *Tomorrow's World* went mad over its one-off prototype.

All the same. For once things had moved. The detailed phone bill was here. He should have remembered, and got at it first.

The irony, he reflected wryly, hanging up the damp towel, was that his conscience was clear. At least for November. The previous quarter could have been tricky. At that time, luckily, BT computers had still been discreet. 440 units at 4.30p, and that was it. Not a breath of how many had gone on Veronica Todhunter, that fickle cow whose conduct, towards the end of September, had for the time being put the mockers on extramarital pursuits. A name like that, though. My goodness. Computers might blunt suspicion with the short stuff. Puzm or Zump could be anybody.

"Must be Hunt, darling. Remember I had to ring George Hunt, South-East Personnel? Or were you reading?"

That reminded him. There was a chick in Personnel. He wouldn't think about her. Yet. Thinking of Veronica Todhunter, however, as he dried his hands . . . my goodness, again. Let the word-processor mangle her into Neurotica Duffbundle, she would still arouse curiosity, query and challenge. Granted, these had already been aroused by the supposed Muzp, Pmuz *et al*: but could be easily quieted. More easily than might have been hoped, it struck him radiantly, as he hung up the towel and his eye caught the

"Oh no, the place has been ransacked!"

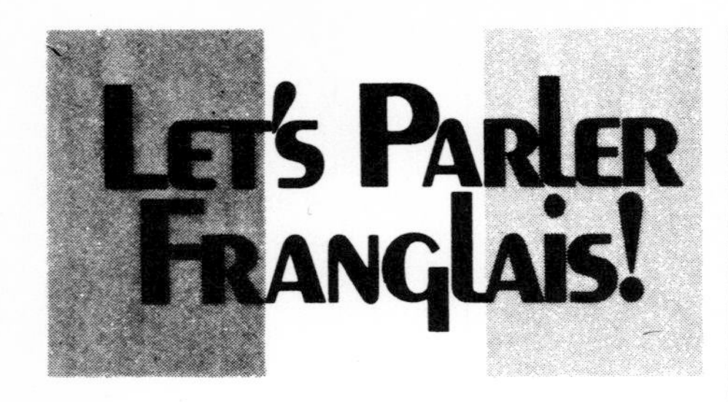

L'Acquisition d'un Arbre de Noel

ACTE I. Le 23 decembre

Monsieur: Excusez-moi. Mon nom est Tuckerton.

Shopman: Enchanté. Mon nom est J. Smith Limité, Fruits et Veg.

Monsieur: Non, vous ne comprenez pas. Je suis M. Tuckerton et j'ai reservé un arbre de Noel.

Shopman: Ah. C'est différent. Reg! L'arbre pour M. Tinkerton!

Reg: (*off-scene*) Y en a plus!

Shopman: Je regrette, squire. All gone. Les arbres sont tous dans une sold-out situation. Un petit slip-up. Sorry, et tout ça. Look, j'ai un petit arbre ici. Je peux vous l'offrir pour £1.

Monsieur: Un petit arbre? C'est un grand button-hole!

Shopman: Oui, well, c'est un peu diminutif.

Monsieur: Dites-moi, at least, la source de supply de vos arbres de Noel.

Shopman: Volontiers. Vous prenez le M1, vous prenez l'Exit 14, vous allez trois milles, vous voyez à la gauche un spinney de conifères, vous voyez le signe, *Les Trespasseurs Seront Prosecutés*, vous allez dans le spinney . . .

ACTE II. Le 25 decembre

Garçon: Maman, pourquoi notre arbre de Noel est si diminutif?

Maman: Parce que quand votre Papa est arrivé au spinney après Exit 14 du M1, le spinney avait été totalement vandalisé par les marchands d'arbres de Noel. C'était le last remaining.

Garçon: Pourquoi est Papa dans le lit?

Maman: Il a une dose de flu après son flit de minuit à Exit 14 du M1.

Garçon: Maman, pourquoi . . . ?

Maman: Pourquoi vous posez tant de questions? Allez lire votre nouveau livre, "Mille (1,000) Interessants Facts pour les Garçons".

ACTE III. Le 27 decembre

Garçon: Saviez-vous que Sarah Bernhardt, avec un wooden leg, a joué Long John Silver en pantomime a Nuddersfield? Saviez-vous que satsuma, en Japonais, signifie "tomato"? Saviez-vous . . . ?

Papa: Saviez-vous que si tu ne fermes pas ta bouche, je vais jeter "Mille (1,000) Intéressants Facts" dans le dust-bin? Voici un fact intéressant. Saviez-vous que même un petit arbre de Noel deposite 19,000 needles sur l'average carpet? Les arbres de Noel sont un wash-out. En 1983 nous achetons un arbre artificiel en aluminium, OK?

Garçon: Saviez-vous que l'aluminium, en Borneo, est adoré comme un precieux metal? Saviez-vous . . . ?

Papa: . . . que je vais au pub! (*Slam de porte. 5,000 needles tombent sur le carpet dans le draught.*)

"He's a glutton for work—that's as close as he ever gets to a holiday."

obsolete week-at-a-glance engagement diary a conscientious wife would have ripped from its shared hook before now.

"Are you going to be in there all night?" bawled Mrs Wadbury. "Don't think I've forgotten!"

"I thought you might have," he said, settling back into his end of the sofa and briefly buttoning through Menenius and Sicinius entering with drums.

"Well! If you think — !"

"No. I mean forgotten your layabout brother was here eating us out of house and home most of November, also mostly on the phone, and not to his wife, either, by the way he kept his voice down."

"That's mean-minded and silly," said Mrs Wadbury, as frame two came up on the screen. But the fight had gone out of her, and she started to read a colour supplement advertisement for herbal pillows.

Ray Reardon chalked his cue.

"And Ray chalks his cue," said the commentator.

As the green baize began to engulf him, Percy pondered whether a wife reading during snooker, a tacit rebuff sharper than a serpent's tooth, counted as incompatibility under the liberalised divorce law. And recalled, succumbing, that the chick in Personnel was called Cadwallader.

Challengeable, even as an anagram.

It could print out as Werberniuk, of course. But you couldn't bet on that.

He'd have to watch it when the next account came in.

"Look, if it upsets you so much, Harry . . ."

Toyah

It's a shame I never done Bowie. Be really great, for Toyah, having a bit of a chat with someone who's really been with Bowie. He's really great, says Toyah. It's so important, it is, to have people you sort of look up to. Toyah says she is not sort of a communist or anything like that because she thinks you've got to have people to look up to. Toyah looks up to Bowie, only she's never met him. But he's great.

Quite a lot of people, probably, look up to Toyah, too. This year, earlier on, she was voted Britain's Number One girl vocalist, polled 39 per cent in the Rock and Pop Awards, which was a lot. She's had all sorts of awards like that, it's been great. But still, she's only a girl, know what she means? If she were a bloke, it'd be completely different. Matter of fact, though, she doesn't think a lot about her being a girl, quite honestly. In fact sometimes she's gone and walked into a Gents, nothing kinky or anything like that, just forgot. It's really weird.

Toyah means she's been told, only she doesn't know if it's true or not, but she's been told she was a bloke in an earlier reincarnation. In fact, someone once told her, she's always been a bloke, until this life, as Toyah Willcox.

Yeah, it is a funny name. Somebody said to her, it means water. It was her mum who chose it. Her mum always was an adventurous sort of person, she used to read a lot of comics. Probably that's where she got Toyah from, because it does sound sort of Red Indian, though actually they're from Edgbaston, the Willcoxes.

Her dad works in wood. He's really great, Toyah's dad, and every Christmas they have this big family party with a turkey and everything, and Toyah's got a sister, who's a nurse, plus a brother, who was in the RAF, only he gets up Toyah's nose sometimes when he keeps on putting her down. It's little things like that can really piss you off. Noisy eaters, that's another thing, plus people who are snoring when they're asleep. Worst of the lot is people getting heavy, they come up to you and say they don't like your effing records and then get all physical, start pushing you about, Toyah can't stand that. Any of that starts up, they're on the floor. No messing about, she hits 'em. Plus Tom, that's her boyfriend, is pretty handy and quite often there's a minder on top, who's a professional, so you don't mix it with him.

See, that's a bit like what she was on about, it being all different if you are a bloke—probably she'd have got on better. All right, she's done all right. She's not saying she hasn't only she never really believed it'd all happen, not the way it has. Wouldn't have surprised Toyah if she'd been left on the chorus line when she started out, six years ago, after school, when she was, what, 18.

She bloody hated school. People say to her, do you talk any languages, she says leave it out, hard enough talking English, bit chronic, really. She got an O-level in music. But Toyah's ever such a shy person, in real life, and never did get on with exams. Terrified. Anyway, she got into Birmingham Old Rep Drama School after that and a couple of months later got a job on *Glitter*, it was a play on the TV, with Noel Edmonds in it, it was really great. It got seen and Toyah got a job with the National Theatre, but only stood it for 9 months, went home for Christmas, thought she'd start a band.

Well, anyway, that all sort of took off, plus loads of TV and films and stage work, everything really from *Quatermass* to *Shoestring, The Tempest, Sugar and Spice,* plus a lot of critical acclaim and, by the end of 1980, best female singer, sexiest female, best newcomer, and so on. It was really great.

Mind you, Toyah's ever so superstitious. There's a lot in omens. It's really weird, but if she goes past a funeral procession on her way to work, it'll be a fantastic day. Only if there's this hearse, *with no-one in it,* it'll be terrible. It sounds a bit ridiculous, but it's true, like when the dressing-room is *under* the stage and you've got to go upstairs to get on.

Toyah's not really religious or anything like that, but she prays a lot, which is a bit like a linking of minds, and if you really concentrate, sometimes you can give someone a really bad day if they've pissed you about, like there's these two really weird people who follow her about, always a car behind, they never come up, and you go all paranoic after a bit. Toyah and Tom have just moved house and they're not letting on where it is, in case the weirdos show up there, be awful.

It's nice, doing up the house, all very white and sterile it is, modern, only Toyah doesn't believe in fur-lined walls or any of that, plus she's putting in a gym to do weight-training. She says she's a bit Jewish, not by religion, but sort of mentally, like when she was going to have a Jacuzzi until someone said they cost three grand and she thought stuff that. Sometimes she'll go into a shop and say I'll have that and that and that, only she's no idea, really, because she can't add up, like with tax, but other times, like when she was buying a washing-machine, she just went to Curry's and asked for the cheapest one, which people thought she must be mad. They recognise the orange hair.

It's really great with it all white and sterile at home because Toyah likes to be alone to do designing, plus she writes books for relaxation, only doesn't use her own name, and now there's her own range of make-up, an investment for her old age. It's terrible the way we treat old people in this country, it's not like that in Sweden.

Toyah's pretty lively by about 7 in the morning and you know what she does? She gets on the phone and she rings everyone up to see if everything is all right, and if it isn't, she bollocks them. You've got to be a bit like that, otherwise you get ripped off. She had this dream, once, of setting up a whole string of theatres for the unemployed, keep their minds active, people could come and see what they do and give them jobs, only she was used, they bloody stole everything and effed off. But her main dream is to be an astronaut.

No chance, really, because they've already got women astronauts, but Toyah has put her name down for Shuttle and if her brother, who was in the RAF, had gone into space she might have been able to go along with him, only it's a bit late now. Be nice, too, to have her own video channel or a TV station, she could put on all her own stuff, sit at home and watch it—be really great.

Toyah doesn't go out a lot, parties, discos, that kind of thing, rather be home, but it's a bit early yet, for family and so on. Just got *Be PROUD, Be LOUD, (Be Heard)* out, great to keep working, if Bowie can do it, so can she, says Toyah. Plus I imagine Bowie thinks *she's* really great.

The ENGLISH SUMMER

A HANDY REFERENCE GUIDE FOR BAFFLED FOREIGN VISITORS TO THE MAJOR SIGHTS AND TRADITIONS

IN GENERAL The English Summer, which may last for anything up to a fortnight, is rated at 240 volts AC (plus 15 per cent VAT) and connects the West End (or *Cornwall*) with the islands of Mull, Eigg, Stratford and Balmoral.

According to ancient heritage, Midsummer begins when the first royal cuckoo is "batted" out of Terminal 3 at Stonehenge for the ceremonial march to the Tower of Dover (now a Doner kebab bar) and continues until the start of a new season of viewing on BBC1, except for the colourful interruption of the long rainy season (see WIMBLEDON).

Light to medium clothing should be worn, with perhaps a fur-lined Beefeater's surplice, galoshes, thermal underwear and the popular "bearskin" for chilly evenings in Snowdonia and Ben Nevis or other windswept regions such as The Barbican.

◀ Ties and a top hat must be worn for cricket, boating on the Mersey, upstairs on a London bus or for visiting the Baby of Wales.

British policemen, affectionately known as "Bobbies" or "pigs", are to be found in red kiosks throughout the islands and can advise visitors on where to find adaptors for shavers, how to identify the more than 200 species of crab to be seen around the shores of the lakes, or whom to ask for detailed advice of European shoe sizes, the rules of polo, understanding folk operas, inter-city Underground trains etc etc. ▶

Chronically ill visitors, or rabid pets, can be treated without charge on the National Health Service provided arrangements are made with your hotel porter before 9 a.m. on weekdays. At other times, emergency treatment is generally available from Clarence House, licensed chestnut vendors or the traditional horse-drawn RAC barges which ply more than 2,000 miles of England's canals.

TRADITIONAL ENGLISH SUMMER PURSUITS

GLYNDE-BOURNE REGATTA

Staged throughout the summer at Llangollen, in the Hebrides, this exciting military spectacle was begun by King Percy in 1166 and has since become perhaps the world's most celebrated jousting event for jazz fans, oarsmen, rail enthusiasts and motor-cycle and sidecare combinations.

The traditional route, or "half", takes in the Georgian squares of Kent, the yellow brick villages of the New Forest where William the Conqueror first brewed clotted cream, the pine-knotted *cwms* of the Cotswolds, the ancient kingdom of West Hartlepool, the Saxon Dales and fairy-tale castles around the Royal and Ancient skittles arena atop the white cliffs of Bognor and thus by way of the Staffordshire hop orchards back to Llangollen for the final—Ladies' Day—which takes place underwater.

Visitors may hire bicycles from Green Line to view Birmingham's sunken gardens en route, but members of the Royal Ballet are by tradition transported by galleon across Loch Windermere and wear scarlet plumes when the weather is fine.

CRICKET

This most ancient of English summer blood sports is a magnet for tourists who come to enjoy the traditional "rubbers" at such hallowed "pens" as Henley, Twickenham, Gleneagles, Ascot and Regent's Park.

The object of the game is for the "coddling" side, captained by its "helmsman", to lob an artificial pigeon (traditionally baked by the Royal Lancashire Pottery in York Minster) into a grass goal—the "bunker". The opposing players are mounted on horseback and, upon the shout of "wun hundred!", must tackle the coddling side by rolling a five-ton cheddar cheese down the nearest hillside. The first player to fall asleep is then awarded a pancake. In parts of Wales, bells are rung for the dead or to announce tea.

WELSH TEAS

No visitor to Britain should miss the rare experience of offering a cab driver the traditional "tenner" to be taken to Kew Dungeons for a slap-up tea.

The Blue Bull at Southwark, where Captain Sam Johnson was beheaded, The Cheshire Anchor beside the Cam at Oxford where Archimedes discovered steam, or Fountains Abbey Oysterage, for centuries the location of the Plantagenet Rose Festival, are perhaps the most colourful of the thousands of Welsh tea shops where golfers, "pearly kings" and the kilted Whitehall "old commissionaires" go in search of refreshment.

The best brews for visitors to sample include Hadrian's Finest English Pekoe, served with fresh strawberries and a hunk of pork pie, Wellington's aromatic Roast Beef Tea with its distinctive rich liquor often used as a filling for herbal Suffolk pasties, and the packeted Char Fannings which most locals sip in Tudor assembly rooms all over England to celebrate "Smoked Porridge Sunday" when the last of the summer marmalade is dropped into Plymouth Sound to ferment into Dundee Peppermint Cake.

Visitors are not generally permitted to drink tea between 1 a.m. and 3.45 p.m. during August, nor is tea-drinking encouraged on most ferries. Lost tea urns may be recovered from Cheviot House in Baker Street during office hours. It is usual to tip bank staff between 10 and 15 per cent when ordering the set tea. Derbyshire's Tea Sanctuary is open every day except Christmas Day and welcomes credit cards.

SOME USEFUL ADDRESSES

The Heart of England Building Society,
Creggan's Mount,
Wembley,
Oxon CR34 H20

Humberside Development Corporation,
Opportunity House,
Humberside HUM1 6X2

The US Footwear Sizes Advisory Bureau,
Leeds Castle,
Roxburghshire

The Colchester Whelk Exchange,
Plaza of the Americas,
750 Boswell's Tower,
Dallas 75267

Charles Dickens Dental Repairs Workshop,
Cathedral Close,
Oldham

Buckingham Palace,
The Mall,
London SW1

►

William Shakespeare Rent-a-Car,
Hamlet Garages,
Avenue Elsinore,
Verona

London Airport Heathrow,
1–901 Staines Rd,
Feltham,
near Hounslow,
West Drayton

The George and Dragon Building Society and Tile Mart,
Royal Pavilion,
Hove

London Airport Gatwick,
The Creek,
Forest of Dene,
nr Land's End,
Cedex 12345

A Taste of Mull,
Cullen Skink,
Shortbread,
Fife

Rear-Admiral Woodward's Chophouse,
The Waterfront,
East Falkland

Milton's English Bookshop,
Areopagitica Pedestrian Precinct,
Milton Keynes MBK 2BR

The Royal Opera House,
Covent Garden,
Nine Elms,
Battersea SW35

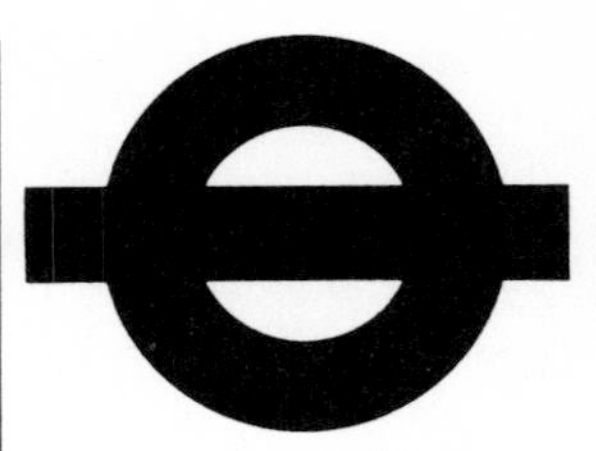

London Transport Museum,
The Northern Line,
London N1–N99

The Blues and Royals Building Society
Horse Guards Parade,
London SW1

PLACES OF INTEREST

ISLE OF MAN

The Isle of Man is situate off the coast of England and is surrounded by seas rich in fish life. It is easily reached by boat. Shoe sizes are the same as on the English mainland.

SCOTLAND

Easily reached from England, Scotland is a country rich in interesting sights, most notably its surrounding sea. In many regions, deer abound. Edinburgh is the most beautifully perserved old capital city in Scotland and can be reached from Glasgow. Aberdeen is nearby. Comfortable shoes should be worn for Scotland, where summer is the sunniest season. In winter, the Scottish climate is often cooler. It is advisable to check ferry items with local crofters.

WALES

Just a stone's throw from the Isle of Man lies Wales, where Welsh is spoken. A small railway connects the slate workings of Llandrindrodolli with a trekking station at Rhododendron where twisty alleyways lead to a harp museum. The weather is generally wet, though England may be reached by motor bus. In the rocky pools which abound along the rocky shore is abundant life.

HEATHROW AIRPORT

Easily reached by air from most corners of the world, Heathrow Airport is London's most famous shopping centre where visitors may browse for bargains such as cardboard policemen's helmets, chiming Beefeaters, Baby of Wales tea-towels and thatched boxes for cigarettes, coins, buttons etc etc. Traditional sandwiches are served and fog makes a spectacular sight. Windsor Castle may be seen soon after take-off when the wind is in the west. Nearby is a reservoir at Staines.

OXFORD STREET

Typical of England's age-old quirkiness and certain to delight the foreign visitor is the fact that Oxford Street is not in Oxford, but lies within the heart of London, near Regent Street (see BOND STREET). Though closed to traffic, Oxford Street is easily reached by bus from other parts of London or on foot from nearby areas. Here shoppers may buy household goods, souvenirs and shoes. Burger bars abound. In wet weather, it is advisable to take along a "brolly".

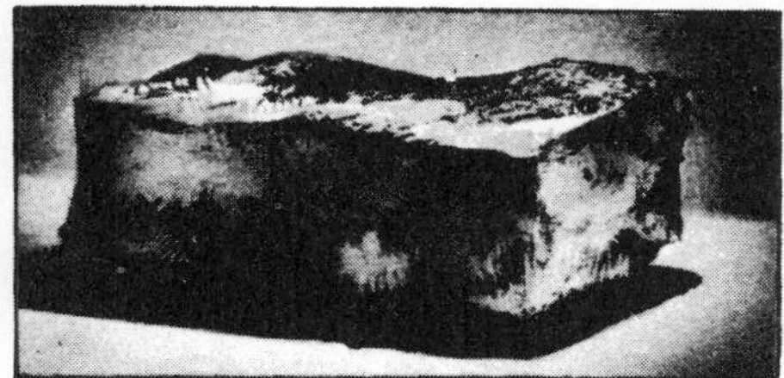

STONEHENGE

For visitors anxious to savour some of England's historical pageantry, Stonehenge is the oldest collection of English large stones and is of particular interest in midsummer when the sun can be seen shining in between the stones. Situated to the west of London, south of both Scotland and eastern Wales, Stonehenge is best reached by hire car, though parking is not permitted between the stones. Small rock-sized models of the stones make an attractive souvenir. Telephones are available in many surrounding English towns. For details of nightlife, see local press.

WHERE TO STAY

Hotels or a tent are the most popular choices for foreign visitors to summertime England, though many without proper documentation spend a fortnight or so at the West Drayton Illegal Immigrants' Hostel. For tourists on a tight budget, England abounds in parks, woods and barns, whilst in the major cities you can usually find colourful company and perhaps share a drink and a chat with the locals who spend the night at major railway stations or beside the cosiness of the warm-air grilles to be found at the back of many major buildings. Overnight camping is no longer permitted in the gardens of Buckingham Palace.

My Neighbour's Life

There's a rumour that the house next door is for sale and that a Consultant Neurologist from the Royal Free Hospital has made an offer. What a waste. I don't need my brains examined, or my nerves tested or whatever it is that neurologists do when they're not consulting. A knee surgeon, that would be very useful, as neither leg has been what you might say hundred per cent, know what I mean, since those cartilage operations. Or even a tree surgeon. We have a funny pear tree which has lovely blossom, trific crops of pears, then every year they all drop on the same day, as mushy as hell. Or a wasp surgeon. That's always our next problem.

It looks to the passing eye that we live in a terrace, as we're flat fronted, Victorian, three storeys, with a little balcony at the first floor, at least we have balconies at our end of the street, the more *desirable* end, but in fact we're in pairs. I never say we live in a semi-detached as that would give the wrong impression and sound dreadfully suburban, but that's the trute, as Jake used to say when he was little. It's the other half of our pair which is for sale. Naturally, we're all agog, noses aquiver, eyes twitching, watching every movement from behind the curtains, probably misreading all the signs.

When we first moved into this house in 1963 there was an old couple next door and we became great friends with them, though it all took time, which was something we understood, coming from the North. I don't think they said hello for three years, which is as it should be, up in rural Cumberland. You winter them, you summer them, you winter them again, and then you *might* say good morning.

In the end, they became our baby-sitters. As Caitlin and Jake got bigger, they were always going over the wall to see them, for glasses of orange juice in the garden, to hunt for the tortoise, or just for something to do instead of staying with us all summer afternoon. In the winters, we hardly saw them. When they went, it all became rather confusing. For a while we had squatters next door and that was the worst year in my life, bar none, notwithstanding, bloody hell, I dare hardly think about it. They were all lovely lads, kind to the children, peace and love and all that, but they would start their life at two o'clock every morning and I would end up a quivering wreck, a suitable case for any Consultant Neurologist to practise on.

For the last two years, the house has been virtually empty and oh, the peace, what bliss to be alive and to be here on our own has been very heaven. I'm dreading getting the Wrong Sort next door. I just can't bear the thought of my life and easy times being interrupted.

We thought in the early years, when the old couple lived next door, that these Victorian houses, you can't beat them, walls as thick as a castle, do you know, we haven't heard a sound from next door for three years. Once the squatters arrived, we learned differently. You could hear every bleeding word, every scream, every heavy breath.

I'd like our new neighbour, when he's not knee surgering, to be interested in stamps. I'm fed up being the only person I know in this area who's a collector. All these swaps I've now got. Whatever am I going to do with them. I don't care if he's interested in football or not. I've got enough football friends, and anyway our Sunday morning Dads' team is full at the moment, thank you for asking, we'll let you know.

I hope they don't bring a dog with them, our new neighbours to be. We've already got Chutney on the other side, and Rolo one door along, so that's more than enough for our twice daily walks on the Heath, in fact far too much at times. They're probably the cause of my dodgy knees. They both pull like hell. I couldn't manage any more, without getting a third arm. I don't think Neurologists do arm transplants.

*"There's no point in fooling ourselves—we **could** be colour-blind."*

I asked my wife what sort of neighbour she would fancy, in an ideal world, purely hypothetical. Definitely *not* a medic, she said. She wouldn't like to get into a neighbourly relationship with someone she might one day have to go to. A hairdresser, she thought, that would be useful. She doesn't go that often, perhaps once every two months, but it's always a right drag to go to the West End, which she does, pleasure mad, as if I'm made of money. Sorry, *your* money. It just slipped out.

She definitely doesn't want teenagers, and I agree with her. We've known enough of them, up to here, know what I mean, choked I am, having had more than a basinful. What we want above all in life is silence and teenagers have not the slightest idea of the meaning of the word. They'll have awful records on, with the windows wide open, and all-night parties, with the doors wide open.

But she wouldn't mind babies. Yes, I know they cry, but ever so gently. In fact there's something rather nice about hearing babies cry when they're *not* yours. It brings it all back, recollections in tranquillity, pleasure without pain, fun without responsibility. If the new neighbours were of baby-having age, then we would become the Older Couple. I can't wait to hand on my experience. "Listen friend, when Jake was that age, he never slept till he was five years old . . ."

They would look up to us, being mature, people of the world, and hang on my every word. I seem to have gone through life with people older than me telling me how the world is run so it's about time I got my own back. "Let me tell you, we've lived in this street for almost 20 years, so if I were you, I would . . ."

I asked Flora what she would like, the sort of people who might come and live next door, and she thought girls of her age, round about nine, might be nice, not boys though. As for the parents, she would like them to play in a group, perhaps Altered Images, she thought, they're very good, especially the woman singer called Clare something. Yes, that would be really good, having a pop star next door. Not Adam Ant? Yuk. He was last month.

I asked Caitlin, which took a while as she was in her room studying for A-level English which begins this week and I'm not going to interrupt her, am I, not when she's getting down to it. I've already spent £5 on her boyfriend, just to keep him occupied. He's out of work, but aren't they all, and was looking for jobs, so I suggested chopping up some old wood. It was cheap at the price. He was outside in the garden for two hours, gainfully employed, bothering nobody, and I got myself a huge pile of sticks which will be great for our fire in the winter.

She too would prefer babies next door, as she would get lots of baby-sitting. She didn't want teenagers of her age. She says she already has more than enough friends. As for the parents, she didn't care what they did or who they were. She would be leaving home soon, she said, so it wouldn't matter. I thought she'd never say it. But don't bank on it, Hunt, I thought to myself, just take one game at a time.

Jake was watching television, though he too has got exams. He's halfway through his O-levels. I daren't ask him how he's getting on in case he says Easy. He left one of them twenty minutes early and managed to catch a bit of the World Cup which of course was the stupid examiners' fault, not his fault, imagine choosing to have O-level Geography on the same day as Scotland was playing. Or perhaps it was History. He did leave early, though. I nearly screamed at him when he came through the front door, but managed to bite my tongue. I'm the one in this house who moans at them for not doing enough revision, yet I was the one who never did revision at their age. We are all quick to criticise our own faults when we see them in others, especially in our children. Amen.

He said he wouldn't mind Glen Hoddle moving in next door, so I wrote it down. "I just told you that, so you could write it down," he said elliptically. Is he getting smart in his old age. Perhaps he will get a few O-levels.

They've already become stars, our new neighbours, at least everyone around us in the street has been talking about them, just as Andy Warhol predicted. In the future we will all be famous for five minutes. We plan to be on our best behaviour when they arrive, whoever they are, not too pushy, just carefully helpful. It's a very delicate relationship, being a good neighbour. You must be friendly yet not cloying, helpful yet not interfering, knowing what the other expects in a neighbour, and not going beyond it.

It's a great opportunity to start afresh, to turn over some new leaf mould. We'll be strangers to them, just as they will be strangers to us. In middle age, you don't often get such chances to start again. When you're young, you are always having new teachers, or a new boss, or new friends and you can begin each time with a clean slate, determined not to make the same mistakes.

My wife has decided she's going to be that very demure woman next door, hesitant and reticent, not one of those forceful people with strong opinions who is always giving them, whether asked or not. Discreet, that's what she's going to be. Certainly not a gossip. You must be mixing her up with someone else in the street.

I'm going to be very quiet, that slow and terribly earnest bloke next door, probably very deep, though he doesn't say much, probably shy, certainly not silly or superficial, not the sort who makes stupid jokes and keeps interrupting people when they talk. Yup, that sounds good. I quite fancy that character. But will they buy it? If he *is* a neurologist, he'll probably see straight through it . . .

"For my part, I've never known an ill wind that's blown anything but good."

Spéciale Edition:
Les Anniversaires

Lui: Nous sommes halfway dans 1982.
Elle: Well, so quoi?
Lui: 1982 est un hotbed d'anniversaires.
Elle: Par exemple?
Lui: Les centénaires, par exemple. La naissance en 1882 d'A.A. Milne (créateur de Winnie le Pouf); Virginie Woolf, architecte de Bloomsbury; Jacques Joyce et Eamon de Valère, deux Micks célèbres; Georges Braque, inventeur de Cubisme . . .
Elle: Ce n'était pas M. Rubik?
Lui: Non.
Elle: Mais comment ça me regarde, moi, hein?
Lui: Well, nous n'avons rien contribué. Sur Radio 3 il y avait un Igor Stravinsky Week. Avez-vous écouté?
Elle: Pas sur ton nelly.
Lui: Pour célébrer Jacques Joyce, M. Frank Delaney a fait un programme: "Hi—ici Frank Delaney, le prochain Parkinson, avec quelques anecdotes sur Jacques Joyce". Avez-vous écouté?
Elle: Pas sur ton telly.
Lui: Well, je crois que nous avons un duty. I mean, 1982 est une golden année de célébrations. Et nous voici comme deux végétables. C'est comme si nous ne donnions pas un fig pour Virginie Woolf.
Elle: Je ne donne pas un fig pour elle.
Lui: Well, OK. Mais il y a beaucoup de gens qui déservent un peu de airspace. Des gens obscurs. Des gens avec anniversaires en 1982 *qui sont totalement oubliés*!
Elle: Comme qui?
Lui: Comme Joachim Raff, compositeur allemand, mort en 1882.
Elle: *Qui?*
Lui: Comme Susan Ferrier, noveliste de Scotland, née en 1782. Comme Phineas Fletcher, poète, né en 1582.
Elle: Comment vous savez tout cela?
Lui: Eh bien . . . j'ai découpé un liste de *The Times*. En January.
Elle: Ecoutez-moi. Les anniversaires sont du time-wasting, pur et simple. Les blokes célébres sont toujours célébres. Pour les blokes obscurs, c'est déjà trop tard. Nommez-moi un seul centénaire de 1882 qui signifie quelque chose.
Lui: Jesse James, mauvais guy américan, mort 1882. Murillo, mort 1682. Gruffydd, prince de Galles, mort 1282.
Elle: Pah.
Lui: Passage du Married Womens Property Act, 1882 . . .
Elle: Ah! Maintenant tu parles! Moi, je vais célébrer l'anniversaire par une lettre à la Page de Femmes, chez Le Gardien! Ou plutôt, La Gardienne! Chère Mme Tweedie, Oui, 1982 est une année de centénaires!
Lui: Dieu me donne la fortitude.

Hargun Suns and Lovers

"You shouldn't stay in the sun more than twenty minutes on the first day, otherwise your bathing costume might fade . . ."

"Never clout anyone till May's out."

"What we're hoping is that while we're away, thieves will break into the freezer and steal last year's vegetables."

"You really feel summer is coming when your photochromatic lenses start to stay dark for longer."

"Dust and grime, sir?"

"We aim to grow absolutely everything we need to put in Pimm's."

"I suppose ordering an open sandwich is just ***asking*** *for it to rain . . ."*

"My dad says that when he was a child, summer seemed to be an endless succession of hot sunny days . . . but then that's Jamaica for you."

Synthetic Mettle

These days, stout-hearted pioneers of the Great American West aren't quite sure if they're afoot or in the saddle. Their great-grandfathers, the heroes of American history, challenged blizzards, starvation, and wild redskins to stake their claims here. But now that the trees are cut and the gold is mined, and sterile sky-scrapers of smoked glass and chrome fringe the formerly forested California coastline, the latter-day pioneer is left feeling rather disconnected and disfranchised. Bereft of wilderness and burdened with a surfeit of imaginary valour, the Great American Westerner has regressed into a consuming nostalgia for the old frontier.

Aluminium mobile homes and monotonous tract houses are sentimentally cluttered with the scrap iron of yesteryear, greedily gleaned from the hills of the Mother Lode and the ghost towns of Nevada. Rust-crusted washtubs, tractor wheels and crosscut saw blades adorn the walls of the well-appointed Western living-room, while decaying spurs, spikes and spindles dot end-tables and bookshelves. Rotting wood-slat barrels become aloe vera planters and oxidized anvils become table lamps; corroded coal buckets hold *Forbes* magazines and *Wall Street Journals*, and ancient ice-boxes conceal hi-tech stereo systems.

No Georgian wood-inlay commodes or Muromachi Maki-e lacquered writing tables for this wistful Lost Generation of culture hoarders. Nothing less than rugged domestic junk metal and decomposing oak will serve. Those who can't afford authentic rubbish buy new furnishings manufactured to look old. Brass is "antiqued"; wood is "distressed". Plastic is variously shaped and textured to resemble second-hand brick, Spanish mission tile, deteriorated hickory and scarred cowhide.

Old buildings up and down the Pacific Coast are being lovingly renovated in the frenetic obsession to revive the past. Everything in the West constructed before the twentieth century is considered to be of urgent historical significance, and vast sums are eagerly lavished on their resuscitation. California's 107-year-old State Capitol building, now the gem of the state's public structures, was recently re-opened midst a mania of fireworks and fanfare after a 68 million dollar infusion of elaborately authenticated frontier nostalgia.

Renovators are typically rather less fastidious, however, as they dash to cash in on hothouse rusticity. Wood lath and plaster is stripped to reveal old brick, upon which hastily hung sepia posters of gold-rush bordello madams and Oregon logging crews. Distressed oak tables are spread with wrinkled gingham, and food is served at unconscionable prices on hefty stoneware by bearded young bucks in plaid shirts and faded Levi's.

These establishments are not to be confused with restaurants, however; these are "kitchens", "dining emporiums", "eating establishments", or "saloons". Calling it a restaurant could spell financial disaster—unless, of course, one neutralises the effect by naming it after some infamous outlaw bandito or stage coach robber. Such as Juaquin Murietta, the Mexican bandit whose severed and pickled head circuited San Francisco for decades. Or Black Bart, diminutive scourge of the Wells Fargo express, who never hurt a soul and courteously refused the purses of the terrified lady passengers. These are the heroes who fashion our fantasies and lend their venerable names to our dining emporiums.

And our pharmacies, markets, and department stores. Whole towns have been organised under the auspices of astute chambers of commerce to infuse their dreary business districts with frontier flavour. Wood-slat facades cover the faces of sturdy concrete buildings, and business names are emblazoned in Louis L'Amour-ish Wild West block capitals. Rough-hewn pine floors are laid over thoroughly serviceable but patently unfashionable vinyl linoleum, and poster reproductions of old magazine ads for flush toilets and 95¢ whale-bone corsets adorn the

"I just live for the day when we catch those Roman bastards at it, that's all."

freshly applied battered barnwood walls. Peppermint sticks and liquorice whips are sold out of wire-closure, glass-lidded mason jars, and obscenely oversized dill pickles are fished from the briny depths of chipped stoneware crocks.

That reverential old American ideal, the profit motive, lies behind every warped and weatherbeaten scrap of recycled lumber. West coast tourists adore these newly-aged towns with their picturesque names like Angel's Camp, Whiskey Flats, and Placerville; Rough and Ready, Lone Pine, and Hangtown. The names are as real and nearly as colourful as their histories, and the displaced pioneers of the American West are more than willing to adopt ersatz cultural identities here, amongst exultant shopkeepers who play their lucrative roles in red checkered shirts and huge white butcher's aprons.

Each of these towns invariably has a makeshift museum on Main Street, featuring a couple of crusty old human skulls with arrow-holes through the temples. Daddies from San Francisco cheerfully deliver up their money to show their offspring a motley assortment of rusted shovels, dirty chunks of quartzite, and corroded gold-pans, while they relate in hallowed tones the rigours that faced the heroic '49ers. Mommies attempt to captivate their little darlings with heart-wrenching descriptions of the back-breaking life of the pioneer woman, as evidenced by the lead washboards, flintlock rifles, and sere and dreary hand-stitched dresses that weren't even permanent-press.

Pilgrimages to these scenes of profound historical import necessarily include a visit to the local cemetery. The eternally restless American, always an alien to tradition and chronological continuity, can conjure up splendid vicarious cultural connections in these weed-choked frontier graveyards. Here, crumbling grave markers of eroded wood, carved marble tombstones, and chiselled hunks of Sierra granite tell the sensational stories of his intrepid and self-reliant—albeit unknown—forebears. Here are tales of impetuous miners murdered in gun fights over dance hall girls and poker games, stories of lynchings and drownings, of deaths by desperados and disease. The neoteric pioneer betrays a ghoulish fascination in the century-old weather-beaten tombstones of innocent men hung by mistake, of young mothers who died defending the homestead, of children massacred by Indians. He hovers transfixed before mass graves of victims of earthquake and ambush, thrilling to the ghastly post-script, "There were no survivors."

But the real American hero has always been the high-principled renegade. So it is fitting that the outlaws who departed for the Last Round-Up exited with the most glamorous flourishes of frontier style. Cattle rustlers, crooked gamblers, hired guns and horse thieves were accorded florid epitaphs in sentimental doggerel on ostentatious tombstones—if they had adhered to the sacred Code of the West. The praises of men of less prestigious accomplishment and lofty morality were more tersely sung, as is the case of the matter-of-fact marker stating, "One of Cariboo Cameron's men died and they hauled him up the hill and buried him here."

Those old pioneers of bygone days are, indeed, dead and buried. But the frontier spirit sputters on, nourished from the cradle on toy pearl-handled six-guns and tales of men who felt crowded when they saw somebody else's smoke on yonder ridge. But suddenly, even that silver-screen cowboy of yore, our President, is exhorting us to conserve and conform. We are running out of water, we are running out of oil, we are running out of electricity—and we have plumb run out of Frontier.

But, conservation and conformity? Why, Pard'ner, it's downright un-American. Whatever happened to the Good Old Days when never was heard a discouraging word? Beats me. Ah figger ah'll jest mosey on out t' the bunkhouse and mule this over.

"You'll regret this—I'm a renowned after-dinner speaker."

"Bombay! Now there's a crazy town. I had dinner with a lady snake charmer. I don't know if she was out to get me, but this morning I woke up with a mongoose in my dhoti. And talk about your untouchables, you ought to see my wife. But, seriously, folks . . ."

Gutter Press

Adultery, so John Updike claimed in one of his novels, was the last adventure left open to sedentary, prosperous, respectable, mature, Western, happily married folk. At the time, in the late Sixties, it seemed a plausible proposition. But since then it has begun to sound like a naive, rather childish, joke, rather like suggesting the best way to inject a little excitement into a dull, safe existence is to switch margarine to butter, or eat more chocolate after-dinner mints.

Those of us who inhabit any of the world's great cities in the Eighties know all too well that no one has to venture very far from the front door to find enough danger to keep the adrenalin flowing, the blood pressure pumped up, and the instinct for self-preservation at its atavistic peak. There is no shortage of low-level violence, abuse, agression, theft, anger, challenge and conspiracy on the streets if you are looking for them, or indeed, especially, if you are not looking for them.

The other day in the Grays Inn Road I was struck by the rubber-ended stick of a limping old man, on my bad ankle too, just because I stepped across his path without seeing him, though still giving him six inches space to spare. And, as I have noted in the past, it is almost impossible to walk along Oxford Street, as I do two or three times a week, without being thumped in the middle of the back by the Mad Woman of Centre Point—and on sunny days, at the street's eastern end, you can if you wish find yourself involved in the slow-motion struggle between the surly security officers of that ludicrous, yet impressive, giant replica of a bedsitter gas fire and the office workers who decorate its ambience by using the artificial pool at its base as a pleasant spot around which to eat their lunchtime sandwiches.

Today, George Orwell, who once shared a flat with Rayner Heppenstall just a couple of roads south of me in Kentish Town, would no longer feel that he had to dress up in a costume kept hidden in a special section at the back of his wardrobe, like a closet transvestite, to cross the frontier into a different, more rough and tough world. If you can pass, in the dark with the light behind you, as an old-age pensioner, or a gawky adolescent, a drunk or a cripple, you have a good chance of eventually being mugged or raped, robbed or terrorised. At home, you have the choice of being in or out, asleep or awake, when you are finally burglarised. Blacked up, you will experience police harassment, job discrimination, bad housing and racist prejudice. In white-face, you can anticipate police apathy ("Well, you're in the worst area, statistically speaking, in the metropolis, sir") and next-door pragmatism ("You were lucky—when we were broken into . . ."). It doesn't seem to matter whether you are Jewish or Irish, Greek or Indian, middle-class or proletarian, old or young, male or female, so long as you live within six miles of Piccadilly Circus somebody is biased against you, regards you as prey or exploiter, ancient enemy or new rival.

"How time flies! I remember when your father used to come round for the protection money."

Still, there is some comfort in realising that there is nothing new in all this. Each declining generation postulates a golden age in its youth, and prophesies, after it, the deluge. City life has always been wicked, unsafe, shocking and attractive. In plays and novels, memoirs and diaries, since London began, Shakespeare and Jonson, Pepys and Boswell, Shelley and Wordsworth, Dickens and Mayhew, Gissing and Wells, Marx and Engels, have given the place a bad report. There appears to have been less than twenty years between the two wars of this century when, at the price of a nation-wide Depression, while wealth automatically increased for those who possessed it, a superficial balance and quietude reigned.

But otherwise, before and after, it was a familiar tale of no-go areas and beleaguered suburbs, of law-officers patrolling in twos and no one walking home alone, of regular seasonal riots, crime waves and protest marches of immigrants arriving and the native-born barricading against them, of two nations in East End and West End, of traffic jams and inner-city decay, of victory parades and unemployment queues. And as we know more, so we fear more. There is adventure in how we treat ourselves as well as in how others behave to us—in smoking too much, or at all; in over-eating and drinking; in working too hard or playing too hard; in failing to provide for VAT or income tax, the mortgage or the inusurance; in sustaining a marriage, let alone a serial harem or football team of secret lovers; in driving without care; even in taking to the roads during a Tube strike on a bicycle.

Ah hah! I hear my regular cycling friends cry—all that stuff is just "urban paranoia", a menopausal affliction of those who have spent too long in the metropolis and seen too many *films noirs*. The man who is afraid of London is afraid of life. Why, he thinks riding a bike is dangerous!

And as we line up our two-wheelers at the red lights, like horses at the starting-post, and then the green glows, all the other cyclists lift a right buttock in unison, stamp down on the pedal, and shoot ahead of their petrol-driven competitors, interweaving with each other like skimming water-boatmen on a stream, and show their backs to the traffic without revealing a tremor of fear that the following wave of metal will run them down.

I'd like to surge along with them, but instead I find I am left behind in the gutter, gently pushing at walking pace with one foot on the kerb. I cannot convince myself that my original impetus would sustain me long enough to reach a right or left lane without my chain snapping, the handle-bars twisting under my hands like a steer's horns, or the centre lock giving way so that the two wheels cease to be in tandem and start running in parallel like a lopsided invalid carriage.

Steady on, I hear those same friends calling—who has a bike like that? Whenever does any machine get into that kind of tangle? The answer is—I do, and that's what happened when I took it out on the road.

I bought this device six months ago as a Christmas present for myself in one of my fits of mail-order purchasing. I am the most suspicious and sceptical of customers when faced by a flesh-and-blood salesperson in a shop, but somehow I am a sucker for anything presented in print, with a four-colour picture and lots of slogans with exclamation marks, which I can eagerly wait to have delivered through the post. This seemed a bargain I couldn't refuse. It looked so neat, and portable, and efficient, half the price of anything I'd seen in the racks outside our local cycle store, and also folding in half so that it could be carried, and tucked away each night, in the back of the car. I could even order it on my credit card by telephone, thus avoiding all the second thoughts involved in cheque-writing, stamp-finding and remembering not to lose the envelope in the porridgy mess of papers at the bottom of my shoulder-bag.

Even then, I left the transaction rather late, five days before Christmas, not telling anyone in the family in case they tried to dissuade me, and baffling them by my eagerness in the pre-holiday week to answer every knock at the front door and rush out on the pavement whenever a large van slowed down in the road. It seemed the best of omens when this huge box arrived for me to open on Christmas Day while everybody else was fiddling with their little presents.

As always with any mail-order goods, there are far more pieces to assemble than you can possibly imagine even in a dyspeptic anxiety-dream. So it wasn't until late afternoon that it stood gleaming and complete, the ideal big-city toy and yet also a perfect gadget to take along on a camping holiday. After years as a non-driver, with only my feet to carry me around town, I was independently mobile. I could already feel the thrill of holding my whole body motionless and seated while coasting along at absolutely no cost in energy, either mine or a machine's. It was the only way to travel—exclamation mark!

All that was needed was the final part, which pinned the two halves together, hidden somewhere at the bottom of the carton. The household waited, bored but indulgent, as for a child's first conjuring trick out of the Ali Bongo Magic Set. Also, as always with mail-order goods, the last essential piece was missing. The bike remained in the attic, a shameful item of jumble, as it might be an inflatable sex-doll with a leak, while I tried every shop that could have a replacement. But it seemed no one else in Britain possessed the simple German-made screw and nut I needed. After trying the obvious places, I was even reduced to being one of those odd, desperate, hermit figures you see in street-markets picking through mounds of metal on barrows. I wrote to the firm and around mid-January received the part. Now we were ready for the first trials, and I put the bike in the car outside the front door, ensuring the shortest distance between it and the open, already-calling road.

"Oh, my God! It's Clyde and Clyde!"

One February Sunday morning, all seemed set for the great launch, and I rose early, chose my costume with care, and went to release the iron horse. The hatch-back of the car had been smashed in during the night, and my Christmas treat was gone. The process began again, the insurance claim, the re-order, the wait—much longer this time—until in April the second big box arrived and the assemblage started—much quicker this time. You won't believe it. I don't believe it. But now a different, but equally vital, nut and bolt was missing. In a lather of manic misanthropy, I connected the parts with loops of wire, hurled the machine into the street and started to pedal the hundred yards to the pub. It was one of the most curious experiences I have ever had. As I moved along, I felt the seat gradually, even majestically, swing out and take up a position alongside the handle bars, so that I was travelling on two wheels, side by side, with my body turned at right angles.

Despite double-tightening every single knob on the entire skeleton, I couldn't bring myself to trust it for months. Then came the Tube strike, and people began dropping hints about wasted money, and useless lumber, and why didn't somebody whizz off to work and back, instead of spending a couple of hours each day trudging through the rain and then falling asleep, exhausted, in front of the television set. Last Sunday, I decided to take a short jaunt to a friend who knows so much about bikes that he won't ride one he hasn't made himself. It went well with just the gears jumping so that even down-hill it was like pedalling through glue. "It's a load of old rubbish," he said cheerfully, but he generously oiled and checked it while I held his cigarette, patted me on the saddle and sent me away.

As I turned to wave, not too shakily I fancied, in the middle of the cross-roads, I had the next most disturbing experience of my cycling career. Just when four cars chose to converge on me from opposing directions, I found I was spinning the pedals in free-fall, yet without moving, as the chain links popped and spat all over the ground.

The chain is fixed and I have been cycling in and out of central London but I cannot summon up that easy, cheerful confidence displayed by all the old ladies and young boys who go scorching past me. I don't like having anything with an engine in its nose behind me, but so long as I stick to the cycle-lane (i.e. inside the yellow line along the gutter) I manage to move fleetly, and so far unharmed, around town.

I have even learned some useful tips. As a cyclist, your main enemy is not the car, or the lorry, or even the bus—though when that great red wall slides ever closer across your path, like a Cunarder pushing aside a row-boat, the heart stops. You are competing against other two-wheelers, especially scooters and small motorbikes, which are aiming for the same gap between vehicles as you are. There is, of course, the car driver who opens his door into the road, slamming a metal barricade in your path at split-second's notice, or the other one who edges out of a side-road, looking straight through you, forcing you into the crowded centre. But worst of all, perhaps because during the strike there were so many of them, was the number of pedestrians who were always stealing your gutter.

I've steeled myself, though after half an hour of thigh muscles inflating and throbbing it doesn't take much self-restraint, not to be competitive. The only time I speed up and follow someone else on a bike is when she is a pretty girl. This is nothing to do with my interest in her, but the general rule that road-users ignore all cyclists, except pretty girls. And if you keep in her wake, you can win a clear path better than following an ambulance or a police car.

Leo Cullum **Dog Days**

"They say this neighbourhood is full of dog thieves."

Leo Cullum

Bad Odour

If you were thinking of visiting the chamber of the House of Commons, you can't. The workmen are in, working on "the smell". Somehow, over the years and especially since our part of the Palace of Westminster was bombed and then rebuilt, the air conditioning inhales the output of the kitchen extractors and there are times when the strongest sensation in the House is the aroma of the fumes that hovered over the chip-pan. Members have raised it on points of order . . . and the Speaker has steadily expressed interest and promised that he would bring it to the attention of the officers of the House responsible for that sort of thing—the implication being that it was one of the few things beyond Mr Speaker's remit.

It is odd that the smell of cooking should worry a political speaker; the vast majority of speeches are actually made at dinners when the smell of this or that lingers pungently in the orators' nostrils. I used to play cricket on Mitcham Green (the only cricket pitch I know on which you can score a duck and be run over by a bus on the way back to the pavilion) and when the wind was in a certain direction, the smell of vanilla was quite overpowering. It never seemed to affect one's performance. Over the Bank Holiday weekend we had a pop concert in a marquee that smelt as if it had come straight from a pig-show . . . yet the music sounded pretty good to most of us.

Why, then, should politicians feel that the gentle smell of bacon or kippers is untoward at Westminster? Why should the country's money be spent on trying to eradicate it? Speaking as the sixth most senior Member to have sat continuously on the side of the duct (it is situated halfway along the Opposition Benches) I shall be saddened to have only the odours of the Great Unwashed to distract me . . . but while I hold no great brief for second-hand smells (like those regurgitated by filters and fans) there *is* something marvellously comforting about having the right smell with the right occasion. In Upper Regent Street there was a coffee-shop from which came so delectable an aroma of burning coffee beans that I took to burning a coffee bean or two under the grill as I served Nescafé to my dinner guests at home. They never failed to enthuse.

When the meal you are about to serve is likely to be a humdrum affair, you can cheer your guests immeasurably by putting on a low flame a pan containing a little butter and a squeeze of lemon juice. "I am really looking forward to dinner," they say, and when the tunnyfish salad dressed with Hellmann's arrives, they have spent so much time anticipating joyously that a few moments of pedestrian food is not going to mar the evening's pleasure greatly.

Garlic and black treacle is another good smell to waft at people; a couple of cloves pressed into a tablespoon of treacle in a cake tin, left in the top of a slightly opened hot oven, will make people nod knowledgeably: "I think I can guess what *we* are getting."

Countries have smells, the way in England districts used to have smells until fungicides and insecticides and bees working to rule put an end to all that. There were hospitals that smelled of TCP and others that were pure carbolic; villages were redolent of the perfume of wild garlic, towns belched flavoured smoke. While the French still manage to combine garlic, Gauloise, sweat and aniseed to give a national flavour that has real identity, the UK smell of the 1980s is impersonally clean. In Greece there is the smell of oil and pungent herbs, in Morocco the musky smell of the stuff they spray on to old goat meat to make it seem slightly less old goat.

In India and Pakistan they make curry in the open, crushing garlic and turmeric and chilli peppers for all to smell, even if only a few get to eat. In Mexico rancid fat, spiced sausages and hot peppers go with the sweaty salty metropolitan smell of tequila. Turkey smells of sour cream cheese—none of which odours has, as far as I know, caused parliamentarians of those lands to raise points of order. Yet at Westminster we get a whiff of burnt toast, or a waft of sizzling bacon and the Public Service Agency is summoned to prepare plans in triplicate. Let us hope, at least, that it brings some much needed employment.

Smells are really a very under-rated social weapon, for just as they can make your guests salivate with the expectation of delicacies to come, so can they be used to make them go racing down the drive, leaving you with nothing that will not go away after opening the windows for a few minutes, and time to watch *News at Ten* in peace and quiet. Fish-based cat food thinly spread on the radiator clears a party in a remarkably short time; and hardly smells at all until you switch the thing on, which you can do by remote control.

If this week's offering has been less than very constructive to my readers, I shall state that a very fast and delicious and good-smelling pudding is produced by melting one ounce of butter, one ounce of sugar and one teaspoonful of lemon juice in a frying pan; stir well and when it becomes tacky, fry in it a slice of white bread. Turn after a few moments, fry the other side and when mahogany coloured, serve on a plate lightly dredged with caster sugar and have a jug of raspberry syrup standing by.

Michael Bywater

Finger-tappin' Good

I used to be a writer; now, I organise text at document level. I am interfacing with the future. Excuse me, please, a weisenheimer I am not; it's merely that this mid-Atlantic stuff is kind of, um, appropriate; though you might postulate otherwise. "We're in an asymptotic approach configuration right now, homing in," you might say; "any moment in time, we'll be entrant on a stable facilities modality with the boys in Silicon Valley"; that makes mid-Atlantic, oh, five years out of date; linguistically, I should by now be somewhere about 500 miles west of the Isle of Wight and getting closer, but I have this conceptual difficulty with the glottals. OK? *Right.*

Here's a clue: Len Deighton has been photographed doing it; Jeffrey Archer gets a girl to do it for him, Anthony Holden wrote about doing it with Charles, Bel Mooney doesn't approve of it and thinks it's sapping our strength, and I'm actually doing it while I'm writing this.

With me yet? This is technology I'm talking about, micro-computing, *word processing*. I'm sitting here deploying 128 kbytes of memory through a 16-bit bidirectional data bus, I've got an INTEL 8086 microprocessor and related support components microprocessing and supporting away, and I'm *still* not getting through?

Let's start again, at the beginning. Imagine me in my study (book-lined, shabby, redolent of manly pipe-smoke and Biro-sharpenings) several Sundays ago. On the ancient typewriter is propped a copy of the *Sunday Times*. In my hand is a fluorescent yellow Geha marker, with which I am striking out passages of which I disapprove. So far most of the paper is looking pretty jaundiced. My eye lights on an advertisement placed by something called Information Technology Awareness Programme—four words which, singly, produce a brassy sort of impotent buzzing in the brain of any civilised Briton, and which could only be yoked together by some aerated bunch of government-sponsored cakebrains—a surmise which turns out to be bang-on.

"Is the technology in the Dog and Duck more advanced than in your Factory?" they demand, which shows what they think of us. I can't answer; firstly, I don't work in a factory; and, secondly, I don't know where the Dog and Duck is. (Will the Old Eagle do? In which case, the technology seems fine to me; it can suck up a pint of stout from the cellar and squirt into your glass, and until they invent digital Guinness I can't see what more is required of it.) "In case you haven't noticed," it continues, "we're in the middle of the most fascinating revolution of all time." Note the offensive tone of patronising over-familiarity half-masking a logical absurdity. "Of all time" my foot. How do they know? And, more to the point, what do they want?

They want us to buy micro-computers. Oh, I see. It's not good enough to write memoranda down in little books, to carry them in your head; these people want us to surround ourselves with interfaces and modems and Winchester technology and horrid humming machines. They're ashamed to be analogue. They must be the same lot that put out advertisements telling us to clean our teeth and wash our bottoms. Out with the yellow marker. The paper is beginning to look like a bad day in King's College Hospital Liver Failure Unit.

Two or three pages further on comes an advertisement for Olivetti word processors. My Geha hovers over the page. I know about word processors. You type stuff in and it comes up on a screen; then you shove it around until you're happy with it, and then you press a little button and it prints it out for you. A mug's game. I'd come across them, once, when an appalling shyster had employed me to act as his Corporate Communications Executive. He was a frightful parvenu gumbo *fedornik* in a Gucci jock, and my job consisted of churning out, on the word processor, a series of boastful vainglorious Press Releases which were Personalised according to the Journalist who was destined to Throw Them Away.

But this advertisement is different. There's a picture of Len Deighton, in *his* book-lined study—and there, on his desk, is a word processor, Take A Tip From People Who Write For A Living. Now Len Deighton knows a thing or two. He's richer than I am. Am I wrong about these machines . . . ?

I spent the rest of that Sunday brooding, and first thing Monday morning I got on the telephone to Olivetti. "I want to be like Len Deighton," I murmured. "I want to borrow a thing." "An ET?" said the public relations girl. Visions of a friendly green Extra-Terrestrial sitting on my desk flashed briefly through my mind. "Not as such," I said. "I was thinking more of a word processor." "That's what the machine is called," she explained gently, "an ETS 1010. I'm sure we can help you."

Next day saw me in downtown Putney. The Olivetti Building was all marble and leather sofas, the kind you sink into and feel small, and then these svelte dames behind the desk look down at you. Somewhere, something was humming. It wasn't me.

What it was, in fact, was a roomful of ETs. They looked a lot less cosy than on Len's desk. A systems expert was waiting for me, and what that means is that she not only knew what the machines could do, but how they did it. "Insert Boot," it said on the TV-style monitor screen. Did they have a large skinhead market for word processors? No. What that meant was: Put in the Mini-Floppy-Diskette (They're the size of an old 45! They hold 200 pages of typing!) which enables the machine to get going by pulling itself up by the *Boot*straps, geddit? Colourful turn of imagery these people have; but already I was feeling less intimidated. "They're very user-friendly," said the systems woman in an American accent. "I'm sorry about the American accent," she then said in a normal English one, "but how else do you say some-

"Yesterday he kicked sand in my face, today he blew his nose on my handkerchief."

thing like 'user-friendly'?" How indeed? And they *were* friendly; the machine spells out what to do in a sunbaked, all-the-time-in-the-world, hang-loose, Californian tone, and after the end of two hours I could do all sorts of things.

A few days later, they delivered one for me to work out on In The Privacy Of My Own Home. It looked a bit odd sitting on my desk, but I soon got used to it. I don't want to brag, but me and ET, we've got a great relationship going. It sits there, quiescent, humming with latent power. Not only can I muck around with articles like this until I've got them how I want them; I can send a long and apologetic letter to my bank manager as often as need be (say once a week) merely by assembling a few pre-written modular grovels; I can send begging letters to editors, ditto; I can find things in its electronic insides merely by typing in a couple of key words; I can save all the bits the Features Editor makes me cut out and glue them electronically together to Make A Whole New Article From Common Household Scraps.

Mind you, you need self-control; last week I spent over an hour mucking about with a television script, watching the machine SRCH for a character called Hector Campbell and RPLC him with Fulminating Extravasated Jejunum and then Sir Hoadly Groark-Groark-Bulldozer until people came up to find out why I, alone in my room at eleven at night, was giggling hysterically to myself. Good fun, and also useful if, for example, you're a solicitor burdened with the sort of crotchety client who's always ringing up to disinherit the Hon. Algernon and substitute her faithful companion Miss Mavis Niblet; a quick prod of the button and Algie's snookered, the client's happy, and you don't have to mention on the bill that it only took thirty seconds.

But the most interesting thing is the way ET has solved the Blank Sheet Of Paper Dilemma which afflicts all writers. The machine imparts a subtle insubstantial quality to the words which means that one can just launch straight in and to hell with the consequences. On the old, macho, Hemingway-style Remington Noiseless, once you'd typed something it was there for ever, no possibility of alteration except after a hefty plying of the Tipp-Ex brush, and even then it was still underneath, retrievable with a razor blade and patience; which was why one spent hours smoking and "thinking" and arsing around, not daring to commit oneself.

Not so on ET, one prod on DEL and it's gone for ever, never to r

See what I mean? It's the modern equivalent of "Once upon a time," gets you past the hard bit and into the main stream. So now I start right in each morning, save a lot of time and a lot of coffee, and Earn More Money, not as much as Len Deighton (yet) but enough so that when Olivetti rang up and said, "Please can we have our machine back now?" I replied, "The hell you can, this machine stays put, send round a man and I'll sign up on the spot."

I have, however, one serious criticism. When one does something particularly crass, the machine, like an irascible park-keeper, snarls from the screen CAN'T DO THAT HERE and *beeps* at one in a peremptory and mechanistic fashion. Surely technology is now capable of reproducing, instead, a discreet subservient cough, like a well-trained butler? Ask Len; I'll bet he agrees with me.

"My relaxation at weekends is a regional accent."

"Miss Gardner, tell the staff they can come in quietly, one at a time, and have a look at my Christmas tree."

ANY ANSWERS?
The replies to the programme you never heard

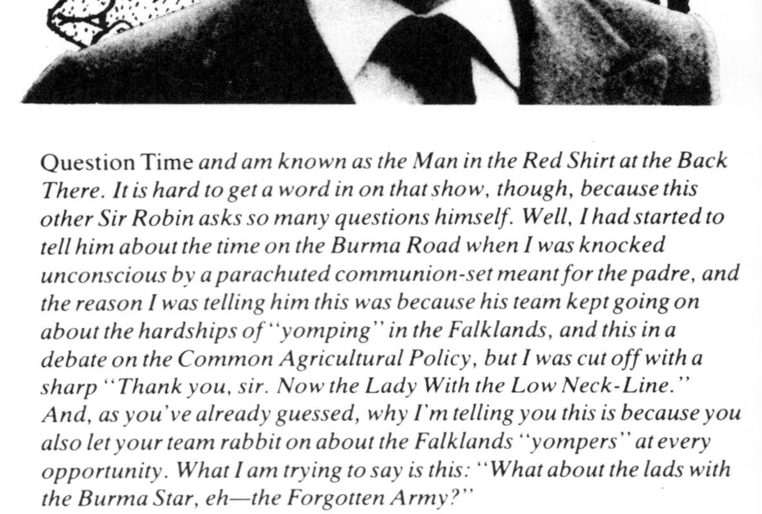

Presenter: Most of you will have missed the last broadcast of *Any Questions?* from the nuclear-free village of Little Clavering. For technical reasons this was heard only by a handful of listeners before it went off the air completely. There were, however, enough letters to *Any Answers?* to enable you to guess what the questions were.

We can hardly do better than start with a comment from Barry Treadwater, of Neck's End:

Dear David Jacobs, I thought the balance of the team was, as always, just right, that is to say, three articulate radicals and one bent Tory left-winger at odds with his party. What a pity the middle-class morons who packed the audience hissed and booed every tentative forecast of insurrection and action in the streets! How anyone could feel menaced by talk of tumbrils and paraquat cannon from a slightly over-wrought polytechnic lecturer is beyond my comprehension. Where does the BBC recruit these audiences—from the National Front and the Home Counties SS? These people ought to be setting up their own revolution-free zone somewhere. No wonder the BBC technicians, incensed by the attitude of the audience, decided to pull out the plugs, which I assume is what happened. Three cheers for democracy!

That was not quite how Peregrine Whitebait saw it:

Dear David Jacobs, Three voluble tub-thumping rascals and one superannuated reactionary! No wonder the loyal audience pulled the plugs out. Here in Harrogate they were dancing in the streets and my own staff handed out free drinks at the tradesmen's entrance. PS. Be sure to have this read by someone with an upper-class neigh.

Well, we obliged, didn't we? But other listeners were puzzled to know what happened in the British Legion Hut at Little Clavering that night:

Dear David, I have been a faithful listener to the BBC since the "ether", as we called it, was infested with "uncles", as we called them. May I say I have always admired the brilliant way in which you change the subject whenever the speakers show signs of becoming relevant or controversial. I expect you will be cutting me off any moment, ha! ha! Anyway I was very pleased when you ended that discussion on the importance of maintaining indiscipline in the Boy Scouts so that the team could discuss whether they would let their daughters marry a doe-eyed "ugly" from Outer Space. I thought the snippy-snappy young woman from the National Council for Taking Liberties, whatever her name is, the one who is always on your programme, was very wrong to denounce this as a frivolous topic unsuited to a non-nuclear zone and her offhand remarks about "uglies" seemed to me not only racist and sexist but speciesist and spacist as well. I like to think it was an Extra-Terrestrial Influence which eventually put an end to the broadcast.—Marcus Aurelius Jones, of Stopcock Common.

And here, for a change, is the sort of letter we often get from listeners like Herbert Merryfeather, of Batley Bridge:

Dear David, How your programme loves to ignore the ruling topics of the day! The other night your team actually got round to discussing rape, but it seems they thought rape was some sort of oil-producing turnip. Is this what I pay my licence for?

Well, if people *will* tune in to *Gardeners' Question Time* . . . Somebody else who likes to watch a rival programme writes as follows:

Dear Sir Robin Jacobs, I frequently appear in the audience of BBC1's Question Time *and am known as the Man in the Red Shirt at the Back There. It is hard to get a word in on that show, though, because this other Sir Robin asks so many questions himself. Well, I had started to tell him about the time on the Burma Road when I was knocked unconscious by a parachuted communion-set meant for the padre, and the reason I was telling him this was because his team kept going on about the hardships of "yomping" in the Falklands, and this in a debate on the Common Agricultural Policy, but I was cut off with a sharp "Thank you, sir. Now the Lady With the Low Neck-Line." And, as you've already guessed, why I'm telling you this is because you also let your team rabbit on about the Falklands "yompers" at every opportunity. What I am trying to say is this: "What about the lads with the Burma Star, eh—the Forgotten Army?"*

Well, the Man in the Red Shirt at the Back There has made his point. Now, as the festive season is a time for nostalgia, let us hear from Albert Wagshaw, of Hove, who is cross because the *Any Questions?* team seemed to be sneering at the 1930s:

Dear David, I can assure your team that the 1930s were far from being a decade of misery. Why, there was one magic year when toilet rolls had a joke on every sheet. Surely Lord Soper can remember that, even if Paul Foot can't? Let us again show the world what our manufacturers are capable of!—Harry Loam, of Sadbreth.

And the memory of Alice Springs, of Rye, goes still further back:

Dear Mr Jacobs, The reference in the discussion on defence spending to "twelve inches of cold steel" reminded me of the days when every woman carried a unilateral deterent of her own—a twelve-inch hat-pin. We didn't hear much about rape then.

I knew we should get back to rape. Finally the BBC wishes to apologise to Horace Warblefly, of Kelton Hall, whose set of fine Venetian wine-glasses shattered during an animated discussion of Mr Heseltine's policies by two lady panellists on this programme on September 1. Mr Heseltine asks to be joined in this apology.
And *Any Questions?* also apologises to its favourite panellist Arthur Scargill for using the phrase "vanished like Arthur Scargill up the M1". This should have read "vanished like a scalded cat".

Another One Along in a Minute

SEPTEMBER 1

Ms Clewhumble, being liberated, wishes to give birth under water.

I say in surgery, Fine, if you're a mermaid. She says, But doctor, birth in water relaxed and beautiful, has seen photos in papers of joyful mothers and babies awash. I personally do not care if Ms Clewhumble has her little one in deep end of municipal baths, or while performing transcendental meditation or free-fall parachuting. Am becoming exasperated at women who read smart articles in the Sundays and demand give birth in trendy positions like all fours, standing up, or as Chinese peasant squatting in paddy-field.

She says, Surely baby get oxygen through umbilical cord like North Sea diver? I say, Yes, but must land pretty smartish, and newborn baby slippery little thing, might lose it like soap in bath. Why make maternity branch of aqua-sports? Assure her tenderest care under Mr Bertram Taverill FRCOG available free at Churchford General, she says, *No thank you!* Had two there, they put you in stranded beetle position and use drugs to make a 9-to-5 job of it for doctors' convenience, every morning fire all mothers off like barrage of guns.

Ms Clewhumble big comprehensive schoolmistress, seven months gone, founder member SDP, feminist always kicking against the pricks. She says, At General, treat me as suffering from a disease called pregnancy, why cannot I enjoy natural childbirth in own home? I say, Giving birth not domestic duty as cooking Sunday roast, natural childbirth like natural appendicitis, needs expert attention. Believe me, doctors have same caring feelings towards labouring mothers as lifeboat men to shipwrecked mariners, will similarly spare no effort to bring them through harrowing experience. But obviously must use efficient lifeboat, latest safety gadgets, expect floundering sailors to obey megaphoned instructions for own good. See?

Unimpressed, says male obstetricians simply feel threatened at losing birthing process, will take it up with Birth Right (headquarters Islington).

Reflect to Sandra (wife) natural childbirth only retrospective, when all goes as smoothly as hen laying egg. She says nervously, Hope patient won't upset Bertram, remember he's lending us his villa in Cannes (all obstetricians rich), so superior to your rotten old Costas.

SEPTEMBER 6

Mr Clewhumble (bubble-haired, runs garden centre) at morning surgery announces will deliver infant at home himself. Exclaim, Will really open tin of wasps! He says, If giving birth not a family matter, what is? We are serene, caring couple, people were having babies long before doctors were invented, anyway the gypsies do it. I say, Well, I cannot stop a man delivering his wife's child any more than cutting her corns. Also remember to order Gro-bags for the greenhouse.

SEPTEMBER 10

Mrs Bryanston-Hicks, queen bee midwife, seems six foot tall, tits the size of goldfish bowls, enough to make any newborn baby bolt back to its burrow, slaps on my consulting-desk morning's *Churchford Echo*. Front page full of Mr Clewhumble defying the General by doing own thing with own baby, encouraged by Dr Gordon, traditional GP full of loving care. Appalled, try explaining *Echo* no more reliable than *Pravda*, Mrs Bryanston-Hicks going to prosecute Mr Clewhumble under Midwives Act (1951), cannot allow whole country have babies wherever they please making mockery of midwives, is prosecuting me as accessory before the fact.

Bertie Taverill leaves (from Rolls) at teatime pained letter, saying surprised letting myself liable to hauling before GMC on four counts—advertising, inciting lawbreaking, denigrating fellow-practitioners, associating with unqualified midwives—assumes am seeking martyrdom. Adds, as the knocked fellow-doctor, old fellow-student, neighbour always furthering my professional interests, social life and family happiness, hopes GMC take lenient view, though cannot see how they avoid instant striking-off for life.

Ashen-faced, trembling-handed, pass to Sandra over teacup, who cries Oh, God! I cry, What do? She says, Well, I suppose try Rentavilla for something in dreary old Spain. I shout, Trivia, trivia! When my career, livelihood, honour imperilled. She says, not at all trivial, all my friends know we're going to Cannes and are dead envious, though would admit in preference adultery with milkman. I slam down cup, bite ginger-nut. Break tooth, shall have to go to bloody dentist as well.

SEPTEMBER 11

Anxiously shuffle morning post, nothing from GMC. Indignantly phone Ms Clewhumble, who says just off to Saturday morning demo outside General for Birth Right, coaches hired from Manchester, Birmingham and York. Afternoon in greenhouse can hardly keep mind on disbudding chrysanthemums, when Sandra shouts phone call. Is Bertram, saying Ms Clewhumble and little boy fine, Mr Clewhumble delighted. Say, ??. He says, She went into labour making impassioned speech outside, pity GPs don't help us by getting their patients' dates right, ha ha, hope you enjoy the villa, have just installed a jacuzzi. Tell Sandra, who says, Pity, had just arranged with that diplomatic couple to rent their house in San Francisco, much more fun. Thumbscrewed between private and professional life, cruel torture for doctors.

Jam Yesterday

I didn't become a Londoner until quite late in life. Living down the road at Windsor, there were frequent excursions up to Town—visiting relatives, seeing shows (every Christmas holidays from the mid-Thirties on it was Leslie Henson, Fred Emney and Richard Hearne in some new romp) and attending school functions and outings. There was the annual Eton and Harrow match at Lords from which, in case you haven't heard, I played truant to buy my first trumpet. And, although it doesn't really count as a metropolitan jaunt, there was a memorable trip, with other senior boys, to Croydon Airport to watch Neville Chamberlain waving his piece of paper. In the car back to Eton, our housemaster, in a burst of wishful-thinking rather than optimism, said, "This means there'll be no war in your lifetime." A year later, we were in it up to our armpits.

So it was as a newly-demobbed twenty-five-year-old that I first took up residence in London. I started off rooming with another ex-Grenadier in his mother's house somewhere off the Buckingham Palace Road, but it soon transpired that we were not on the same wavelength. To underline the point, it was about 30 years before I saw him again, when he popped up on the television as a deputy chairman of the Conservative Party Conference. So I moved into a bed-sitter in a rooming-house run by a gay couple in Smith Street, Chelsea. (I was studying at Camberwell Art School then, and Chelsea was suitably arty, though somewhat far-flung.)

After a sheltered life on the borders of Bucks and Berks, and despite six years in the army, my awareness of homosexuality was confined to the rather hearty goings-on embodied in public school gossip. I spent the winter of 1947—allegedly the coldest since the century began—huddled in an overcoat in my top floor room, deterred by all the giggling and romping behind the landlords' door from asking how the meter worked.

To anyone who knows the King's Road today, with its boutiques opening and closing like nervous eyelids and every Saturday looking like the annual conference of the Last of the Mohicans, it may seem odd that my abiding memory was of the quietness. The dead of night in Smith Street was punctuated by sudden sounds from afar—a brawl at World's End, squabbling cats in Sloane Square. Once I was woken by the sound of female weeping and the crescendo and diminuendo of a voice repeating, "David . . . oh, David," in tones of deep tragedy. It was probably just an overwrought deb tottering home brainless after a flop party, but to my active imagination she was heading, Ophelia-like, for the river.

After Chelsea, I moved to Hampstead (where else?) and a bed-sitter in the Vale of Health, that little enclave of houses and pubs sunk into the middle of Hampstead Heath. I found it spooky, and still do. Returning from a gig or a party late at night, one had literally to wade into the nocturnal mist rising from the Hampstead ponds. The mere appearance out of the gloom of another human being would cause an explosion of adrenalin.

And here's a funny thing, as Max Miller used to say. Haunting the Heath at that time was the rotund, shambling and perpetually soliloquising figure of a local down-and-out. Though seemingly tuppence short of a shilling, to use an old phrase and an old coin, he was quite harmless, but I always hoped to make home base before he loomed out of the darkness. After I married (twice, in fairly rapid succession) and settled in Belsize Park through the Fifties, his daily peregrinations would often take him past our window. Then, in 1959, we migrated northwards to Barnet. Ten minutes from us, in Mill Hill on the route into London, there's a Roman Catholic institution of some sort which provides shelter for what used to be called tramps. We hadn't been here six months before he turned up in the area, and I still see him, now snow-capped and puce, trundling self-absorbed around the local lanes. For 35 years now he has hovered, in a disturbing, Pinteresque fashion, on the fringes of my life.

"I've been dropped!"

In my art school days I made no secret of mildly anarchist leanings, and the thought has more than once passed through my mind that I may have been under surveillance all this time by a supernaturally patient undercover man from MI5. A more sensible observation would be that, for all its eight million population and sprawling acreage, London is to long-term residents no more than a village. Buildings and environs may change, but the *dramatis personae* of one's life remain peculiarly constant.

That profoundly philosophical thought leads me to another. The pent-up horrors which used to assail me when I walked alone at night across Hampstead Heath were no more than an extension of a childish fear of the dark. Mugging was then many years from becoming established as a national sport, and so far as I recall, the upper, NW3 reaches of Hampstead Heath did not represent Teddy Boy country. Experiences elsewhere in London prompt me to denounce as rubbish the often-heard assertion that the London of 30 years ago was a much safer and less violent place.

Most of my early memories of London involve mayhem of some kind. The Nuthouse, a subterranean club in Regent's Street where I served my jazz apprenticeship sitting in with Carlo Krahmer's band, boasted a clientèle split evenly between the London underworld and the US armed forces, a mixture that guaranteed a fight most nights. The Yanks used furniture and fists, the gangs razors, which was messier. Either way, the band followed the golden rule for survival, which was to keep playing at all costs. One night we flogged *Who's Sorry Now* for 45 minutes while the blood flowed. One of the first venues at which my band played regularly was a building in Windmill Street called Mac's Rehearsal Rooms. If Mac, the owner, was not a petty gangster, he certainly did his best to look like one, with his rimless glasses and flinty, restless look. There were occasional scuffles during our sessions for the London Jazz Club, which rented a big room at street level. But most of the action took place outside. Piccadilly Circus teemed with prostitutes, and if it wasn't the pimps fighting it was the girls themselves, an altogether more formidable sight.

Once, when a party of us were relaxing in a café next door after a session, a cat fight started up at the far end of the narrow room. The late John Cooper, then sports editor of *Autocar* and a man of peace and sweet reasonableness, decided to intervene. As he stepped between the two enraged ladies, making papal gestures of peace and reconciliation, a third woman stood up behind him and, raising a chair aloft, took aim at the back of his head. For a moment the action froze in a menacing tableau and then John turned away and returned to us with his usual unhurried step, quite unaware that the chair which splintered itself against a table a second or two later had been designated for him.

It was from this same café, on another occasion, that Trog, in his role of Wally Fawkes the great jazz clarinettist, emerged one night almost into the arms of a team of "heavies" lined up outside the door. One of them moved towards him saying, "Is dis der geezer?" In the nick of time someone put his head out and confirmed that the geezer was still inside, awaiting whatever retribution he had incurred. Today, the nocturnal hubbub that surrounded Mac's Rehearsal Rooms has been replaced by the monastic tranquillity of the porno cinema.

What, some unsuspected maiden aunt out in the shires might say on reading this, were we doing frequenting such rough places? The answer, in a couple of words, is "eating cheaply". Students and jazz musicians (and I was both simultaneously) were as penurious then as they are today. The difference is that, until Terence Conran came along with his soup kitchens, offering cheap and wholesome fare in what we used to call "contemporary" surroundings, no self-respecting catering entrepreneur bothered with the bottom end of the market. To the Londoner, Wimpy and his hamburgers existed only in Popeye cartoons, "pizza" referred to an Italian city famous for its leaning tower and McDonald was still a Scottish clansman on his farm.

Out in Camberwell during the working day we used to eat at Charley's, a caff run, as many of them were, by a Greek-Cypriot family. There was nothing ethnic about the food—mostly, we ate heated-up meat pie with chips and peas which, with a mug of tea thrown in, set us back one-and-ninepence. In today's joke money, that's about 8p. If we couldn't run to that (my annual grant for board and keep was £163), there was a place round the back of the Art School that did tea and rolls. The owner made up the rolls with the use of a forefinger perpetually swathed in old bandage. We used to order cheese and ptomaine rolls, please, but he assumed we meant tomato and prodded away without concern.

In Central London, things were much the same. A favourite after-hours place for musicians—and without late buses, Tubes or private transport, after-hours meant about 11 p.m.—was The Rex in, I think, New Compton Street. This was another family affair run by Greeks, and again, the only notably Mediterranean aspect was the Turkish coffee, to which I took a shine in those days. A vast lady with a grey bun, carpet-slippers and a consoling bosom used to brew the wasteful mud in little copper jugs in the back room, while we held an earnest post-mortem on the night's music in the front. London closed down incredibly early then. At 100 Oxford Street, in the hired basement restaurant where I had the Humphrey Lyttelton Club during the Fifties, a toothless member of the Corps of Commissionaires used to bellow, "Ain't you got no 'omes to go to?" so hot on the heels of *Get Out Of Here And Go On Home* that many of our customers must have thought it was part of the tune. But there was always somewhere you could go afterwards to lie about chewing the fat (literally) over cheap and usually nasty food.

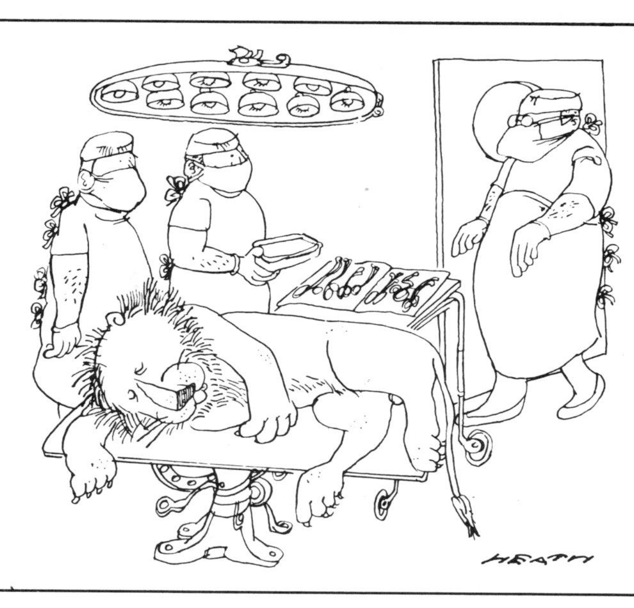

"It's Doctor Androcles. He's a thorn in the foot man."

Of course, when one starts comparing prices over the decades, one surrenders oneself to the mysteries of higher economics. I have never understood about inflation. If prices, wages and the rest go up together so as to remain proportionately the same, wouldn't it be a fairly simple matter to arrange for them just to stay put? In 1937, the food columnist of the *Daily Telegraph*, Bon Viveur, wrote of Kettner's in Soho ". . . The restaurant acquired a good name for excellent food in quiet surroundings. Some years ago it shattered this reputation by going in for music and cabaret and Heaven knows what. Now the quiet surroundings have come back again and, better still, the prices have been reduced. Lunch is at 4/6 and dinner at 7/6. It is not cheap yet, certainly, but the food is first class." In 1968, the *Good Food Guide* quoted Kettner's at 25/- for table-d'hôte lunch—that's £1.25 in today's money. By that standard, dinner would have been about £2. The *Guide* commented that this was reasonable for the West End, but not cheap. Just lately, Kettner's was taken over by Peter Boizot of the Pizza Express chain, and once again they go in for music and cabaret and Heaven knows what. (The American guitarist and surrealist singer Slim Gaillard was there a week or two back.) Serving what Peter Boizot calls "haute cuisine populaire"—that's steaks, pizzas and so on—at around £8 a head for a full meal, Kettner's can now claim to be cheap by 1982 West End standards but no longer first class French. Perhaps that's just as well since Le Gavroche, the modern equivalent of the old, chef-founded Kettner's of the Thirties, is today quoted in the *Good Food Guide* at £28 for a table-d'hôte meal. From 7/6—call it 37p—to £28 in 45 years is an impressive leap. My pocket calculator tells me that by AD 2001, when I'm an octogenarian on a dwindling pension, even meat pie, peas and chips at the equivalent of Charley's will cost around £8. And I'll be down at the Roman Catholic place hobnobbing about the good old days with my chum from Hampstead Heath.

"He was leaning on a lamp-post at the corner of the street until a certain little lady passed by."

BAYEUX REVEALED

It's easy to see why the row about cleaning the tapestry remains unresolved. There could be almost anything underneath the muck

Much publicity has attended the imminent appearance in Britain of the Reader's Digest condensed Bible. But nobody has said anything yet about the marketing of it . . .

MIRACULOUS INTRO-DUCTORY OFFER!

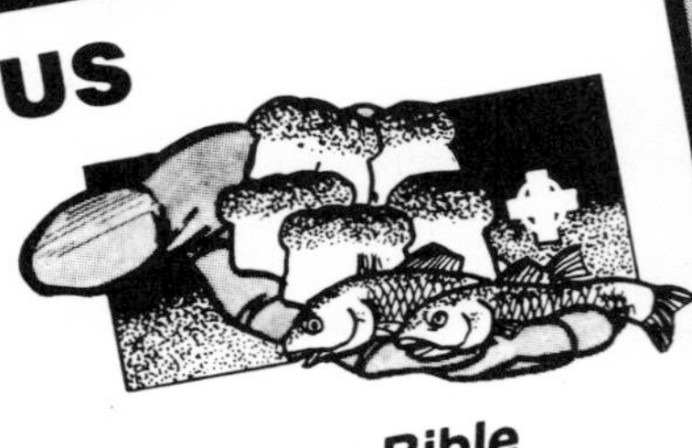

Open to purchasers of the new Bible ONLY!

BUY FIVE LOAVES AND GET TWO FISHES ABSOLUTELY FREE!!!

Hard to believe? It's true! When you have finished admiring your superb machine-crafted RD Bible, simply turn to Mark 6, xxxviii, tear it out, fill in the coupon on the back, and mail it to us in the handy Freepost envelope provided on Jeremiah 15, and we will send you five (5) elegant matching loaves (Large Tin, Small Tin, Family Sliced, Rye, and Wholemeal) for only £2.95 the set, PLUS two (2) handsome fishes **ABSOLUTELY FREE!**

These fishes (choose from cod/skate/hake/brill) could cost up to £4 the pair in your local fishmonger's. Each fish has a smart head and tail and is finished in elegant silver-look scales. As your family and friends tuck into these magnificent items, they will be amazed at your faith!

Allow 28 days for delivery.

Introduce a friend to Jesus, get a wine-making kit for yourself, FREE

2,000 years ago, it wasn't easy to spread the Gospel: disciples had to battle against everything from primitive advertising techniques to getting beaten up (or worse) by potential customers. Even the boss had ascended to Heaven before the campaign itself was properly off the ground!

We Christians have learned a lot since then. Today, YOU can convert the person of your choice simply by sending us his/her name and address on the form provided on the back of the Lazarus Discount Health Insurance leaflet gummed to the Sunsoaked Vatican Holiday For Two Offer facing *The Acts of the Apostles* in your terrific new RD Bible. He/she will then receive his/her very own Bible and permission to feel its rich texture in the privacy of his/her own home for seven days ABSOLUTELY WITHOUT OBLIGATION, and *you* will receive from us the amazing Cana Winemaking Kit, consisting of three handsome bottles, individually labelled Red, White and Rosé, three litres of high-quality water, and a prayer available to RD Bible-owners ONLY! Say it right (instructions provided) and within minutes you and your family could be settling down to an evening of drinking that could cost £££'s in any public house!

Introduce TWO new converts, and we will send you, COMPLETELY FREE, a handsome folding bed you can actually take up and walk with!

SUFFER LITTLE CHILDREN

Parents:

Like Jesus, we at Reader's Digest believe in getting kids interested in the good things of life at an early age! So to all purchasers of the wonderful new RD Bible, we are offering the golden opportunity of receiving a second Bible, at an enormous discount, to give to the child of their choice.

This will arrive as part of a terrific Bratpak containing not only a Bible, but also the fully-illustrated **Plaguespotter's Handbook,** ***a handy stick which turns into Wriggly Snake at the touch of a concealed button*** **(batteries not included),** ***a cut-out-'n'-float ark in laminated digesterene, and a miniature John the Baptist whose head comes off to reveal a valuable pencil-sharpener.***

AND REMEMBER—introduce *two* children to the kingdom of God, and we will mail you, via the Automobile Association, an exclusive set of Apostle Feeler Gauges COMPLETELY FREE!

My Part in the Cuba Crisis

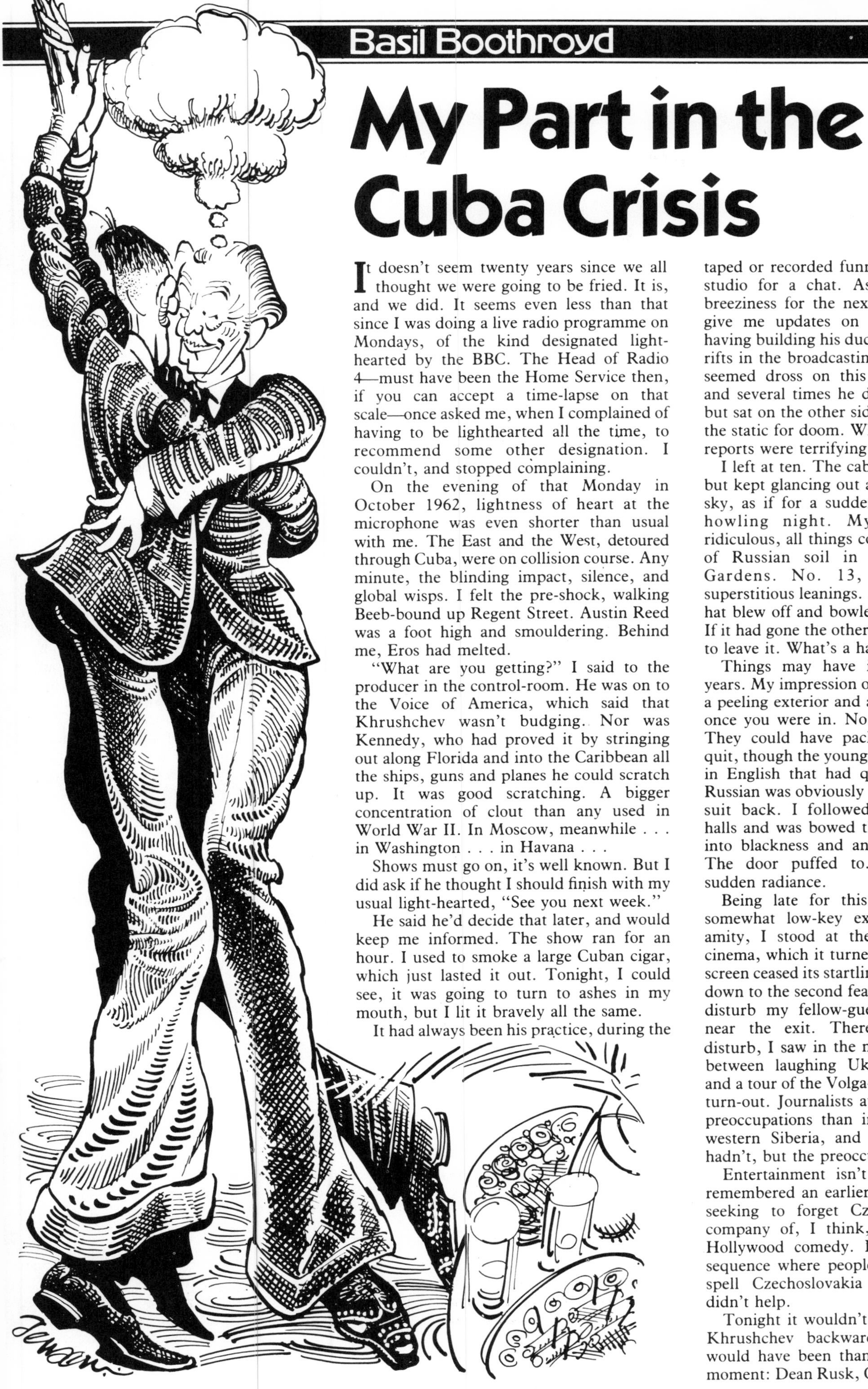

It doesn't seem twenty years since we all thought we were going to be fried. It is, and we did. It seems even less than that since I was doing a live radio programme on Mondays, of the kind designated light-hearted by the BBC. The Head of Radio 4—must have been the Home Service then, if you can accept a time-lapse on that scale—once asked me, when I complained of having to be lighthearted all the time, to recommend some other designation. I couldn't, and stopped complaining.

On the evening of that Monday in October 1962, lightness of heart at the microphone was even shorter than usual with me. The East and the West, detoured through Cuba, were on collision course. Any minute, the blinding impact, silence, and global wisps. I felt the pre-shock, walking Beeb-bound up Regent Street. Austin Reed was a foot high and smouldering. Behind me, Eros had melted.

"What are you getting?" I said to the producer in the control-room. He was on to the Voice of America, which said that Khrushchev wasn't budging. Nor was Kennedy, who had proved it by stringing out along Florida and into the Caribbean all the ships, guns and planes he could scratch up. It was good scratching. A bigger concentration of clout than any used in World War II. In Moscow, meanwhile . . . in Washington . . . in Havana . . .

Shows must go on, it's well known. But I did ask if he thought I should finish with my usual light-hearted, "See you next week."

He said he'd decide that later, and would keep me informed. The show ran for an hour. I used to smoke a large Cuban cigar, which just lasted it out. Tonight, I could see, it was going to turn to ashes in my mouth, but I lit it bravely all the same.

It had always been his practice, during the taped or recorded funnies, to drift into the studio for a chat. As I pumped up the breeziness for the next live link he would give me updates on the trouble he was having building his duck-shed, or rumoured rifts in the broadcasting hierarchy. All that seemed dross on this particular Monday, and several times he didn't come in at all, but sat on the other side of the glass, sifting the static for doom. When he did come, the reports were terrifying.

I left at ten. The cab-driver said nothing, but kept glancing out and up at the starless sky, as if for a sudden radiance. It was a howling night. My destination was ridiculous, all things considered: that patch of Russian soil in Kensington Palace Gardens. No. 13, for anyone with superstitious leanings. As I paid the taxi my hat blew off and bowled through the gates. If it had gone the other way I was in a mood to leave it. What's a hat without a head?

Things may have improved in twenty years. My impression of the Embassy was of a peeling exterior and a vast, chilly vacancy once you were in. No frills. No furniture. They could have packed things ready to quit, though the young man who greeted me in English that had quite an edge on my Russian was obviously keeping his best blue suit back. I followed it along the silent halls and was bowed through a heavy door into blackness and an even heavier hush. The door puffed to. Nothing. Then a sudden radiance.

Being late for this culture evening, a somewhat low-key exercise in East-West amity, I stood at the back of the small cinema, which it turned out to be when the screen ceased its startling flashes, and settled down to the second feature. I didn't want to disturb my fellow-guests. Besides, I was near the exit. There weren't many to disturb, I saw in the next blinding interval between laughing Ukraine tractor-drivers and a tour of the Volga-Ural oilfields. A thin turn-out. Journalists at this time had other preoccupations than irrigation progress in western Siberia, and had stayed away. I hadn't, but the preoccupations remained.

Entertainment isn't always the cure. I remembered an earlier brinktime, in 1938, seeking to forget Czechoslovakia in the company of, I think, Cary Grant. Some Hollywood comedy. I know there was a sequence where people were challenged to spell Czechoslovakia backwards, and it didn't help.

Tonight it wouldn't have helped to spell Khrushchev backwards, trickier than it would have been than other names of the moment: Dean Rusk, George Ball, now long receded. Or just ordinary words. Minuteman. Nuclear superiority. Incineration.

After the films we danced.

Eerie.

It was a better room, if my memory serves. There could have been chandeliers. Dancing was not immediate, because there was certainly food and drink. I see a long buffet. Had the waiters behind it actually white gloves? The vodka was, as to be expected, the real thing. None of your alien labels, conning the unwary with English characters reversed. Diplomats plied us. They were in the lower reaches, His Excellency in person having, I imagine, other commitments. The music, from a hidden source, was waltzes and foxtrots. Quite old. The wind battered the windows. Nobody mentioned Cuba, not even a short woman journalist I took an early turn with, representing a do-it-yourself weekly. We agreed that the films had been interesting.

It must have been some time later that I partnered, and became intimate with in the most proper sense, a cultural attaché and strong waltzer. He led. His name, which surprised me less at the time, was Romanov. I know that because we exchanged cards, and I still have his. After arming each other to the vodka bottles once or twice, he holding me up, we also exchanged neckties. Whether he still has mine, an early *Punch* design with gold Mr Punches on a green ground, I don't know. I like to think of it now perhaps taking the eye of passers-by on Gorki Street. His was tiny red stars on black. When I was well enough to look at it a day or two later I saw the label had been scissored out. A microfilm cache? That was a thought I might have had if I'd examined it before.

But I had other thoughts as we danced the last waltz. *Kiss Me,* I believe it was. Even without that, I felt that the barriers were down, and told him so. I expanded, obviously with some coherence, on this. When such bonhomie between nations was clearly the only way of life, what was all this ludicrous nonsense about rockets? Who wanted to blow anyone up? What was the point? Let Khrushchev be told now, for time was short, that dismantling was the only course: any Romanov of vision and resolve, with access, however tenuous, to the Kremlin ear . . .

I don't know where he went. I know we hadn't finished the dance, and I had to lean on what could have been an associate editor of *Pottery and Glass.* But he went, looking damned serious.

It's daft to make extravagant claims. Detail of history could prove me wrong. All I can say is that when I somehow got home and turned on the television it was in the middle of a news flash that the rockets were pulling out. What if Kennedy did get all the credit, a bit spilling over on Dean Rusk and George Ball?

So I was back in the studio next Monday, smoking my large Havana as if nothing had happened. As nothing had. Except that even now, I'm told, twenty years on, it's still illegal in America to import cigars from Cuba.

These silly old feuds.

"If I looked like that, I'd at least try to be pleasant."

"That's nothing. You should have been here five minutes ago when the dish ran away with the spoon."

Angus McGill

Best-sellers, still at the planning stage, revealed for the first time . . .

A curious thing happened to me last week. I dipped a madeleine into a cup of tea and raised it to my lips. At once the entire plot of a fine autobiographical novel unfolded before me.

A train sped through sleeping Europe and a great French detective was called from his *wagon-lit*. A rich and powerful man had been murdered. Who had done it? Good eh? But there's more. The other passengers are assembled and the truth emerges. They had all had a motive. Indeed they'd all done it, each one shoving in a knife. What a wheeze and what a film! But I don't know. French detectives. Trains. Are they what the public wants? You have to think of these things.

Proust did better with his madeleine. He got twelve books out of his but then he was French and had a moustache. Still revelation, inspiration, those are what we want, also some help with the typing. Otherwise you have to sit down and force the plot out like toothpaste.

I can't remember which method I used for my first novel, "Brown Michaelangelo". (This was just a working title you understand. Another was "Brown Leonardo da Vinci".) It was mostly inspirational, I think.

It was set high in the Himalayas, a place I had not actually been to but had Tolstoy? It was a place of profound stillness and very nice views and this traveller arrives, British, naturally, leading a mule. There was a lot of good stuff about this mule who had a name and wouldn't budge on narrow passes and things like that but to get on with the story, this traveller discovers a simple village in which a simple villager sits outside his simple hut painting a marvellous picture of a Chinese girl with a green face.

Well, this traveller, his name was Quartermaine or Fieldhouse or perhaps it was a girl, you get romantic interest with a girl especially if she wears one of those khaki outfits open at the neck and boots, anyway this traveller says to the simple villager, Have you got any more? And the villager, very wrinkled with wise slanty eyes and a long thin white beard, says, "Yes, heaps," and takes him into the hut which is stacked high with pictures, cardinals in crimson robes, seaside scenes, everything.

So Quartermaine or Fieldhouse gives the old painter some beads and mirrors or whatever it is you give simple villagers in the Himalayas and ties the pictures onto the mule and sets off back down the mountain.

He feels really pleased with himself. He thinks ho ho, I have saved these great paintings for posterity and I've made a packet, but all the time as they descended to the sweltering plains below the pictures were just fading away to nothing. Something to do with the supernal air of the mountain village or perhaps he'd been sent a poor batch of paints.

Meanwhile, back in the hidden valley far above—did I mention the village was in a hidden valley?—old Yo Ho Fu, for it was he, was turning out another patch of Chinese girls and cardinals for the next traveller.

I wrote all this down in the poetic prose brought out by Himalayan settings and it only filled six quarto sheets, even with a lot of padding about the mule. So I put it in a drawer somewhere and I suppose it's still there. It just needs fleshing out a bit that's all.

I might do this on Tuesday. On the other hand I might get on with the book I've been planning for the past three years about the double life of the Queen. I actually got round to discussing this idea with a publisher in Joe Allen's and I think he thought it was a great idea. He had the Caesar Salad.

The idea of this is that the Queen has a double life. By day she is the Queen and loved by all but every now and then she changes into an outfit she has bought from a mail order firm and slips out a side entrance to have adventures among the people.

You can see the possibilities, lots of good plot about her having no money and not knowing what to do when you get on a bus and so *many* loyal subjects in Oxford Street and the cosy bed-sit in Earls Court and the lady in the lift who is *SURE* she's seen one before. Oh yes, and there can be a revolutionary student saying unsuitable things and what about a job? She will have to have a job but she's got no shorthand or typing. A temp perhaps.

Yes this would be good, a best-seller surely and I'll be able to achieve my dearest ambition which is world peace and one of those penthouses overlooking the river that Jeffrey Archer lives in.

I'll call it "Majesty II". That's it exactly, so hands off "Majesty II". I'm starting it this afternoon.

"I'm not sure a London correspondent is such a good idea."

A Game of Skull

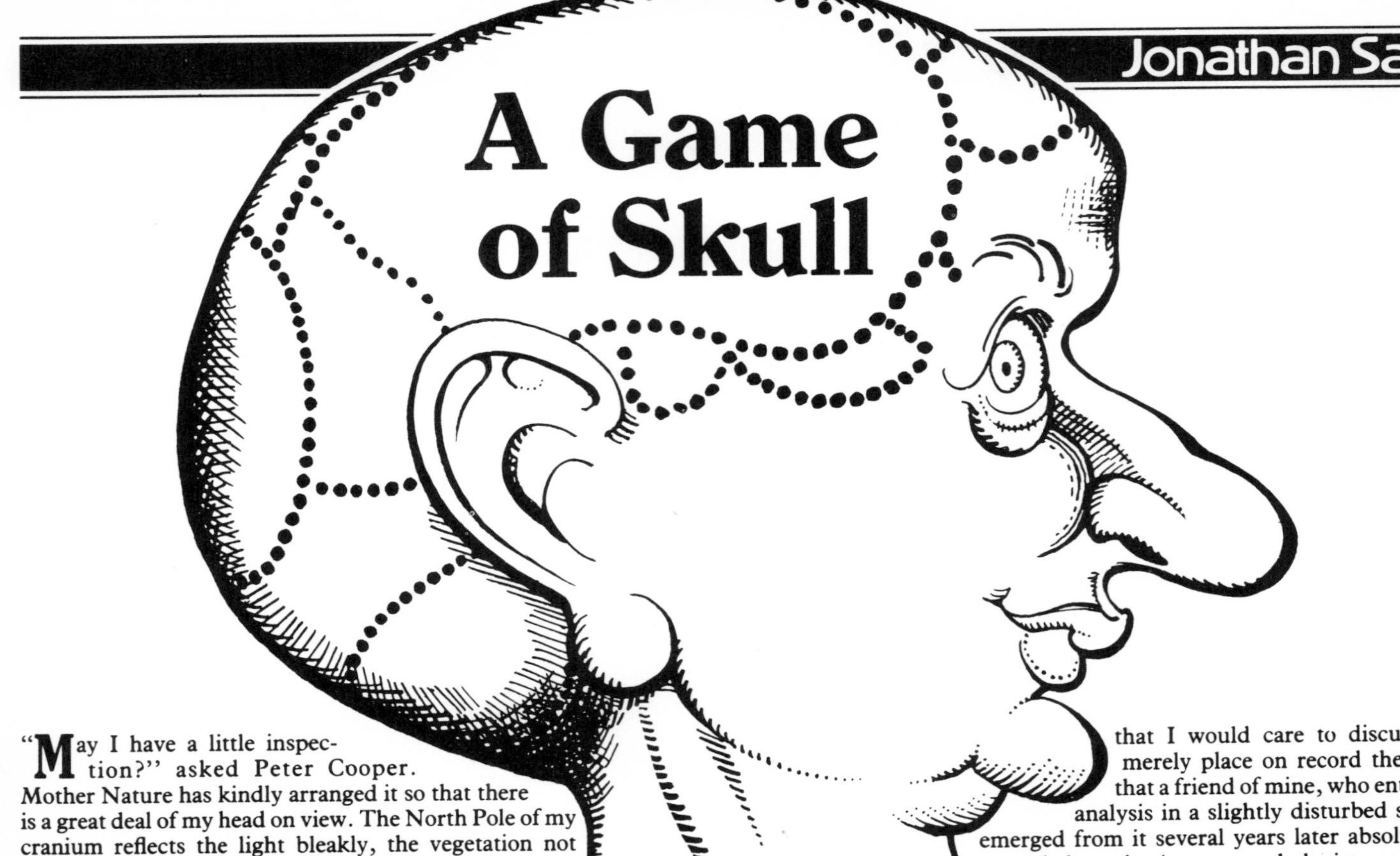

"May I have a little inspection?" asked Peter Cooper. Mother Nature has kindly arranged it so that there is a great deal of my head on view. The North Pole of my cranium reflects the light bleakly, the vegetation not commencing until much lower latitudes, say about the equivalent of the British Isles. It is not generally an advantage, unless you call it advantageous to arouse mirth in less sophisticated colleagues, who pretend to be dazzled every time I stand underneath the strip lighting, but it was handy now.

"This is a perfect head," explained Mr Cooper, who is a psychologist and director of the London Phrenology Company Limited. He was referring not to the container of my grey matter but to a bone china bust being sold by the London Phrenology Company Limited at £120 plus 18% VAT, differing from mine by having the top mapped out into tiny allotments, each labelled "Tune, Modulation" or "Humor, Mirthfulness, Wit."

"You are strong out here," he decided, fingering somewhere round behind my ears which is as unknown to me as the far side of the moon. "This is the so-called 'selfish' area signifying self-display, extraversion and ambition. You are also strong here, denoting obstinacy." I restrained a desire to stand on a table in the middle of the Savoy's Pinafore Room, where the London Phrenology Co was promoting its busts, and yell, "If there's one thing I'm not, let me put you absolutely straight, it's obstinate," for Mr Cooper had shifted his grip slightly and was saying, "You are also quite strong here." He pointed to the relevent part of the map on the perfect bone china bonce: "Love of children," "Sex drive" and, a new one on me, "Amativeness".

He didn't spell that out, going on instead to bits where I am weak in the head. "Where you're weak is in the spiritual area, on top. Your Bump of Veneration is in need of exercise." Again, he didn't go into precise details of how one takes the top of one's cranium for a bracing stroll while leaving the overdeveloped amativeness at home, but then Peter Cooper is not a Victorian phrenologist, who would have spent an hour taking calipers to my skull and charting things that go bump in my head. And then reading my character from the undulations of the bone. And getting it completely up the spout.

"The Victorians were wrong in terms of contemporary neurosurgery," explained Peter Cooper, who has himself a rather fine head but don't make anything of that. "They believed the brain was symmetrical; we know it has a left and a right side with different functions. Phrenology was based on a fairly easy answer to the question: Who am I?"

It is a question that is, of course, still being asked, mainly in the early hours of the day, as sensitive folk in fashionable parts of town head for couches to start the day with their analysts, with only office cleaners for company on the Tube. Whether they receive any more sensible answers—the analysees, that is, not the cleaners—than Victorians consulting their local phrenologist, is not an issue that I would care to discuss. I merely place on record the fact that a friend of mine, who entered analysis in a slightly disturbed state, emerged from it several years later absolutely round the twist (as we psychologists put it), which is not something that happened if you had just been told that your Bump of Veneration was not quite up to scratch.

Rephrased slightly, the question reads: Who is he? That is what we like to think of as Positive Vetting, and once again the nineteenth-century phrenologists had the answers. The wrong answers, as it happened, but still something that would stand up in a court of law. A phrenologist's report would be brought up as evidence in much the same way that a psychiatrist's is today and, considering the confusion over the Yorkshire Ripper's mental state, it is hard to see which method deserves higher marks for accuracy.

According to *Heads, or the Art of Phrenology* by Helen Cooper (out this week at £7.95 or free with one of London Phrenology's perfect bone china busts) the question "Who am I?" was first asked by prehistoric man. As soon as he evolved the sense to find a cave and go in it out of the rain, he drew a rudimentary picture of himself on the wall and cried, "That's who I am!" After that, he always knew who he was if he met himself in the cave entrance.

Afterwards the study of the subject rather went downhill. The place where the soul, brain or mind was situated, was thought to be the abdomen, as the origin of the word "phrenology" betrays: the first five letters derive from the Greek for "midriff". However, there is not a lot to be learnt from close study of the navel, although it is a harmless enough pastime in its way, and scientists soon realised that the body's computer centre was, of course, in the heart. One man's breast-bone is much like another, and no one was prepared to get up early in the morning to lie on a couch and have a specialist count his ribs; the theory was soon dismissed as invalid, certainly not financially valid as far as the rib-tickling expert was concerned.

It was Aristotle who continued with this upward progression, finally locating the brain in its present place. Since he confined his dissections to animals, his discoveries did not progress much further; in fact, Greeks, Romans, Jews, Arabs and Chinese were among those whose medical professions were barred from taking a scalpel to human beings, which didn't leave many cultures free to start the long trek towards heart transplants and other spare-part surgery.

It was not until the second century AD that Galen, who counted as an expert because he had actually *seen* two human skeletons, worked out how the nerves were plugged into the command centre in the skull. But he too had a licence to carve up only pigs (as opposed to male chauvinists) and tripped over a part of the brain that controls a pig's digestive system; he decided that this must be the site of the immortal soul, as indeed it may be in porcine terms, but alas it was and indeed is lacking in humans. The theory persisted into the nineteenth century, that is, until not long before the publication of *Doctor in the House*.

It was perfectly rational when compared with some of the other theories that went the rounds over the centuries. Some held that the way in which the face was put together was highly significant, since the different features referred to various astrological signs, thus multiplying one erroneous belief by another. Others held that the lines of the forehead forecast a person's fate. Others again held that the angle of the nose demonstrated the owner's "angle of intellect"; according to this, a baboon's snout gave it a 50% rating, while a typical American clocked up 74%—percentage of what is not specified.

This was poo-pooed by Johann Lavater as ignorant mumbo-jumbo. The answer lay in considering the area between the forehead and eyebrows, which gave away the amount of intellect; the nose and cheeks, which showed the moral virtue or otherwise; and the eye, which summed up the whole farrago.

This in turn gave way to the observation of a man who noticed that great talkers had prominent eyes, while a great space between the pupils meant a good verbal memory. He then felt the bumps in the craniums of some 200 prisoners and, as soon as he had got his wallet back, produced what we know today, or rather don't know, as phrenology. It was a sincerely held and interesting theory, spoiled only by the complete absence of any connection between bumps and brain lurking beneath.

Oddly enough, this fad of compartmentalising the surface of the skull into Ordnance Survey-type contours had a useful effect. It suggested that people couldn't altogether help the way they were, being born that way, and pointed out the areas upon which people should work to improve themselves. A nymphomaniac, who could be spotted by her cranial mountain denoting excess "Amativeness", would know that she should improve herself by concentrating on moral aspects and thus tone herself down—however much her lovers might doubt that this was in fact an improvement.

More usefully, phrenologists wanted candidates for Parliament to have their heads examined for bumps, a screening process that would have been a sort of Victorian lie-detector. This never caught on, possibly because any filtering process involving sanity would result in an empty House of Commons, but phrenological salons, schools, foods and instruments were as popular as encounter groups, est and bogus gurus today. In fact, more so.

George Eliot had her head shaved twice to allow of easier access to passing phrenologists and Queen Victoria had her children's skulls scrutinised. On her death, a stamp greeting the accession of Edward VII was denounced by a phrenologist on the grounds that it depicted the royal head as lacking in intellectual bumps and overloaded with Amative elements.

That was the end of the Golden Age of Phrenology, which was knocked on the head, as it were, by medical science. In seeking to revive it, the father and daughter team, the Coopers, hold no brief for bumps. They believe that the busts with the engraved charts make an agreeable object to have about the place. They also believe that the 42 elements marked on the china skulls are important of themselves, and recommend us to jot them down in a circle, the individual placings depending on our possession or otherwise of the mental element in question.

While accepting that this do-it-yourself psychoanalysis saves you having to get up every morning to lie on a couch, I retain my doubts. Put it down to a lack of Bump of Veneration.

ALPHABESTIARY

TSETSE FLY

Two-winged, blood-sucking fly whose bite transmits all sorts of horrid diseases to cattle, horses and dogs and vice versa. The bite of the Tsetse causes sleeping sickness in humans and, in the days of Empire, colonial civil servants were particularly susceptible to the disease, often prolonging independence talks for years on end. Returning to the UK, the ex-colonials infected in triplicate the Home Civil Service by both word of mouth and by memo. Sleeping sickness has proved almost impossible to eradicate in the Foreign Office and it is endemic in the higher echelons of the Intelligence and Security services, as recent events in Cheltenham have shown. Constant purging is a possible cure.

TURKEY

The Wild Turkey was discovered, prairie-fresh, by the Pilgrim Fathers whose descendants, by cross-breeding, butter-injection and machine-plucking, have ended up with an overweight, all-white, drug-addicted monster, far wilder than its ancestors. The New York-dressed Turkey is rightly regarded as a tasteless joke; *Vogue* compared it to eating roasted denim. Happily, most English butchers now find the cost of flying Turkeys to the USA for slaughter prohibitive since Laker's demise. Cold Turkey is a painful, but necessary, withdrawal symptom which can last up to three weeks after Christmas before the onset of Salmonella poisoning.

TURTLE

Aquatic elder brother of the Tortoise but much quicker to come out of its shell and therefore has a far superior breast-stroke action. Prized as a source of meat and handbags, it is now extensively farmed by soup manufacturers, who have overcome its irritating tendency to rise and float on the surface by chucking away 99% of the Turtle after boiling, and inserting little bits of handbag in each tin of soup. The eggs of the Turtle are eagerly sought and when hard-boiled make excellent billiard balls. The Florida Turtle lays its eggs ready-numbered and this accounts for the invention of American billiards or pool.

Arnold Roth

The High and The Might

America has been shocked and shaken by scandal. Professional athletes have admitted to using drugs. Small boys' hearts have been broken. On the other hand, so have some long-standing records.

September Song

You will have to search hard in the literature of autumn to find a better threnody for lost summers than the one which appeared in the *Sunday Times* last week

> Ringing the field, the chestnuts were heavy with conkers; and after all these years, I discovered the pear tree near the pavilion full of massive fruit. Perhaps I'd become more perceptive of such peripheral details, as two weeks before I'd noticed for the first time the apple trees on the Hove ground.

Thus Michael Brearley reflected on the final day of his 22-year career in first class cricket. Since Mr Brearley is a gentleman (and would have been a Gentleman if that status had not been abolished by the MCC) there can be no question of the passage having been lifted from the collected works of Neville Cardus. But I mean it as an unequivocal compliment to the quality of the writing when I say that anybody who confused large parts of his "Memories from the journey's end" with extracts from *Cricket All the Year* or *Days in the Sun* would make an understandable error.

Mr Brearley's talents as a writer were first revealed to me when he wrote an article about success for this magazine. It is a difficult subject (as many of the contributors to the series discovered) to write about without appearing arrogant or ridiculous or both at the same time. But Mr Brearley managed it. He did not tell boastful tales of little boys with autograph books or women's underwear being sent through the post, but simply described the complicated psychology of batsmen. Cricket is unique amongst sports because it is a contemplative game in which a moment of frenzied action is followed by a pause for reflection. It is to be hoped that the ex-England Captain will spend some of his now surplus energy on recording what he thought during the lulls between the six-ball onslaughts. After all, Basil d'Olivera made him feel that "Being forty is only the end of adolescence." Writing about cricket will keep him out of trouble on the streets.

Cricket is also a game of reminiscences and nostalgia: indeed, its critics would say, of sentimentality. The Cardus caricature concerns the pavilion shadows lengthening across the pitch and the John Arlott imitators write of reminiscences in Hampshire taprooms. The strange contented sadness that comes at the close of a good innings is felt even more keenly in September when a successful season ends. And mortals must assume that when a great career is finished, there is the same sensation of falling leaves and roses which will never be in bud again. It may be the unaccustomed feelings of mortality running in his veins which made Brearley such a clear authority on the autumn of cricketers' lives. Michael, it is yourself you mourn for.

Take, for instance, his article in the *Sunday Times* of August 15th. It concerned the return of Raymond Illingworth from retirement and described the exploits of Yorkshire's fifty-year-old new captain under the title "the middle age of Mr Illingworth". Michael Brearley, psychoanalysis student as well as professional cricketeer, was obviously fascinated by the reasons that brought a man (at least approaching the sear and yellow) back into the Oxford Blue, Cambridge Blue, and gold-edged sweaters of the Yorkshire CCC:

> . . . it was a rich challenge (irresistible when it became clear that virtually all the players welcomed the idea) to lead the side out at fifty, to be able to put his cricketing brain to full use once again, to run his own train set,

A month later he reported how long it had taken him really to understand that his own long summer had finally come to an end:

> Wayne Daniel, who had a hamstring injury, was not going to field and was packing his bag. "So I shall never have the chance of cajoling you into one final effort, Diamond," I said, punching his massive chest. He reckoned I'd be back—"Unlikely," I said, "and certainly *not* in that role!"

I am almost tempted to add that "I should hope not." For normally I would argue that anyone who writes as well as Michael Brearley ought not to be wasting his time on anything else. But then he is something of an exception. Anyone who has scored over 25,000 runs in first-class cricket ought not to be wasting his time on writing whilst his hands can still hold a bat.

My suspicion is that Michael Brearley really does intend to lock his bag. Certainly the newspapers thought that they had seen him climb the pavilion steps for the last time. "Wherever he goes now," wrote the *Guardian*, "his are the qualities which should serve the game in his middle age as usefully as in his prime." Ignoring for the moment the notion that a man in his forties is not in his prime, the idea of cajoling Brearley "into one final effort" is clearly attractive. What he ought to be doing now is writing about the game and not administering it with the other old gentlemen at Lord's.

I offer in evidence his description of how Illingworth "clearly protected himself as a bowler". It involves Jack Burkenshaw who "played taster at Leicestershire to Illingworth's Nero. He would be sent out like a faithful Indian scout to find ambushers. 'Is it turning, Jack? No? Well, carry on then—your flight is excellent.' Though if it was turning, Illy rarely missed out." Consider his account of the temptations to end it all with six. "Perhaps I was almost exaggeratedly cautious this last innings, living up or down to an image, conscious at this stage of what was expected of me. Not that another slog would have been an assertion of existential freedom. But I can't see Botham going out without a bang."

Nor can I see him ending a valedictory article with a little enigmatic story about a spectator mysteriously asking his weight. On that puzzling note Brearley "drove through the gates into the one-way system". A lesser man might have deviated into a pun about keeping right and keeping writing, but that would dishonour my subject's elegant prose.

£5 spectacles

Sales over the counter of spectacles, without a prescription, are recommended by the Office of Fair Trading. A report suggests abolishing the opticians' monopoly, and sale of spectacles for only £5

The Times

PUNCH BARGAIN GLASSES MART!

WANT TO GIVE UP SMOKING?

Of course you do! But have you found a foolproof, guaranteed, and utterly safe method? Of course you haven't!

Until NOW:
Our all-new rock-bottom cut-price D-I-Y spectacle kits, specially imported from Taiwan, can be gummed together **in seconds** to give you a pair of elegant spectacles through which, thanks to an exclusive cost-cutting system specially developed for our customers, you will be unable to see a bloody thing! Try to pick up a packet of fags—**it's the cat!** Run down to the tobacconist, suddenly you're forking out for a couple of lamb chops and a bag of giblets! Offer your boss, shop steward, VATman etc one of yours, and there you are with your finger stuck in his eye!

Within weeks, days in some cases, you'll never want to see another cigarette! Even if you could.

Recommended RP £2.25, at most vegan outlets.

BLACKHEADS? ACNE? ECZEMA? DANDRUFF? HALITOSIS?

Yes, all these things *can* be absolutely revolting! But why go on suffering embarrassment and ridicule? If you wear a pair of our really horrible glasses, no-one will even notice your unsightly personal blemishes. Comments a satisfied user from Lymeswold:

"My skin was so bad, I used to be afraid to go out of the house in case people laughed at me. But now I wear your wonderful spectacles, they cross to the other side of the street while I am still fifty yards away. Thank you, Dept. G78!"

Prices start at around £5.50 for the Fairly Horrible range, rising to £49.95 for the top-of-the-market Janet Street-Porter, for which a special licence may be required during daylight hours.
Catalogues from Yegh International, Dunmow.

Due to Ministry of Defence over-ordering during the recent Falklands Crisis, we are now in a position to offer the public 10,000 pairs **ONLY** of fabulous

GENUINE EX-OFFICERS' SPECTACLES

similar to those worn by top names like Montgomery, Auchinleck, Wavell etc. etc.! Not just things to stop you walking into walls, but also a piece of this island's glorious history which could be sitting on your nose by return of post! Exclusive khaki eartapes ensure these will not blow off, even in the heaviest bombardment or family row, and the durability of the lenses has been proven in innumerable engagements. During the last lot, in fact, many of these tough no-nonsense manly specs were the only means of identifying where their former owners had been standing!

DON'T DELAY, TEST YOURSELF TODAY!

Simply snip out this handy chart, gum it to the door, if you can find it, take ten paces backwards, and see how much you can read. You'll be glad you did!

H
E G R L M
K P D B H Y X
F J U T P O C V B

Cheques/POs/Cash (£4.99) to:
Bat Products International Box 478.

ASTOUNDING LO-LO-COST ROOF CONVERSIONS ARE OUR SPECIALITY!

Yes, but are they *yours*? Could it be that there is something in the small print of your loft-conversion contract which, when your new granny-snooker-darkroom falls off in a light breeze and flattens your carport, allows the crooked bastard who built it to slide out of his responsibilities?

Why take risks?
Even those who think they have good eyesight cannot read loopholes which may be contained in microdots at the foot of page 27! Our all new horn-rimmed bottle-bottoms will change all that, plus enable you to engage in all manner of hitherto impossibly fiddling, but profitable, hobbies, such as headlice examination, gerbil sexing, etc., etc.
Send your rush order NOW to Dept. 1, Optico, Basement House, Stag Lane, W14., enclosing credit card no. or personal cheque for £2.99. Trade welcome.

AMAZING UNDETECTABLE TOUPEE AND SPECTACLE SET!

Yes, it's true! You could look not only years younger but also amazingly more distinguished with our combined hairpiece in elegant shower-resistant stoatene and fabulous executive glasses colour co-ordinated to match your sexy new thatch! Choose from Fashionable Ginger, Zesty Custard, Sleek Welshnut, or the new Gay'n'Gray Pincurlo.

Our prices start from as low as £9.95 (to include valuable monogrammed Jiffybag)! Why worry about looking like a prat when we can help?

Write **NOW** to:
WIGOGGLE HOUSE,
14a Keir Hardie Buildings, E.4.

FARG VIDEO CLUB

Amazing New Year Offer!

Are you having trouble getting all you should out of such all-time video greats as **HEAD EATERS OF MORDEN, CHAINSAW NUN, I MARRIED A DONKEY, VIBRATOR FROM THE BLACK LAGOON,** etc. etc.?
Squint no more! We are now, as the result of the new legislation, able to offer you ABSOLUTELY FREE a handsome pair of tri-focals with every three cassettes ordered!

Please send me FREE details! I am over 12 years old and for some reason something is going wrong with my eyes.

NAME..

ADDRESS..

Farg Genuine Collections, Greek Street, W1.

HAEMORRHOIDS ARE NO FUN!

But You May Not Need Painful Surgery!
A doctor writes: Many people mistakenly believe themselves to be suffering from what the medical profession calls piles, simply because they have been unable to get a good look at the seat of the trouble, ha-ha-ha! But now, with the abolition of the opticians' monopoly, Tongspex Ltd. have been able to come to their aid with these truly amazing extendable glasses which enable sufferers to take a good look without the embarrassment of involving a second party. I thoroughly recommend them!

Thank you, Tongspex! Yes, something is bothering me Down There, and I should like to take a closer look in the comfort of my own home. I enclose £3.95, which I understand includes p + p. I undertake to seek professional advice in the event of not being sure, e.g. could it be a boil, say?

NAME ....

ADDRESS ....

....

Tongspex, Erzanmine, Laburnum Villas, Bromley BR1 2AX

Professor Patterson's Christmas Package for the Poms

passed on by
BARRY HUMPHRIES

ADVERTISEMENT FOR AND ON BEHALF OF THE COMMONWEALTH GOVERNMENT OF AUSTRALIA

I'm wearing my marsupial ermine-trimmed academic hat now and dictating this Chrissie communiqué to my Secretary-cum-Research Assistant Friday, Roxanne, as she hammers out my prestige press statement with her frosted green finger nails on our Government issue IBM daisy wheel. New paragraph, Roxy, and whaddia doin' in the luncheon recess?

You could have knocked me over with a hard-rock, Ayers Rock didgeridoo when I was suddenly seconded from the Commonwealth Cheese Board the other day and head-hunted for the prestigious, cushy sinecure of Vice-Chancellor, Provost, Treasurer and Food and Beverages Supremo at the upcoming Australian Research and Studies Establishment (ARSE).

"Money is no object, Les," came the firm, prematurely vacillating voice of our Prime Minister over my de-coding scrambler. "Just help us put across to the poor old Poms a broad-based, grass roots, multi-faceted, wide-spectrum picture of our wonderful sun-drenched sub-continent. Dish out a few flash degrees in Dingo Studies, Possum Pathology and Rogue Wombat Handling—you name it. Get 'em swotting up on who was up who in our last award-winning, internationally-acclaimed feature fillum, and if the Poms won't buy that, tell the bastards they can stick their heads up a dead bear's bum.

"Australia's international image needs a bit of spit and polish and you're just the man to put his mouth where Australia's money is. Let's face it, Les," our lanky leader went on to infer, "London's choc-a-bloc with ex-pat knockers making a fat quid selling Australia's credibility short. Smart alec galahs like Germaine Greer, Clive James and that old Sheila, Dame Edna, who dresses up as a man and tips the bucket on our incomparable cultural attainments in front of the crowned heads of Europe.

"The Australian Government has lashed out and bought a nice old period-style maisonette a stone's throw from prestigious Bloomsville Square with ample parking facilities outside for visiting Australian academics y'know, and post-graduate ponces in their pre-owned, as-new, VW campers. We've given this assignment to you, Les, because you're that smart you could sell soap

e Poms. Rustle up a horny little Yuletide
ıotional package, get off your campus
your skeleton staff, take a firm grip of
syllabus and stick it up 'em." End of
e, Roxy, and how about a nice juicy
in the Chips Rafferty executive dining
tory? You look like a girl who could do
something hot inside her. New para.
'ell, I'm here to tell you lucky *Punch*
ers our venue is looking pretty good and
u want to crawl in out of the cold for a
Christmas indoor Aussie style shark-
, or a simulated bush or beach barbie
all the liquid trimmings, activate our old
d entry-phone and one of our spunky,
back, outback hosties sporting their see-
ugh shortie black lace-trimmed aca-
ic ra-ra gowns and kinky PVC mortar-
ds will give you a guided walkabout of
facility and the disciplines catered for
ein. There's the Dame Nellie Melba
sh courts, the Rolf Harris solarium, the
ick White hot tub, spa pool and jacuzzi
plex, the Colleen McCullough cold
ge, as well as our extensive "Seekers"
orial lingo-lab and the Ned Kelly audio-
al inter-active, laser-scanned, antipo-
crash course Community Input System
sored by the Tasmanian Boomerang
rette Paper Conglomerate.
his Christmas there's been no shortage of
est from impoverished Pom Professors
've been queueing round the clock for
chance to chip in on the odd lucrative
inar. When we're fully operational in '83
e expecting such guest luminaries as For-
-Sir Anthony Blunt on "Baroque Abbo
oes in the Murrimbidgee Basin", Dr
than Miller's post-mortem on the first
ralian convict production of *Fidelio* and
last Abbo *Aida*, Dr Pamela Stephenson
Australian Wit and Humour in the Post-
dial Period" and "Undressing as Sat-
, *plus* Sir Harold Wilson's sell-out lecture
he Aussie diplomatic community on
w To Be Successful *and* Common".
ne of my old drinking cobbers from the
igration Department who has assisted
e passages than I've had chilled break-
will be counselling on "Ways and Means
rviving the Pommy Christmas" in close
ciation with a top Qantas ticket writer;
a spokesperson for the Australian
men's Civil Liberties Association will be
fing local Brit housewives on "Animal
bandry Down Under" and "Outback In-
icide—The Do's and Don'ts".
o front up at ARSE House anytime over
festivities and plug into some of the most
isticated promotional hardware this side
he black stump (an old ethnic Abbo ex-
sion meaning SFA).
'ours Truly is Santa this year and I'll be
ing out the dried apricots, Joanie Suther-
d EPs, Sid Nolan dinner mats and
wanese tea towels featuring the map of
mania—and talking of the map of Tas-
ia, have you worn them crotchless
ties I gave you yet, Roxanne?

"No, really, the tap-dance makes a fine finale—don't bother about the striptease."

"No, I'm Father Cooney's receptionist."

'Lack of sex killed dinosaur'

DINOSAURS may have ruled the Earth—but their sex lives seem to have gone from bad to worse.

The Observer

WHOS

BRACHIOSAURUS was the dinosaur with the largest body and the smallest brain: such was the immense distance between its reproductive organs and its tiny cranium, it tended to have sex without realising it, and then immediately forget what had happened. Even if it had enjoyed the experience enough to want to repeat it, it could never remember what it was that it wanted to repeat. Males would often meet females, and both would experience a vague sense of occasion, staring desperately at one another until their heads began to droop. They would then part, wondering which one of them had been the tree.

TRICERATOPS was perhaps the most tragic of the dinosaurs, being unquestionably the most repulsive, even by its own poignantly undemanding standards. A victim of its own evolution, it continued, pointlessly, to refine its disgusting physiognomy from something which sensibly repelled its enemies into something which finally repelled itself. A male triceratops would meet a female triceratops and, quite frankly, refuse to believe what it saw. For a while, each would make polite noises about minds being more important than appearances, they would discover all sorts of hobbies they had in common, they would agree to meet for a second date, and then they would go their separate ways and throw up.

Alan Coren: A SHORT HISTO

The Triassic Period

Two hundred and twenty-five million years ago, there was not a l of a lot to do.

The earth consisted of one huge continent, covered in moss a surrounded by a single ocean. It was from this ocean that th creatures emerged which were ultimately to evolve into the f dinosaurs, and they were a pretty happy and undemanding crow Most days, they either looked at the moss, or they made love. It w only much later that they found themselves doing both at the sa time.

Basically, these first animals were fish with little legs, and tha itself was no small contributory factor to their contentment: hopp about was a whole new experience. Not that they hopped far; the itself was a new enough phenomenon for its owner not to be entir certain that it might not vanish again, and nobody wanted to fi himself as a legless fish stranded far—it could be yards—from loved ones. Gradually, however, confidence grew, legs lengthen and strengthened, and, within a mere eon or so, more protrac hopping began, followed rapidly by adultery.

Not that this was any major cause of social or marital division. T sexual act had no great significance to the prehistoric reptile, it w simply the thing that wasn't moss. But perhaps the most important f to remember was that all these creatures looked exactly ali marital misconduct proceeded not from dissatisfaction but fr unawareness. You might as well view the movement from one pa of moss to another as being unfaithful to dinner.

All this, however, was to change by the second half of the Trias period. Primitive seed plants called cycads had evolved, and tr began to grow up along the river banks, and spread inland, evolvi as they went. Pretty soon, there were bushes everywhere, and m than a few flowers.

The flowers looked good to eat. They weren't, but that didn't st the Triassic citizens taking a crack at it. What motivated them w called desire.

And the citizens themselves were changing. Having been fish w little legs for millions of years, some of the smarter ones had h enough. Apart from anything else, they wanted to look over t bushes, to see if there were any more of those good-looking flow about for lunch. So legs grew even longer, and the great plant-eati sauropods began, during the next thirty million years or so, to r above the bushes and peer over them with their new long necks

Whereupon they discovered not only new and good-looking fo they also found new and good-looking sauropods.

With their new big legs, they jumped over the bushes, and beg to run.

The Jurassic Period

By one hundred and fifty million years ago, much had changed. T climate was wetter and hotter, the seas were warm and clear, a there were some really fashionable swamps.

And suddenly, almost, the Earth was full of millions of differ creatures: sexually speaking, choice had taken a quantum le forward. There were camptosaurs and coelurosaurs and carnosau there were apatosaurs and ornitholestes and protoceratops, a there was nothing to do all day except work your way through th alphabetically until either (a) you found something that took y fancy, or (b) you found something that took your head off.

This, then, was the highpoint of the saurian culture. The dinosa of the mid-Jurassic, big, dim, and cheery, lived a life of sybar experimentation, spiced with risk and free from guilt. Life was, short, like an eon in Benidorm.

It was not, of course, to last.

'AURIAN NOW?

F MESOZOIC SEX

'he Cretaceous Period

round one hundred million years ago, the first dark clouds started gather above the saurian Eden. The continents began to assume eir modern shapes, locally specific climates and flora emerged, ıd major physical and personality differences opened up between e reptilian sub-species. Rapid and fundamental changes in habitat red insecurities, fears, and neurasthenic twitches: a sea would ıddenly appear beneath your feet, a redwood forest would spring behind your back, a big bang would take the top off a favourite ountain and nasty stuff would gush out. Seasons developed: stand ound ruminating too long, and you would go white and vanish.

Thus it was that more and more dinosaurs had trouble sleeping; it ay be argued that, compared with what besets us his heirs, the ɔove worries do not seem much to have on your mind. But with a ind the size of a cobnut, it doesn't *take* much. Naturally, the saurian x-life was the first thing to suffer, their new preoccupations and eir inability to adapt to environmental changes being compounded the sad truth that after sixty million years of copulatory fun, the hole thing was beginning to pall, anyway.

Couplings became far more infrequent: the paucity of fossil re-ains from the period c.90,000,000–c.80,000,000 BC suggest that any dinosaurs chucked in the sexual sponge altogether, probably favour of canasta and flower-arrangement. From the disposition of ɔnes in Southern Arizona, we know that a measure of dinosaur-opping went on, since there is no other way in which evolution uld have arrived at the corythosaurus, which was a duck-billed nithopod with the tail of a brachiosaur, the hindquarters of an uanodon, and the forearms of a psittacaurus. It was not unlike the ɔrd Edsel, and almost certainly gay. We can infer this from the ssilized footprints, which show a marked mince.

Further evidence of sexual disorder and decline may be gleaned ɔm the remains of Cretaceous females, which for the first time have eth equally powerful with the males. Clearly, they were no longer ppy about role-imprinting, wanted an equal part in an ongoing eaningful relationship, and almost certainly took casual work snap-ng things off and rooting things up. The teeth would also have been no small value in backing up headache claims. Similarly, sexual rassment would have been given short shrift: fragments of male ɔne appear with depressing frequency after c.60,000,000 BC.

What is beyond question is that the dinosaurs of the late Cre-ceous were growing rapidly more ugly. The smooth, lissom, many ɔuld say fetching, brontosaurs of earlier eons had by now dis-peared entirely, leaving the planet populated by giant horned, aled, fanged and clawed grotesqueries like stegasaurus, styraco-urus, triceratops, polacanthus, tyrannosaurus and monoclonius. ıey were walking arms complexes, they looked like something odled on his sketch-pad by Rommel after a night hitting the mestos bottle, any sexual encounter which any of them was dumb, sperate, or suicidal to risk took on most of the salient features of the ttle for Stalingrad. Copulation, already, as we have seen, infre-ent through a variety of social stresses, now became a thing of en mortal fumbling, as the giant panzers sought desperately to find eir own or their partner's relevant parts in the armoured impregna-ity of their fearful undersides.

Once a year was about par for the course.

Naturally enough, the dinosaurs attempted to convince themselves at the new conventions were an immeasurable improvement on the d, and that the progression from love between males and females to med conflict between males and females was a natural evolution-y step to be welcomed and encouraged in the name of moral and iritual health.

As far as we can judge, it was a belief they held until the very end.

PTERANODON was the largest of the winged dinosaurs, and was always flying abroad on business. What with the inevitable worries and pressures of this stressful career, the permanent flight-lag, the strange foreign food, the constant preoccupation with the whereab-outs of its luggage, and the not inconsiderable fact that its style of flight (*see illus.*) exposed its private parts to every inclemency of weather and altitude, the pteranodon eventually gave up sex altogether. For a time, it continued to bring perfume and small breakable souvenirs back to its mate, but these were of little evolu-tionary help to either of them. Recent fossil excavations suggest that the last pteranodon died of exhaustion over what is now Gatwick.

TYRANNOSAURUS REX was, as its name indicates, the most power-ful, the most arrogant, the most domineering, and the most egocentric of the dinosaurs. It is interesting primarily for the fact that it was probably the first animal (though not the last) to evolve sexual condescension into a suicide weapon. For 99.9% of the Cretaceous week, tyrannosaurus rex would kill anything that moved, eat anything that didn't, break up the landscape, laugh at its own lousy jokes, belch, scratch, snore, pull the hairs out of its nostrils, and go to lodge meetings. In the five hebdomadal minutes remaining (usually on Saturday night), it would suddenly leap on tyrannosaurus regina with terrible ineptitude. Finally, tyrannosaurus regina left, saying she had had enough. Or, in some cases, not enough.

THE CLEOPATRAS RICHARD GRIFFITHS *as Pot Belly* AMANDA BOXER *as Cleopatra Tryphaena*
JAMES AUBREY *as Grypus*

Jensen/TELEVISION

THE IRISH RM PETER BOWLES *as Major Sinclair Yeates*

BRITISH ACADEMY AWARDS
JOHN MILLS
RICHARD ATTENBOROUGH

KING LEAR
JEREMY KEMP
as Cornwall
LAURENCE OLIVIER
as King Lear
LEO McKERN
as Gloucester
COLIN BLAKELY
as Kent

BANX Dr FRANKENSTEIN'S CASEBOOK

"That's another thing I can't stand about him—he never stops complaining."

"Personally, I blame metrication."

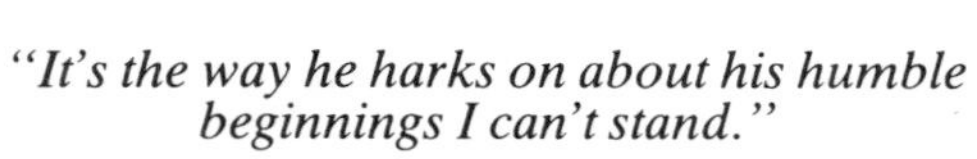

"It's the way he harks on about his humble beginnings I can't stand."

"I got sick and tired of him losing his gerbils all over the place."

"I had to make one to comply with the Equal Opportunities Act."

Melvyn Bragg

Poverty Trap

The report of the Theatre Writers' Union, *Playwrights: An Endangered Species?*, is et another shot at educating the establish- nent and the public in the hardly difficult esson that few writers make a living while all round and all dependent on them do. The ast majority of novelists in the United King- lom do not, annually, from their novels, nake as much as the lowest-paid secretary in he publishing house which exists because of heir labours. The overwhelming majority of laywrights in television earn less than the lirector, the cameraman, his assistant and owadays almost certainly the film or video ditor. Most stage playwrights earn far less han reviewers and the actors who perform in heir works. The Theatre Writers' Union is aking up the cause and good luck to it.

History is against them. Great victory in rinciple though PLR is—and all praise to 3rigid Brophy, Maureen Duffy, Francis King and their unpaid cohorts—it was so rilliantly fashioned by the civil servant con- erned (as he admitted in the TLS in an stounding letter which he clearly considered o prove him some sort of clever old chap: are *ll* bill-drafters as insensitive and conceited s that?) that few of us will make more than 0p.

The fact is, although we would all deny here was any more truth (if ever there had een) in the fairy story of the Writer in the Garret—the assumption that the writers ome for nothing is deeply set. Nor is it nerely based on philistinism, hypocrisy and neanness: although students of public life in he UK will not be too pushed to discover examples of these unattractive characteristics ittered around, clogging up the concourses of decency, jamming honest connections and generally polluting the moral and social environment. We are, indeed, in need of a Dickens to be bold enough to show that the old failings are still there, though camouflaged in new Emperor's clothes. No, the idea that the writer should not be considered as someone who does a job at all is held tenaciously and at many levels in our society. And if it is not a job, then why should he/she receive remuneration for it?

No one asks you to write: that is the first accusation which carries the anti-vote of most of the nation. And, therefore, it is not a real job. A job is something you are required to do; generally speaking, it is something you are likely to dislike; it is, however, necessary for bread, butter and holidays. To be without a job is not only an economic penalty but a social anxiety and often the cause of serious personal distress. The job, the wage, the salary, the occupation, the profession: our society is glued together with work. Nobody asks anybody to write—not plays and novels. (Moreover, using an argument from the department of dirty tricks, there are plenty written already and so if there's nothing new, there's always the cast from the past to turn to.)

What is meant by this, of course, is not really that nobody asks anybody to write: nobody asks people to make Chinese meals or pink striped shirts or four-foot high fluffy pandas. But those who make them know that *they* have a job because people will pay for those objects at a rate which gives them a living which proves that they have a job. In other words, the fact that the market exists is a valid enough reason for those employed in however ludicrous a profession to claim that they are doing a job.

But, you may exclaim, a market does exist for writers. Theatres sell tickets; people read novels; writers occupy valuable space in newspapers and journals. How have certain types of writers—most notably playwrights and novelists—mismanaged their affairs to such a pitiful extent? Journalists can make a living, sometimes a very fat one: feature writers can do it; writer-reporters on television manage it. What about the wordsmiths?

We come back to the same point which can be reintroduced by way of common lore. Few writers have escaped the early, kindly enquiry from a benevolent acquaintance: "Are you still writing or have you got a job?" How many have been told, "It must be marvellous just to write and do what you want,"—the clear implication being that the freedom itself is sufficient reward and the income is immaterial in such a spiritually satisfying pursuit. And who has not been told, "There's a book/play/novel I could write if only I could find the time." Finally, "You're so lucky to be a writer. I'm just a stuntman/international executive/banker . . . " While *you*, so the silence reads, have all the fun in the world sitting alone looking at that empty white paper.

No: in this country anyway, writing is considered a luxury which, by some magic (shades of inherited wealth and the long corrupting association of the Higher Arts and the Higher Society) *gives* luxury to those who "indulge" in it. Simply by setting up as a writer, you inherit all the supposed life-style not only of writers but of those they write about. For that is another snag. Many people read to discover worlds richer than their own and once again the writer is lumbered with a

BANX

"Bloody hell, Jeanette, I thought ***you'd*** *cancelled the Jehovah's Witnesses."*

*"Try and think carefully **exactly** what the angel told you."*

false label: the inventor is included in the cast of characters he invented.

And those, perhaps culturally imposed, reasons rest on an even sterner rock which will see writers batter themselves to a typewritten palsy rather than pay them. That is the solid conviction: "Anybody can do it." Which is true. That some do it better than others is, in the end, a matter of opinion. Are we then, the public says, to pay people job-rate and job-style for a matter of opinion? The resentment of individual Arts Council bursaries—which is widely spread and deeply held—is based on the same point: why writers? Why should he or she get £5,000 gratis? Why not an apprentice plumber or a motor-cyclist or a road sweeper? Not only is it elitist, so they complain, it is also unnecessary. Indeed, the Literature Director of the Arts Council has publicly doubted whether any book has been unfinished for lack of a bursary or any book essentially aided for receipt of one.

Anybody can do it: anybody does. There's no school for scribes, no college of penmen; you can do it whether or not you have been to university or art college or even school; whether or not you are good at exams or can recite poetry or remember the full list of Euripides' plays; you can do it however and whenever you want. You can take ten days; you can take ten years; you can give up everything for it; you can do it on the side; it matters little. The final effectiveness of the finished work is all that counts. And with such a widespread trawl at the beginning of the process, it is no surprise that at end of the process, or one end, a number of "established" writers find it difficult to convince the public that they have a firm enough base on which to found a claim on job-rate.

That they have a claim is undeniable: that they ought to be written into contracts at a much higher level and at a much earlier stage is surely only fair; but there is a long way to go before the public, even the educated public, will leave aside its conviction that if some writers stop, others will start up. The basic freedom of a writer is so wide, so goes the deep assumption, that it must carry the penalty of arbitrary and not regulated reward. Anybody who wants to write takes a chance and is somehow breaking the pact which society likes to have with a writer by demanding proper wages.

CIRCUS
THE GREAT JUMBO
"Let's face it, he doesn't pull the crowds anymore."
Haldane

VET
"Oh, no! Not Mrs Blenthorpe and her chihuahua again."

Arthur Marshall

Tea Shoppes

Much of my happy childhood was spent in Devon and at my grandparents' deous but comfortable house (if you want feast your eyes on architectural horrors ıd really fearsome coloured brick patterns, unter through the North Devon seaside wns). My grandfather being a devout ergyman, one spent quite a lot of one's time ıeeling and fervently praying. Like the lady ho bought two of Ernie's premium bonds ıd couldn't understand why her £25,000 dn't arrive almost by return of post, I could ever get the hang of prayer. Why bother to ay for a new tennis racquet and a 2lb box of ft-centred chocs if the wretched things ever turned up? Why waste the time, a view which I have always adhered.

But in point of fact there was available mething almost better than chocs, for sixty ears ago you could not venture far down a evon lane without coming upon a cottage or rmhouse with, outside it, a notice saying EAS. In those days it never said CREAM EAS, for the cream, scooped out from a ıge and gloriously golden-encrusted basin, as taken for granted, together with plates of ıose fresh scones that some Devon people ıll "cut-rounds". And in those days when ıe sun seemed always to be shining, you ıade your way to tea down a cottage pathway ordered with nice and now slightly old-ıshioned flowers—hollyhocks and vast umps of pinks and sun-flowers and stocks ıd snap-dragons.

With the arrival of tea and home-made rawberry jam, one might almost have been ı an Eden Phillpotts comedy, *The Farmer's Vife* perhaps, where the farmer's name was amuel Sweetland, his serene housekeeper ıd wife-to-be was called Araminta, and the ıcal spinster was twittering Thirza Tapper. Vhen we met her (tea was often outside) the ottage's Araminta always looked like one of er own cottage loaves, pleasantly rounded ıd considerably rounder and larger below ıan above. Uninfluenced so far by the BBC's arefully modulated tones (the early announ-ers could have read selections from Jack the ipper's Diary and made them sound taste-ıl), she spoke as she had always been accus-omed to speak: pretty was purty and cream as crame and we were "M'dears". Tea was /- a head, all in.

A recent and prolonged search by car has ıiled to locate a single country lane TEAS otice among the proliferating caraparks and amping sites and tented communities. To nd once more TEAS it is into the towns that ou must go. Here tea establishments are ıirly easy to find, and they often progress, ıter in the day, to the sale of hamburgers and hips. Teas cost on an average 90p and no ramintas serve them, but Cindy-Lous and 'racys and Lorraines instead, here just for ıe season ("Well, it's a job, isn't it?") before eturning to devote the winter months to cquiring the skills needed to become a Iome Counties trainee-coiffeuse. Tea usually consists of two saffron-yellow scones and dollops of cream and jam large enough to ensure the proprietor a hearty profit. The tea itself is boiling hot and is in one of those metal tea-pots with the totally untouchable handles (I can only think that they are known in the trade as Watch-Them-Wince).

Teas in the old days were not confined to country lanes. They existed in Devon towns as well and the tea-shops often sold home-made fudge and were flanked by a draper's shop, those things of the past, and, perhaps, an antique shop. Gone, for the most part, are the latter. The people who patronised them and who appreciated Staffordshire figures and Coalport plates and possibly-Chippendale chairs, don't come here any more. They haven't the money, for one thing, and for another there is a social gulf fixed. The retired couples of Torquay now take pains to retire elsewhere. Or, if here, they achieve whatever may be the opposite of hibernation (aestivation, actually). No good blinking at the fact that the merry coach parties are not for them and vice versa.

The antique shops have been largely replaced by places specialising in Take Home Presents. In the world of which we are speaking, it is absolutely vital to take a present to somebody left behind at home. Apart from anything else, it proves to everybody that you have Been Away and preserves your social status. So, which shall it be? A personalised T-shirt (in this genre, KISS ME QUICK would be considered very feeble and tame) or an invitation to LOVE YOUR LOO by purchasing a porcelain crinoline lady concealing a lavatory paper roll in her petticoats? A ruby crystal sweet basket or a maize "bit-bin"? An article in "fancy bamboo" or a coconut-and-sea-urchin-spine wind chime? There are, rather touchingly, ashtrays labelled TO THE BEST OLD DAD IN THE WORLD. Enormously and inexplicably popular these days are vast china cart-horses in full harness and hauling, what else, carts.

What to buy besides a present? Of course, a saucy postcard must be sent and here in seemly Devon and unlike some Welsh towns that censor them, there is no dearth of the sauciest. There are numerous hilarities connected with nudist camps (often called THE KOOLBUMS), there are vicars' wives complaining about the smallness of their husbands' stipends, and when a notice outside an ironmonger's announces a Sale and ALL TOOLS REDUCED there is an agitated lady shrieking to her husband, "Blimey, don't go in there, Fred!" Elsewhere there are Joke Shops featuring Cigarette Stinkaroos ("Oh What A Pong!"), the well-known NAUGHTY FIDO replica in brown chinaware, and an especially ghastly Laxative Tea-bag with a brand name that I really cannot bring myself to pass on to you.

What my clerical grandfather would, saintly man, have made of all this I really cannot imagine. We would have been on our knees the entire time.

"Your mother and I have something to tell you, son. You're adopted."

LAB LIB

"If it wasn't for the first cigarette of the morning I couldn't face the day."

"Well done, Haskett—the research grant is yours."

"I must say, this one's as bright as a button."

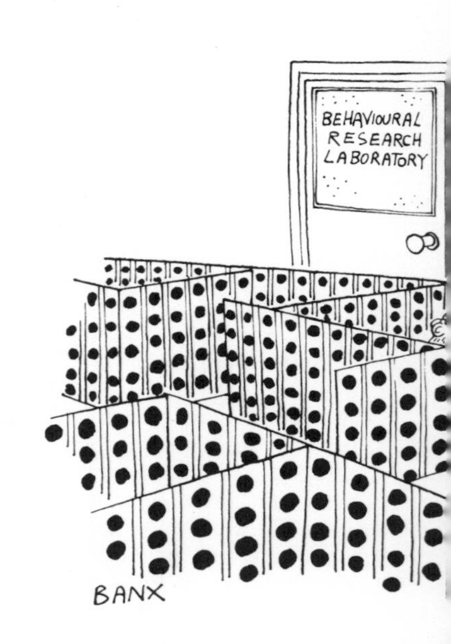

"This dummy hasn't even twigged how to use a maze."

"Those mice were devoted to him."

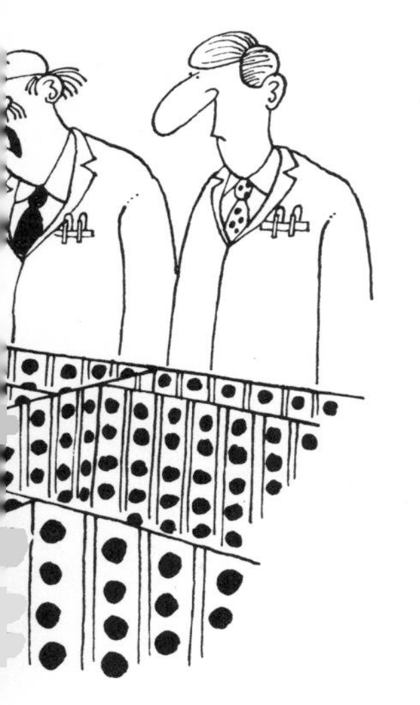

n worried—he chose that bloody awful wallpaper himself."

"Ignore him, he's just the caretaker."

Russell Davies

A Christmas Channel

It had been a poor Christmas Eve for Ebenezer Scrooge. Of course it had. There was no doubt about that. Scrooge knew it; he knew it all too well. Nay, he repeated it to himself as he sat frozen to his Parker-Knoll austerity put-u-up in the small hours of the morning. "Ah, a poor Christmas Eve," said Scrooge, "a poor one indeed." And since there was nobody present to contradict him, we must concede that a poor Christmas Eve it had been in very fact. (*Oh get on with it—Thackeray.*)

In the scanty light afforded by his ancient Ekco television, upon whose dim and dusty screen the pictures had ceased to play some hours before, at midnight, Scrooge contemplated the coming day. A desolate prospect! Very. Tiny Tim was away on the Variety Club outing; and the rest of the Cratchits had betaken themselves to Tenerife again. Even his great-nephew Fuzzy in Ohio, whom Scrooge would fain have rung, had flown to Hawaii to accomplish a glamour-gatefold photo-assignment for *Skinflint* magazine. Alas! The old sinner wrung his bony hands. No reply. True, the doors of the Conservative Club would still be open at this advanced hour, but not to Scrooge. Oh no, not to him! Too benificent and philanthropic by half, Scrooge was, and a member of the SDP withal. He settled his scrawny fundament deeper into the chair—or the Lionel Blair, as he had been taught to call it by the boys, those remarkable, intelligent boys, at the Ebenezer Scrooge Home for the Children of Destitute Professionals and Deferential Prostitutes—and thus he prepared for a long and largely wakeful night among the shadows of his Barbican apartment.

Scrooge might have been asleep, or again he might not, but certainly he was shaping in his mind the picture of a man, assimilable to himself in stature and impatience, dumping Britoil shares by the bin-load into the Thames, when, on a sudden, his stomach gave a gurgle. A most musical gurgle it was, not unlike the chiming tinkle of a Japanese pocket calculator lying forgotten in a drawer, and yet not like it at all. Scrooge regarded his waistcoat with amazement as the tinkling began again. It went hard with him to admit it, but his exiguous old innards were playing—there was no doubting it—the signature tune of *Crossroads*. "Tumbug!" cried Scrooge. "Bah!" And he beat himself soundly in the region where a generous observer might have supposed his belly to be.

Upon the instant, Scrooge's television screen became a blaze of light. Coloured light, it was, now streaming hither and yon in a confusion of ribbons and streaks, now composing itself into a face, but always shimmering in a cascade of sparkling hues.

"But I have only a black and white licence!" cried Scrooge in terror. Convinced that it was a trick, an imposture, on the part of the infamous Telecom, he wished dearly to switch off; yet move he found he could not.

"Hello, good evening," said a voice, "and welcome."

Scrooge sank to his knees.

"Oh no! Not that! Not David Frost!"

"Fear not, old man," said the screen. "For I am the Ghost of Channel Four. Look on me, and try to ignore the adverts."

"The Ghost of Channel Four?" said Scrooge, remembering his investments in a faltering voice. "Must this mean that Channel Four is—dead?"

"I didn't say that," said the voice amid the coloured lights. "Nor can it die, while one benighted soul, such as yourself, is still awake and watching."

"It is very true," returned Scrooge, who was anxious to be allowed to stand up, for he was kneeling on a collar-stud. "What have you, then, to show me?"

"So it's over to Gus Hamburger for this week's edition of *Sounding Off*," said the voice; and without intermission (for once) the screen was filled by a kindly bespectacled face and a Glasgow accent.

"The title of our discussion todee is *Whither Father Christmas?* and I'm joined in the studio by Barbara Vogue-Smith, fashion editor of *Velveteen*; Rodney Struth, Equality Correspondent of *The Guardian*; Victor Goose-Greene, alias 'Frogmarch' of the *Daily Telegraph*; and Arthur Curbishley who's a practising Father Christmas. But first we're goung to be hearing from Anna Domino, editor of the radical journal *Spare Prig*, who will make the opening statement. Anna." Aglow with a sulphurous resentment, Anna's face suffused the screen.

"Basically," began the woman, in fateful tones, "I see the Father Christmas image as a

"Just choose what you fancy from the catalogue and my assistant will see if it's in stock."

frontal attack on the self-image of women in a caring society. That is to say, it dramatises the male as the provider and benefactor and distributor of goods, to the total exclusion of the female. It offers facial hair, which women are discouraged from cultivating in our society, as the symbol of kindliness and generosity. Moreover, it is a fraud practised upon children, obtaining from them normative bourgeois behaviour on the promise of material gain. It usurps the red colouration which we instinctively associate with egalitarian socialism and makes it serve a completely capitalist end. To go further into the symbology of the so-called Father Christmas figure, we can see that the sack he carries his presents around in is freighted with scrotal implications—"

"Enough!" cried Scrooge, "Oh enough! Spirit, release me from this torment!"

"You can stand up now," said the screen.

"It's not my knee," Scrooge pleaded, "it's the programme. Can you not take it away? Have you no more channels? No ghosts of Channels Yet To Come?"

"Picky, aren't we?" said the spirit, gravely miffed. "Nevertheless I shall oblige."

And from a swirl of colours there emerged the jolly rubicund visage of a young clergyman, dressed in the collar of his calling, plus Lurex jumpsuit with sewn-in mirrors.

"Hi!" said the apparition. "Well the cock has crowed thrice, so here on Channel 13—Three in One and One in Three, bringing you 24-hour non-stop Worship 'n' Witness from your swinging Church of England—it's time for our Christmas Carol service. So it's over to the Stevenage Sports Centre!"

At once the screen was filled with merry children's faces, alive with song.

While farm employees watched their sheep
Upon a rocky shelf
A flying object, swooping low,
Identified itself,

they sang, to a familiar lilting tune.

"What delightful voices," muttered Scrooge. He could have done without the ukulele accompaniment, but still.

"No, don't get up," it called (for they
Were all about to split).
"I have a message here for you,
So listen: this is it.

"If you nip down to Bethlehem,
You'll find, I kid you not,
A baby who's the son of God,
Or, in the German, Gott.

"He isn't in the hospital
Or in the nursing home,
He's at the garage, out the back,
All wrapped in plastic foam."

The Thing signs off; but straight away
A load of other Things
Comes shooting up into the sky
And everybody sings:

Scrooge had covered his ears; but the spirit turned up the volume so that the last verse shook the room.

"Terrific praise to good old God,
The Topmost of the Pops.
He seems to like us after all;
Let's hope He never stops!"

"Oh no, no, spirit," wailed Scrooge, leaving his false teeth shamelessly embedded in the carpet. "Less, less! Not another channel!"

"But of course!" bellowed the spirit, bulging the tweeters of the set. "I have not shown you Channel Ten, the Dog-Owners' Channel; Channel Elevevenen, for people with speech impediments; Channel Twewve, the Channel entirely run by toddlers—"

Scrooge, distraught, was shredding his TV licence. Now, with a whimpering cry, he leapt to his feet, coursed across the room like a ten-year-old, and seized the television in his claw-like hands. In a rage of sparks he wrenched it from the wall-socket, staggered to the window, and beat open the casement with a desperate fist.

"Ahoy down there!" he yelled, to a boy wandering anachronistically about in Sunday clothes.

"Eh?" returned the boy, distinctly—which was a marvel, for he was seventy-six floors down.

"You know the turkey in Dewhurst's window? The enormous plastic one, just for show, completely inedible?"

"I should hope I did," replied the lad, who was of a bookish bent.

"Well," called Scrooge, "I've got something even more useless than that!" And with a heave for which a stevedore would have been paid double-time, he hoisted the TV set out of the window, closing the latter with a bang.

Where it fell he knew not, and cared not, for that matter. Presumably the boy got out of the way. Yes, he did, he definitely did. Anyway, that's how Scrooge became a theatre critic.

"Strange, these British. No security leak the whole damn thirty years it's been playing here."

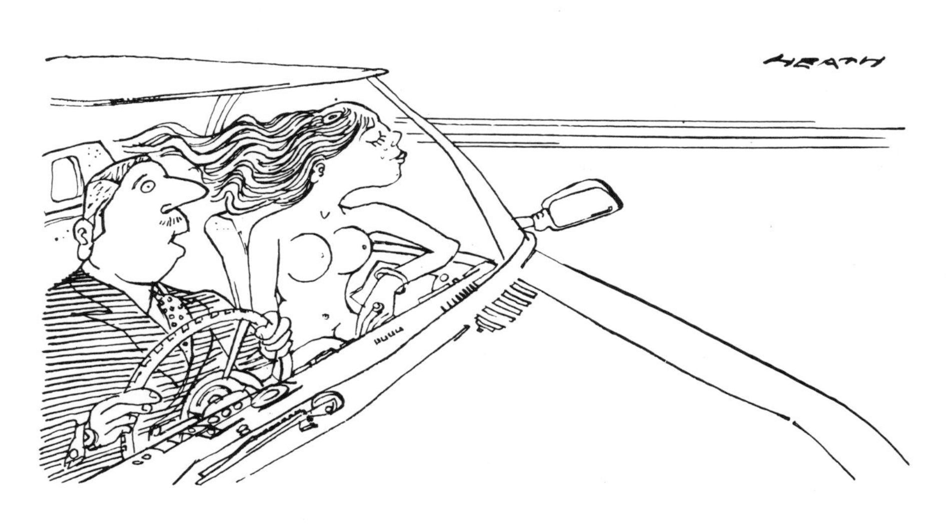

"I don't normally give lifts."

BUSINESS  **William Davis**

Where to, Guv'nor?

I am not surprised that Mr Robin Leigh-Pemberton has come under fire from the Left before he even starts his new job. The Governor of the Bank of England has always been one of the Labour Party's favourite targets, and the temptation to lash out at a former Tory councillor with an unmistakably upper-class name must be irresistible.

Harold Wilson used to have fearful rows with Lord Cromer in the early days of his administration. Cromer, an Old Etonian who owed his appointment to Harold Macmillan, infuriated him by publicly voicing his objection to high Government spending and restraints on overseas investment. Long before the Governor's term expired it was made clear to him that he had no chance of being re-appointed. He was replaced by Leslie O'Brien, a mild-mannered chap who had been educated at a grammar school and had come up through the ranks. He wasn't a die-hard Tory, and it was confidently assumed that he would keep his mouth shut, but within a year O'Brien, too, was faced with noisy demands for his dismissal.

He had told an audience of bankers in Rio de Janeiro that Britain "needed a rather larger margin of unused manpower and resources than in the past". Harold and his Chancellor had been saying much the same thing for months and the Governor felt that he was simply stating official policy. But the Left thought he was advocating mass unemployment (he was doing nothing of the sort) and called for his resignation.

Callaghan gallantly defended him. "I do resent this suggestion that I am nothing but a cipher in the hands of the Bank of England, the Treasury or anyone else," he declared. "The Governor of the Bank of England is carrying out a policy laid down by the Government. This is his job and responsibility and it is also his responsibility to tell me when he disagrees with it."

O'Brien was eventually succeeded by Gordon Richardson, who kept such a low profile that even the most publicity-hungry Labour MPs found it difficult to have a go at him. Richardson has now been given a peerage, and I look forward to his maiden speech in the Lords: perhaps he will at last feel able to tell us what he really thinks when he gives up his job at the Bank.

Robin Leigh-Pemberton is another old Etonian, a former Guardsman and all that. He takes a keen interest in politics, and is a great fan of Mrs Thatcher. He has been a competent non-executive chairman of the National Westminster Bank and it is not hard to see why she chose him. But he will clearly have a rough time if Labour should win the next election.

In the eyes of the Left, the Governor of the Bank of England embodies all that is wrong with bankers. He is seen as a remote, Scrooge-like figure who sits in a sumptuous City parlour and tries to manipulate the levers of power without a mandate from the electorate. Jim Callaghan's long-forgotten assurance that this is not so has clearly not dispelled that feeling.

At one time, to be sure, the accusation was close to the mark. In the early part of this century, Governors frequently took major financial decisions without consulting the Government of the day.

Lord Cunliffe clashed with Bonar Law, then Chancellor, when he instructed the Canadian Government that no more Bank of England gold, large stocks of which had been transferred to Ottawa for safekeeping should be delivered to the Treasury. Bona Law was furious. Cunliffe, he said in a lette to the Prime Minister, had committed "a act of extraordinary disrespect towards th British Government and a direct insult t me".

Montague Norman, another autocrati Governor who ruled the Bank for years showed equal contempt for politicians (and for that matter, public opinion) and defie successive Chancellors. Churchill onc threatened to "hang him".

But that was before the Bank was national ised by the Attlee Government. Today it i simply not open to a Governor to go int public revolt against his political masters—a least not if he wants to keep his job. He i much less powerful than his colleagues i countries like the US, where the Federa Reserve enjoys a considerable measure o independence.

Robin Leigh-Pemberton is, of course, wel aware of this. "I am not going to initiat political decisions," he says. "I am more tha willing to leave that to the politicians." Wha has made the Left angry, though, is his insist ence that Governors have a duty to protec the nation's currency and that he is therefor entitled to resist the thirty per cent devalua tion proposed by Peter Shore.

His choice of words may have been unfor tunate: it would have been more diplomati to say that he would "argue against" devalua tion. But there would have been protest anyway, and there will certainly be more if h should find himself having to work wit a Labour Government dedicated to im plementing socialist policies. There hav already been hints that he might be remove if Labour came to office.

The trouble is that, unlike the Treasur mandarins, central bankers tend to be in th limelight. Treasury officials are just as likel to resist policies which they regard as mis guided, and they often do so far more effec tively. But they are not required to mak speeches at public functions, and they don' give interviews. The Governor of the Bank o England traditionally does both. It some times works to the Government's advantage he can give his authoritative backing to poli cies and, in times of crisis, his credibility is useful asset. But he can also be an embarras sing critic, and there are no prizes for gues sing where Mr Leigh-Pemberton's sym pathies lie.

Leslie O'Brien once told me that he sav himself as head of a nationalised concern rather like the chairman of British Gas o British Rail, rather than as an arm of Govern ment. He was not a civil servant, and there fore had as much right to speak his mind a any other chairman of a nationalised in dustry.

It is an interesting argument, but it is no one which carries much weight with politi cians. The Governor's pronouncements o financial matters obviously have more impac at home and abroad than those of, say, Pete Parker.

The real question is whether it is in th public interest to silence him. I think not: h speaks for the City and there are times whe its voice should be heard.

"Can we manage an instant book on the Hundred Years' War?"

An Exclusive Transcript

Good evening.

Good evening, ma'am.

And what do you do?

I do premises, ma'am. I am what is called in the profession a Second Storey Man.

How very interesting. What exactly does your work entail?

It entails nipping in, doing the second storey, and nipping out. It is extremely skilled work, ma'am. I would not, for example, be caught dead doing a first storey number. And may I apologise, ma'am, for the fact that I do not have a small child with me who might be prevailed upon to shove a bunch of African violets at you, also enquire as to the welfare of little Wossname.

William.

—little William, due to coming out in a rush, plus a small child being something of an encumbrance in my work, it could drop off the guttering and cause no end of a row when striking the concrete, you could be looking at the wrong end of three years.

I quite understand.

Also, I am unable to issue you with special clothing. I know you like to wear, e.g., pit helmets etcetera, when engaging in professional visits, but I only have the one striped jersey with me, due to turning left at Forest Gate.

I beg your pardon?

I should have been doing upstairs at the New Cross Ladbroke's, only I turned left instead of right. I did not intend to be here at all. If I had intended doing *this* drum, I should naturally have brought a spare striped jersey for your own good self, ma'am, also flat cap. However, you may have a go holding my bag.

Thank you. It appears to have SWAG written upon it.

It belonged to a cartoonist, ma'am. They often do a bit of moonlighting. Basically, you are holding it very well, although personally I would carry it so's the word SWAG was concealed by my body, pardon the familiarity, ma'am, due to where walking up a second storey corridor holding a bag labelled SWAG might very well draw undesirable attention to oneself.

I see. How very clever. And by walking up my corridor with the word SWAG concealed, nobody seeing you thought twice about it?

Exactly, ma'am. It is what we call a trick of the trade. It is something you only pick up by experience, also keeping your eyes open. I do not expect a civilian to know this, but there are a lot of bright coppers about, well, one or two, and soon as they see a bloke walking about a corridor in the middle of the night with a bag labelled SWAG, they begin to think *Hallo.*

Hallo?

Right. It is something they train the better ones to do up Hendon. Also, it is usually a mistake to wear a stocking mask.

Hallo?

You do not half catch on quick, ma'am. Of course, it is frequently possible to explain it away to the average copper by saying sunnink of the order of *I dressed in the dark, didn't I, I have probably got a collar and tie on my left leg*, but I prefer to avoid engaging the filth in conversation altogether, hence flat cap only. It is also why I wear plimsolls.

For climbing?

Climbing? I try to avoid climbing, ma'am, it is melodramatic, I am not Errol bleeding Fairbanks, I prefer to ring the front door and explain about reading the meter. If you examine this jemmy, ma'am, you will find it has GAS BOARD written down the side. Most Special Branch men accept that, I find. No, the plimsolls is on account of avoiding bootsqueak. The last thing you want when walking down a second storey corridor in the middle of the night is a squeaking boot. Before you know it, you've woken a copper up, and he's out of his chair in a flash, and it's *Do you know what bloody time it is, I am on early turn tomorrow, I suppose you're after bloody autographs, well some of us have got a job to etcetera etcetera.* You could be stood there jawing all night, ma'am.

Fascinating. Well, I shan't keep you from your work any longer, it has been most interesting talking to you, but I'm sure you'll want to get on now, won't you?

That is very considerate of you, ma'am, I ought to be moving along due to where there is a bloke holding the bottom of a ladder up New Cross who is doubtless on the point of growing choked off, he will be sick and tired of explaining to passing coppers that he is waiting to elope with a turf accountant. It has been a pleasure and a privilege describing my work to your good self, ma'am, I trust it has been of some interest, not too technical, etcetera?

Not at all. One has been quite fascinated. Shall I get someone to show you out?

Thanks all the same, ma'am. I know the way.

Mahood's ART QUIZ

IS THIS
The Last of England by Ford Madox Brown?
The Last Supper by Dante Gabriel Rossetti?
The Last Whale by Edward Burne-Jones?

IS THIS BY
Hans Holbein the Elder?
Hans Holbein the Younger?
Hans Holbein the Practical Joker?

IS THIS
A Self-portrait from memory?
A Portrait of a hat?
An Irish Photofit picture?

IS THIS
Salvador Dali in drag?
The Mona Lisa in middle age?
The Laughing Cavalier in pain?

IS THIS PAINTING BY
Landseer? Schulz? Keating?

DOES THIS PICTURE SHOW

The first "knock, knock, who's there?" joke?
The first salesman of light?
The first Jehovah's Witness?

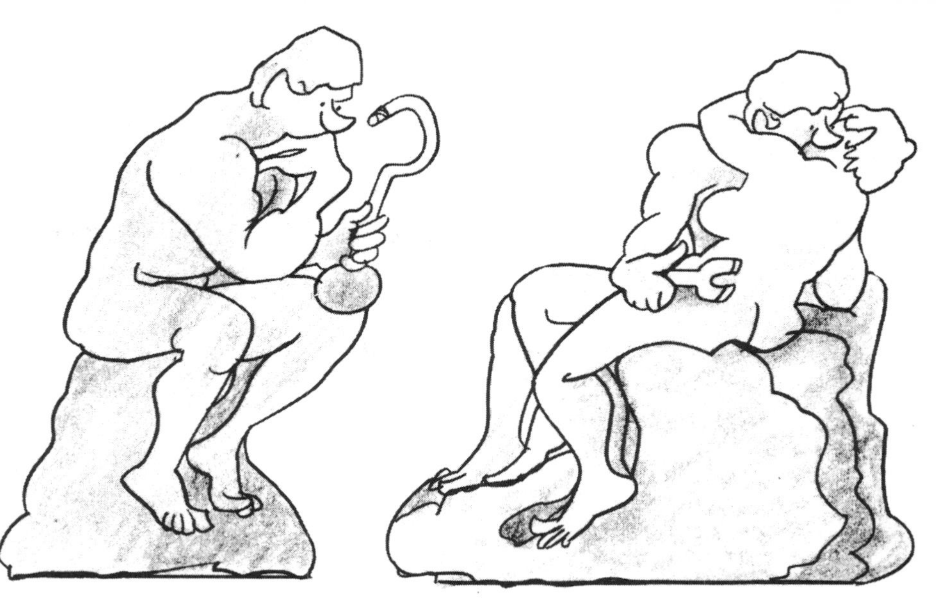

WHICH OF THESE IS

Larry's Plumber by Rodin?

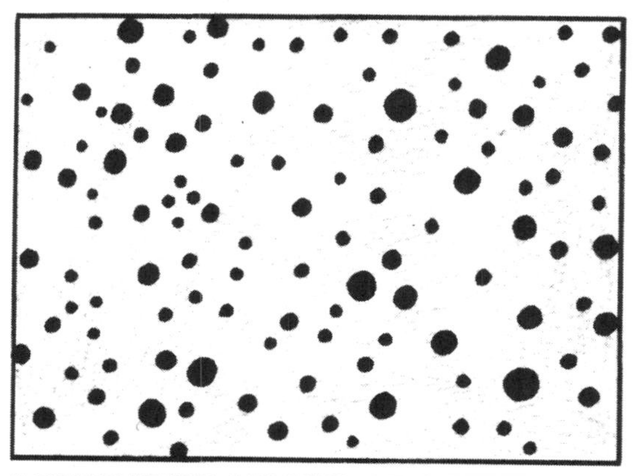

ARE THESE AN ENLARGEMENT OF

Pointillist dots by Seurat?
Ben Day dots by Lichtenstein?
Blackheads by Leger?

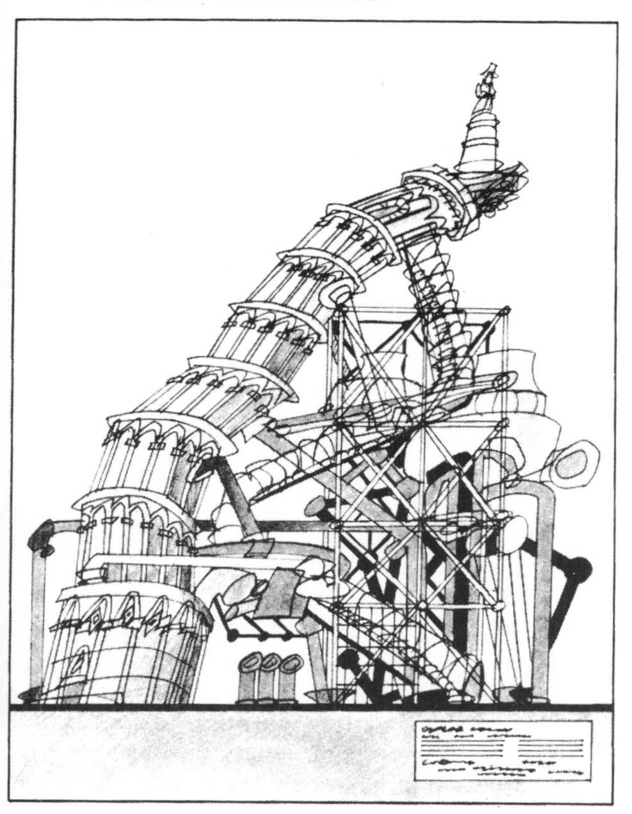

IS THIS

Richard Rogers's plan for the National Gallery Extension?
His plan for saving the Leaning Tower of Pisa?
His plan for saving the Pompidou Centre?

IS THIS A TYPICAL EXAMPLE OF

Leonardo's sfumato?
Verrocchio's chiaroscuro?
Correggio's incompetence?

DONEGAN
Trouble in Toytown
The makers of Matchbox models have called in the receivers
"Four-wheel drive, power steering, cruise control, air conditioning, push-button radio, electric windows, central door locking, made in Hong Kong, sells for two quid. Just for laughs, let's call it a challenge."
PILLBOX TOYS LTD
HORNLEY
Ghost Train
"It's always the same. The children don't get a look in."
"Naturally, we would have preferred them to smash British."

*"Good thinking, Trimble, but what exactly will the microchip **do**?"*

"Wait, Mr Higachi, we'll sell!"

"Tell me, is it true what they say about Taiwanese dolls?"

Alan Coren

Metamorphosis

We must accept that authorship has become a part of show business. Hype and hoopla, personal appearances on radio and TV, book signings and lunches, are all an integral part of the publishing game. One wonders wryly how a Kafka or a Dostoyevsky would fare under these modern conditions. *New York Times*

12 February. They come for me very early, perhaps five am, I cannot say, I have no watch. After I purchased the scarf, there was no money for a watch. I cried for a long time before making the decision, in the middle of the store in Hothrolnyczy Street, with many people staring at me. They would steal my watch if I bought one. Perhaps they will steal my scarf. Who can say? At nights I dream of the watch. I am wearing it around my throat to keep warm, and people walk by me, and each one tightens the watch one more hole on the strap. I hear the ticking grow louder. My eyes pop out. So they come for me at perhaps five am, it is dark in the mean little hotel room, beyond the window London is a black mass crawling with aliens, why am I here, why are they knocking on the door at five am?

There are three of them, a publisher in a black coat of very expensive material with a red carnation in the buttonhole, it is as if he had been shot in the left breast, blood wells out; a person in a striped suit and a spotted bow tie who is in something called public relations, obviously a policeman of some kind, perhaps a government inspector; and a woman who says that she has been assigned to me, who touches my arm with scarlet claws. I am terrified a claw will catch in my new scarf, will pull out a green thread; it will all unravel, and when the last thread runs out, I shall die.

I ask them if there is time for me to vomit, and they all cry har-har-har, and I am bustled out and into a steel lift, and we drop to music, perhaps they wish me to go mad, it would make things easier for them.

They put me into a blue car, the publisher in the front, and I in the rear between the government inspector and the woman who wants to destroy my scarf, and we drive very fast through black streets, I try to scream but my throat is dry. All the time they are asking me about my flight, it is clearly very important, I must have done something wrong on my flight, but what could it have been? I sat in the lavatory holding my scarf all the way from Prague to London, I did not cough on anyone, I kept my passport in my mouth so that anyone breaking down the door would be able to see it and not take me away to kick me for losing my papers, my conduct was exemplary. I did not squeeze my spots.

The car stops at last, beside a cold canal. They are going to drown me like a dog in a sack for something I did on the flight. No, they are taking me into a building. It has giant eggs all round its roof. What is this place? Are they going to feed me to giant chickens?

They hurry me down corridors. My scarf is flying out behind me, it could catch in something, my neck could snap like a wishbone. Suddenly I am in a room filled with lights and cameras, they push me into a chair, they put a microphone around my neck, I am to be interrogated! The interrogators are a girl with a big mouth and a slit skirt, I cannot take my eyes off her leg, *I must take my eyes off her leg*, they will beat me, and a terrible man with a yellow face and tiny eyes who keeps touching my knee, who keeps saying *Hallo, good morning, and welcome, Hallo, good morning, and welcome*, over and over, perhaps he is not a man at all, perhaps he is a robot he will crush my knee with his steel hand, I wish to vomit.

The robot speaks: "Hallo, good morning, and welcome to this hour of *Good Morning Britain*, with us now we are very very privileged to have my very very good friend Mr Franz Kafka who is a Czech, and if there's one thing we're always glad to see at TV-am, it's a cheque, hner-hner-hner, hallo, good morning and welcome, Franz, tell me . . ."

I cannot hear his words any more, I am staring at the thing in his hand, it is a clipboard, he has information about me, it is something I did on the flight, it is something I did in the car, the girl is showing more leg, I have to get up, I get up, but my microphone wire holds my neck down, they are pushing me back into the chair, when will they start hitting me? The robot is still speaking ". . . a little excited, and why not, tell me, Franz, are there wedding bells in the offing, are you, hner-hner-hner, leaning on a lamp-post at the corner of the street until a certain little lady . . ."

I faint. When I come round, I am in the car again, we are speeding through wet streets, the government inspector is saying it went well, the girl is saying it was terrific, really terrific, no, really and truly it was terrific, it was a wonderful idea to start screaming and

"Oh, all right then, we'll jump when your headache's better . . ."

"Drop it! It could be from the Animal Rights Militia!"

fall over, that is exactly the kind of break a book like this needs, he made a really terrific impact, especially with his eyes sticking out and his cheeks hollow, a lot of old ladies will rush out and buy the book, good, good, good, says the publisher, where is the first signing?

What are they talking about?

They take me to a big store, it is full of books, many of them forbidden by the authorities, they put me in front of the books and my books are among the forbidden books, and men begin taking photographs of me, I am being set up, I am being compromised, I begin screaming again, but all that happens is that the girl says it is terrific, it is really terrific, screaming is now my trade mark, they can do big things with that in the gossip columns. Then a man I do not know pushes something in front of me and gives me a pen and asks me to sign! I refuse to incriminate myself, I break his pen, the man grabs my scarf, books fall, I am being pulled round the shop, everybody is shouting, police are called, I fall on my knees and beg them to beat me about the head, the girl shouts that this is *really* terrific and makes them take more photographs, I pass out.

When I wake up, I am staring at soup. I am at a long table, up on a platform, in some kind of banqueting room, there are a thousand women in big hats at a hundred round tables on the floor below the dais, they are all eating soup but not taking their eyes off me, is this a dream, what is the significance of soup in a dream? I cannot stop trembling. Someone has taken my scarf. I look around wildly for my scarf, I see a sign that says *Welcome to Foyle's Literary Lunch*, what does this signify, are these women going to eat my book, are these women going to eat *me*? I pinch myself, accidently jogging a huge man on my left, he tells me he is an actor, he has written a book which is propped up in front of him, it is called MY BIG BOOK. It has the huge actor's face on the cover. The man on my right then introduces himself. He is the huge actor's son; he is just as huge as the huge actor and he has written an even bigger book. It is called MY BIG FATHER. It has a photograph of the huge actor on the cover and a photograph of the huge actor's huge son on the back. Suddenly, a chicken bone from the soup sticks in my throat. The huge actor is telling a story about his huge son and cannot hear me choking. The huge actor's huge son is telling a story about his huge father and cannot hear me choking, either. I fall forward into the soup, and it is only when the huge actor's huge son leans heavily across me to ask his huge father which of them is going to use the one about their huge cousin in their after-dinner speech that his weight projects the chicken bone from my throat.

After lunch, they both tell the story about their huge cousin. A thousand women laugh and cheer. Then suddenly everyone is looking at me. There is a long silence. At last, the government inspector runs across, and pulls me onto my feet. Clearly, they want me to confess something. I refuse. From the floor, a voice shouts at me to say something.

I tell them that I have a bad chest, that I have an infection of the pleural cavity, that the State has stolen my scarf so that my lungs will be full of phlegm. I show them my handkerchief. There is uproar, women shriek, tables are knocked over, the government inspector and the girl grab me and drag me off the platform, my feet are off the ground. Suddenly, I am outside, I am in the car again, the government inspector is saying "wasn't that just a teensy-weensy bit over the top?" and the girl is saying "no, no, *no*, it was really terrifically impactive, it had a really amazing upfrontalism, it . . ." I put my head out of the window, I vomit.

I am in a cellar, it is some kind of broadcasting studio, it is clearly subversive, all the people have beards and sandals and vests with filthy words on, this is not a government broadcasting studio at all, I have been put here to incriminate myself, my head is swimming, a short woman with huge breasts across which runs the legend LBC WOMEN AGAINST RAPE drags me into a tiny plasterboard cavity and puts headphones on my head, they are going to bombard me with some form of sonar lobotomising, but no, a voice is coming through the headphones, a man is saying "hallo, Frank is it, this is Brian, a long-time listener but a first-time caller, I have not read this book of yours but what I want to know is what are you doing over here, you black bastard, why don't you get back to Praguolia or wherever it is, why don't you climb back up your bleeding tree . . ."

I curl up into a ball. They are winning: they have my scarf, soon they will have my sanity, my soul. I am carried out to the car again, this time nobody is smiling, something terrible has happened. I fall to my knees beside the back seat and beg to know what is wrong. They tell me that I shall not be doing wogan. The girl is weeping. What is wogan? They do not tell me, but I discover that it is something Fyodor Dostoyevsky has done. He has been brought here because of his new book *Crime and Punishment* and, during his interrogation, he was, apparently, asked if he would like to sing with the band. At this, he took out his axe and embedded it in the head of his interrogator. Obviously, wogan must be a form of murder.

LIFT OUT OF ORDER
THE NEAREST ALTERNATIVE PUBLIC CONVENIENCE IS SITUATED AT
Hawker

Playing Ball

Last month we were booked for several Oxbridge May balls. I've never found anyone to explain why they are called May balls when they are held in June. It's the kind of semantic conundrum which finds its way into the letters column of *The Times* provoking equally convincing, entirely contradictory explanations. One thing is certain. It always drizzles. It is a rule, or at any rate an inevitable coincidence, that May balls and drizzle go together. Perhaps they should try holding them in May and calling them June balls.

The last one we did this year was at one of the grander Oxford colleges. As is also usual we weren't due on until 3.30 am. We left London therefore at 11.00 pm. This may seem to be over-cautious but, as we know from previous experience, it was not.

Our first problem, as always, was getting in. Two elements are involved here: the right gate, and the Volkswagen in relation to the marquee in which we are to appear. The obvious answer is to go to the Porter's Lodge and ask. It's not as simple as that, however, because the night of a May Ball has the same effect on College servants as the full moon on Lon Chaney Junior. Anyone approaching the Porter's Lodge not brandishing an engraved ticket is presumed to be a gate-crasher. On this occasion it was Chuck Smith. This is not usual; it's Barry Dillon who is in charge of arrangements on the road, but Barry has bought a new bass which he appears to believe is made of glass and, until a suitable foam rubber cradle has been built in the back, nurses it across his knee. It was Chuck therefore who, slamming the driving door, strode towards the lodge for information. Chuck, knowing he would probably have to manhandle his drumkit across several acres of damp lawn, hadn't changed. He was dressed like a rather dashing Victorian burglar with a bold cap, a leather waistcoat and a silk scarf knotted at the throat; not exactly what anyone would choose to try and gate-crash an elegant college ball. This failed to modify the suspicions of the porter, a small but aggressive man with his hair parted in the middle. He rushed at Chuck brandishing a pick-axe handle and shouting archaic abuse.

"Be off with you!" he cried. It was perhaps as well that Barry was pinned behind his bass. While both conscientious and tenacious when persuading a reluctant promoter that we qualify for VAT, he is less suited for dealing with potential violence. Only the other day the blundering approach of a bumble bee outside a Somerset public house caused him such a paroxysm of anxiety that we feared him to be in the throes of a fit. Chuck is less easily intimidated. He is also rather large. Eventually the porter was persuaded, reluctantly, to divulge in which tortuous side-street our entrance lay.

The gates, as we expected, were exactly half an inch wider than our van. The street on which they opened was about a comfortable width for a tanked-up eighteenth-century Doctor of Divinity on a scrawny nag to amble up without brushing the walls. A great deal of manoeuvring was necessary, but that came later. First the guardians of this portal had to be persuaded that our presence was justified. "No tickets," they said, "no admission." The night of the Jobsworth.

Chuck tried giving my name and pointed me out in person in the back of the van where I sat trying to look every inch a celebrity. He argued that if we were trying to gate-crash we would be unlikely to drive up in a VW full of instruments. No joy. Finally he lost his temper. Four-letter words bounced off the ancient walls and scorched the ivy. Strangely enough this did the trick, or at any rate partially. Barry was allowed to toddle off nervously into the college in search of the tickets and returned with them some ten minutes later. They had been left in our names at the desk of the same porter who had brandished the pick-axe handle. We were home and wet. Inside the walls were patrolled by a regiment of men in paramilitary uniforms with walkie-talkies.

"At the third stroke it will be . . ."

It was then, it is always at this moment, that Mark turns up. He isn't always called Mark. Sometimes he's called Simon or Nigel or Jeremy. He is the member of the Ball Committee who booked us, and apologises profusely for not being there to meet us. He is always a bit drunk; white tie adrift, face flushed, eyes a little glassy. He reiterates his regrets as he leads us through a Lewis Carroll-like maze of archways in old walls, cloisters and quads towards the appropriate marquee. Here Chuck and Barry vanish through a tent-flap to set up their instruments behind the stage and the rest of us follow Mark, Simon, Nigel or Jeremy as the case may be, to be shown our bandroom, until tonight and from tomorrow the quarters of an undergraduate. Usually it's at the top of a steep and narrow staircase far from the scent of gilly-flowers, and we have never encountered Morris papers or Arundel stuffs either, and certainly no plover's eggs. A Van Gogh print and Orwell in paperback are the norm.

On this occasion we did rather better; a beautiful room on the ground floor belonging to the organ tutor. He looked in on us once, introduced himself and said he "was in the business". Our stock must be rising.

There was still an hour before we went on so I took a stroll to see what Mark, Simon, Nigel or Jeremy accompanied by Emma, Caroline, Lucy or Henrietta were getting for their fifty quid. There was supper (free): avocado, salmon, roast beef, salad, strawberries. There was champagne (not free). There was "Bad Manners", a fashionable rock group, a disco, a dance-band, us, and a West Indian steel band, *de rigueur* at posh thrashes ever since I can remember. There was also, in the middle of one of the lawns, a recent but ubiquitous feature; a huge blow-up mattress in the form of a mediaeval castle on which Mark and Emma and their friends can noisily bounce off the effect of the champagne. Everyone now wears evening dress. There was a time in the Seventies when punk fashion predominated, but it's gone together with the scent of pot. It's all very traditional again.

They are always a good audience. They were when I was almost their contemporary. They are now that they could be my children. Usually a girl climbs up on the stage and dances in an ambitious but unco-ordinated way, but she means no harm. We finish, pack up and drive back to London through the moist dawn.

OF THE BRITONS, WHOSE DOMAIN LAY NEAR THE RIVER WYE, MET A HORRID STRANGER ON THE HIGHWAY...

MORAL: Make no bargains with the immoderately ugly.

What business is it of hers

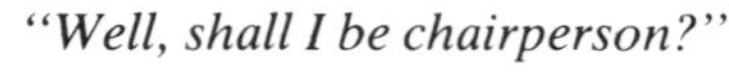

"Well, shall I be chairperson?"

"I'm sure you're right. I'm sure it **is** *important for a sales director to retain an element of mystery."*

"I've been longing for a seat on the board—it's lovely to get the weight off one's feet."

"As soon as my nail varnish is dry I'm going to claw my way to the top."

"She feels she can improve on the time it takes to boil an egg."

"An executive toy? It looks suspiciously like housework to me."

"Frankly, Mr Forsyth, I could do this job standing on your head."

"It's my wedding anniversary. Telephone my husband and tell him you're going to choose me a present."

Can't Say No

I am beside myself. Schizophrenic. Doppleganged. Two-in-one. I'm living, as it were, in the house next door. The world may know me as the bearer of an only son but secretly I used to think a genuine Big Mama wallowed within me. You've met the type: many kids of my own, and neighbours' offspring running in at all hours for my wholemeal doughnuts and goat's milk, and, yes, of course, I make my own maternity smocks out of army surplus parachutes. 'Tis true, I always believed I was a closet earth-mother, a *mère-de-terre-manquée*, a *mama mia* missing her vocation. But all that was when I lived in a house of my own. All that was before every American Kurtz south of Los Angeles (and one from New Jersey) decided to spend their holidays in London. The California Kurtzs (and one from New Jersey) are now established at number 26, where I used to live, and I'm in number 24 while Emily, formerly my neighbour, spends a few weeks in Wiltshire. Am I making sense? It's hard to be sure. After three days with my family, I'm finding consecutive thought elusive.

What was I saying to you? Forgive me, but my six-year-old nephew, David, has just rushed in to tell me he's sighted his 375th double-decker red bus.

"Listen, kid," I said, "when you see a purple one with yellow spots, let me know, but don't bother me again for a red one."

"Aren't you interested in red buses?" he asked, his little "r's" even harder than his Auntie Irma's heart.

"No," I replied. Whereupon he burst into tears. My nephew has this peculiar allergy, you see, just mention the word "no", and he cries. This affliction arose because his mother, my sister-in-law, Rosario, during her pregnancy with David's eight-year-old sister, Myra, lost faith in centuries of wisdom passed down the distaff generations of her Mexican family and decided she had to be a good California mum. To this end, Rosario enrolled in a course called Parental Effectiveness Training, or—can you believe this?—PET. There she learned that to say "no" to a child is to blast its chances of ever becoming a doctor. Say "no" to a two-year-old Californian when it tries to fill the swimming-pool with lighter fluid or to put your avocado tree into the "garbage compressor", and—hey, presto!—you've got a junkie on your hands, or maybe even a liberal. Anyhow, what you're supposed to do instead of saying "no" is engage the little imp in Socratic dialogue and bring it around to your way of thinking. For example, this is the way it sounded in the children's bedroom late last night when my niece and nephew were raising hell:

Rosario to her children: If you do not stop making a noise and go to sleep do you think you will be able to enjoy the British Museum tomorrow?

David: What is British and why do you have to keep it in a museum?

Myra: I don't like museums. Museums always make my ribs hurt. When my ribs hurt somebody has to carry me . . .

Awfully sorry. I must ask you to bear with me. I've lost my train of thought. Little Myra has just come in to ask me where my other bathrooms are. She was horrified to hear I didn't have any other bathrooms so I told her it was against the law in London to have more than one.

Now, where were we? Oh, yes. So there I am in the garden late last night sitting with my mother and my brother and listening to poor Rosario upstairs trying to reason her children to sleep. In my own experience it is a very bad idea to engage these miniatures of ours in rational dialogue because they are better at it than we are. I remember the first time I told my son that he was half American.

"Which half?" he asked.

Which half indeed? The half that has ridiculously big feet? Or the half that cannot hit the high note in *The Star Spangled Banner*?

"Don't be such an ass," I told him, as I always do when he asks a question I can't answer.

"Oh," he said, "*that* half."

My sister-in-law was faring no better than I usually do, and finally she had to retreat, humiliated, to join us in the garden.

"Okay," said my brother with a sigh, "I guess it's my turn . . ."

I do apologise. I've lost the thread. My

"I thought Norman had been looking a bit depressed lately."

"At least he doesn't worry sheep anymore."

brother has just come into the house next door which, you understand, is my house for the time being, to tell me that the British Museum was fabulous and he thinks he may have seen the Elgin marbles.

Oh, of course, I was telling you about my brother. Actually, he's my brother-the-doctor.

"Look," my mother said those decades ago when she returned from hospital carrying a blue bundle, "look, little Irma, I've brought you your brother-the-doctor!"

My brother-the-doctor is called Michael and only I on earth am allowed to call him Mook, a privilege I earned a long time ago by feat of arms. Frankly, Mook is a very moody man, generally taciturn, who only comes to life in cemeteries. Take Mook to a graveyard and he flits from stone to stone like a sparrow. Or a vulture. Cemeteries are pleasant enough places, I guess, but given my brother-the-doctor's profession his interest in them could be considered a wee bit sinister. Anyhow, it was his turn to cope with the children. He went upstairs and stood in their room and fixed them with a steady eye.

"Don't you guys think you should go to sleep?" he asked.

Immediately, they threw pillows at him, knocked him down and jumped on his stomach. Parental Effectiveness Training would probably call this a positive response and that may be so in California but, between you and me, here in Shepherd's Bush it's not the norm. At least, not for children under eighteen and even then they rarely do it to their own parents, generally preferring to do it to old age pensioners on their way home from the post office.

"Usually," my brother said when he'd caught his breath, "I leave the children to . . ." he glared at his wife, "Rosario."

I'm sure you will agree that the last thing anyone wants is for her brother's marriage to break up on her patio, so I realised it fell to me to cajole the little . . .

Whoops! Mom has just come over to tell me not to work too hard and to let me know she has put the tea left over from breakfast on the stove to keep it warm for me.

What was I saying? Oh yes, to cajole the little . . .

Sorry. My son has just come in to put his head on my shoulder for a few moments. "They say their swimming pool is bigger than our entire house," he said, and sighed. "They say they have a pool with Jack Oozey." He paused. "Who is Jack Oozey, anyway?"

To understand my condition when I saw two pygmies turning my upstairs bedroom into a California disco, you must know it hadn't been easy preparing for the family's arrival. It was no walkover converting a slum into a Potemkin paradise, stocking a freezer, scrubbing floors, while also tapping out "Unwed Motherhood: Take It or Leave It?" for *The Guardian* and "Is Sex Good for Marriage?" for *Cosmopolitan*. I was tired and ready to explode.

"Shut up, you brats!" I heard myself bellow. "Shut up, you noisy little brats, or I'll cut your . . ."

My sister-in-law has just run in crying, "Oh, my God!" because it has started raining and, apparently, she is worried about my orange crop.

Where was I? Where the hell was I?

"Good morning. I can see that you believe in looking and feeling attractive in the life hereafter, Madam . . .

Springing a Leak

Last week *Press Gang* began with a paean of praise for Adam Raphael of *The Observer* who anticipated the contents of the Franks Falklands Report by 48 hours. Mr Raphael's coup would have no place in a column which, today, deals with leaks, were it not for one extraordinary aspect of his exclusive story. For the triumphant author argued that he had no prior knowledge of the report's contents, but simply pieced together the opinions of sundry witnesses and came to the conclusion that their evidence would exonerate the Prime Minister.

Now that we have all had the opportunity to digest the Franks Report, Mr Raphael's achievement seems even more spectacular. For after weeks of careful sifting, *he actually came to the same conclusion as the document's two final paragraphs*. The rest of Franks—as all the serious newspapers have now explained—is highly critical of the Government's performance. It takes a journalist of real talent to conduct an independent enquiry and come up, not with the opinions expressed in the body of the report which his investigations mirrored, but with the conflicting judgement with which it ended.

But as Mr Raphael's story was not based on the sight of a secret document it is not part of this week's subject. Today we examine the publication of private papers: the sort of thing that I vividly remember from my days in the Cabinet. All Cabinets leak. And I suspect that all low-grade Cabinet Ministers react as I always reacted to the Prime Minister's Thursday morning denunciation of the known but unnamed culprit. I always feared that although I was wholly innocent, I was the principal suspect. The intonation, the choice of pronouns and the careful textual analysis of the offending extract all pointed to me.

No doubt someone at New Scotland Yard felt very much the same on the Monday morning after the *Mail on Sunday* published its "EXCLUSIVE: On a plan to devolve the police". Certainly the story made Fleet Street buzz. For it was written by Chester Stern, Crime Correspondent. And not only is Chester Stern a real person, he is an ex-information officer of the Metropolitan Police. It was assumed that Mr Stern was in the know. So his story was dutifully copied into the rival editions of other papers. Unfortunately, he grossly overdramatised the proposals. Innocent politicians who were booked for television and radio broadcasts on the strength of his mountain were told that they were not wanted when the Commissioner of Police unveiled his mouse.

All hope that a second David Henke had been discovered was extinguished. When David Henke was local government correspondent of *The Guardian* he seemed to reveal the contents of a secret document almost every day. They usually belonged to the Department of the Environment, and concerned matters of immense controversy and even greater complication. "Rate Support Grant Formula to be Changed" he would prophesy. And then would follow a passage of explanation which appeared to be written in code. When translated into English the prophecies always turned out to be correct.

Mr Henke clearly benefited from the activities of a mole—a man or woman, deep inside the DoE, who surfaced from time to time bearing a piece of paper. Most leaks are by word of mouth—which is why so many of them turn out to be inaccurate. A perfect example of the fallibility of leaks and the frailty of leakers is to be found in the recent spate of stories concerning the Government's new immigration proposals. Knowing Conservative backbenchers have stopped lobby correspondents in House of Commons corridors and assured them (in absolute confidence) that they know the Home Secretary's secret intentions. The lobby correspondents have confused confidentiality with authority and a lot of them will be proved wrong. They have all been sprinkled by conflicting leaks.

The other problem about leaks is that they are usually spurted out for a purpose. There are in Parliament and the Civil Service genuine enuretics who leak because they cannot help it, contemptible and compulsive blabbers who cannot see a journalist without wanting to reveal a secret. But most leakers relieve themselves for a purpose. The people in the Department of Health who spread around papers which outlined plans for re-organising the Health Service did it because they believed re-organisation to be synonymous with destruction. Stories from the Cabinet are usually spread with the specific purpose of discrediting one faction and promoting another.

In my experience leaks rarely do any harm and are the cause of much innocent fun. Occasionally they do positive good—as in the case of President Nixon's destruction. More often they do no more than prick the bubble of a politician's self esteem. For nothing makes a Minister feel more important than knowing something that the rest of us do not know. Hence all the fuss when a story which was intended for release on a Monday morning appears in the newspapers on the previous Friday. The leak is also the enemy of news manipulation. If the careful plan requires a story simultaneously to explode on every front page and it pops up prematurely in a single paper, the people who planned the megaton presentation are naturally furious. They take refuge in pompous pronouncements about the proprieties of public life.

This is how the Government responded to that very special category of leak, the broken embargo, when the list of Falklands War gallantry awards was broadcast 24 hours before official publication date. Newspapers and television companies had been given an early sight of the names, so that they could prepare their articles in advance. Falkland enthusiasm prompted some of them to jump the gun. The official complaint was not that another reminder of the Government's victory had been dissipated but that the families of medallists had been pestered at the wrong time.

Of course, the more the Government tries to manage the news, the more good journalists determine to tap the leaks. Which brings us back to Adam Raphael's story in *The Observer*—or rather would bring us back to it, if we suspected that the ingenious Mr Raphael had actually caught early sight of the Franks Report.

'AIR STOOD THE WIND FOR 'RANCE

er since the dawn of industrial ations, man has dreamed of ımphing over the annual Cross- annel Ferry Strike. In the hope of eering, even inspiring, thousands future sufferers, we offer this ort selective history of their ıstrious predecessors.

Sir Ernest Gunnell (1862–1909), famed inventor of the self-tapping barometer, the steam watch, the nit-press, and the miraculous hippophone for shouting encouragement to unfancied racehorses from an enormous distance, booked a fortnight in Deauville in August 1909. Arriving at Folkstone, he discovered to his chagrin that a strike by capstan operatives on the grounds that their shanty rehearsal time had been cut by fifteen per cent had kept all ferries in port until further notice. Undaunted, Sir Ernest immediately purchased thirteen sections of drain in graded diameters from Jas. Pome (Fine Bespoke Gutterings) Ltd, and a hinged kedgeree-tureen from the manciple of the Royal Albert Hotel, which items he then welded together to produce the submarine romper suit pictured here.

A non-swimmer, Sir Ernest soon afterwards set off to walk to Cap Gris Nez, an estimated eight hours away, arriving some four weeks later off Scapa Flow, where, in the hysterical Kaiserphobia of the time, he was immediately sunk by *HMS Dreadnought*.

In the summer of 1896, eight hundred members of the NUR and their wives booked a day trip to Boulogne aboard the *SS Golden Duck*, only to find upon their arrival in Dover that an NUS dispute over beard allowance had closed the entire port. After several months of negotiation with the shipowners and the collapse of fourteen separate arbitration committees, the NUR finally persuaded the Marquis of Salisbury's government to intervene rather than precipitate a General Strike, and the shipowners were compelled to winch the *Golden Duck* onto a chain of trucks on the Dover-London railway, so that the day out might proceed, albeit to Maidstone. All might at last have proceeded to a happy conclusion, had not members of ASLEF, incensed by what they saw as unacceptable concessions to the NUR, changed the points outside Canterbury. The *Golden Duck* was thus the first ship to be lost with all hands at the mouth of the Dartford Tunnel.

In 1873, Gerald Pilkington of Hove announced his forthcoming marriage to Miss April Gaveston of Brighton, and that they would subsequently honeymoon in Benidorm. Fearful of that summer's imminent rail, coach, and ferry strikes, Gerald Pilkington immediately set to work on the design of a small flying steamboat able to overcome any transport eventuality the fledgling unions involved might choose to throw at him. It was in the course of the long preparations for this craft, and the close and intimate circumstances under which the two men were compelled to work, that Gerald Pilkington and his welder Brian fell deeply in love. Minutes after they sat for this engraving, the happy couple flew over the Gaveston home to break the news to April. In their subsequent attempt to escape, they were pelted with wedding gifts by the distraught ex-fiancée: two EPNS toasting forks punctured the balloon, and the craft crashed fatally into Brighton West Pier.

THE HOUSEHOL

THE ROYAL BABY

. Quay ...d, Poole, Dorset ... 1HT

ENJOYED BRIDESHEAD REVISITED? Then why not spend a few days yourself in Hertford College, Oxford? Jenny Hall on 01-747 0029 or 01-994 6675 will arrange it for you.

Daily Telegraph

Oh What a Lovely Waugh

Monday Arrived Oxford Station 6.30 pm as requested on brochure. Finding no 1924 Rolls-Royce in multi-storey car park, made my way on foot to Hertford; small college situated some way from the High Street, but tasteful plaque on historic outer wall to commemorate the first arrival of Granada Television cameras early in the summer of 1978. Porter's Lodge closed due to long vacation, but hand-written sign announcing Rooms to Let without breakfast through quadrangle, £49 per night plus VAT no washing. Settled in, rang mother from coin-box on corner, considered possibilities of undergraduate life, tried to see dreaming spire, joined Jeremy Irons fan club.

Tuesday Awoken 6.30 am by sharp banging on window. Man with teddy-bear concession for South Oxon wished to know how many I wanted, also correct spelling of Aloysius. Told him I was awaiting arrival of scout with plovers' eggs in caviare for breakfast. He said scouts nowadays knew a thing or two, not likely to hang around with package tourists trying to recreate lost literary life, not unless good money and/or guaranteed immunity from prosecution under homosexual offences act. By midday, still no sign of breakfast but interesting offer in post of free conversion to Catholicism and/or special weekend rates at large country house in Yorkshire also used by Granada Television as background for same television series, and still complete with ancient housekeeper called George able to do cooked breakfasts for usual consideration.

Wednesday Still not much sign of 1920s college life, but have located cornflake box in library with interesting special offer on back of North African Holiday Special, two weeks of free alcoholism in sanatorium of own choice or full refund if not satisfied with physique of all male nurses. Also signed photograph of Diana Quick.

Thursday Decide to complain to local travel agent about lack of amenities for waistcoat-cleaning, picking up young scholars in quadrangles etc. He recommends alternative Waugh Holiday known as *The Loved One* Special: two weeks California, own choice of grave in Forest Lawn plus usual funeral concessions etc. Alternatively fourteen days mid-Somerset, meeting with Auberon Waugh almost guaranteed, plus permission to wear rimless glasses and insult people in pubs and television studios. Or, no extra cost, three weeks in the London Library writing letters to *The Times* about sad improvement in habits of choirboys.

Friday Definitely not the undergraduate life as described by Waugh; have twice been asked by large American ladies off coach to point them towards Oxford University itself, and so far been picked up by nobody except talent scout for *University Challenge* asking if I would like to answer questions on great tourist-rip-offs of the twentieth century. Am seriously considering taking the *Decline and Fall* tour of English preparatory schools.

Saturday Fed up with student life, no sign of degree ceremony or free BA Hons so have decided to join army instead; it was that or the *Vile Bodies* coach tour of Chelsea by night £74.50p including free glass champagne, and I decided on the army on account of it being the trilogy, therefore better value all in all. Two weeks *Men At Arms*, two weeks *Officers and Gentlemen*, two weeks *Unconditional Surrender* plus free pass to army social nights and a good chance of being blown up in Northern Ireland. Travel agent says sorry Hertford College a bit boring, but Waugh himself always thought that even in term-time and organisers eager for authenticity. Also it had been hoped week would include special trip to Venice to inspect canal photographed at length in episode three but costs proved prohibitive.

Sunday Not a lot happening. Went to Mass where Catholic priest said he personally hadn't been in series but he understood Lord Olivier had done a wonderful death scene. This, however, seems not to be part of the *Brideshead* package and now have been asked to vacate my room by noon to make way for the *Zuleika* tourists who are due in at 2.30 pm. Granada are, however, offering rooms in Coronation Street for next week plus an autographed refund from Lord Bernstein in case of overcrowding. Next summer am thinking of taking the Robert Graves tour of Majorcan nightclubs. That or the *Gilbert Pinfold* world tour plus madness supplement.

Alan Coren

Moscow or Bust

A claim was made last week that Napoleon died of a hormone-abnormality disease that was slowly turning him into a woman. This, according to *The Journal of Sexual Medicine*, explains contemporary reports of Napoleon's highly feminine appearance.

One of his doctors described the general's body as "effeminate", another said he had "a chest that many a woman would be proud of", while one wrote that "the emperor has small white hands and shows a good leg." Even Josephine compared her lover to a castrato.

The Observer

As soon as the first pale ray of watery spring sun slid through his curtains and struck his beard, Mr Sam Kaminski sighed, eased his elderly body from the bed, shuffled resignedly downstairs, and began to board up his shop window.

For spring, though naturally enough greeted with ecstasy by most of Mother Russia, brought nothing but anxiety to the ghetto of Plotz: as winter thawed, Plotz, on the barren banks of the River Niemen, gritted its teeth, prayed its prayers, and waited for the worst.

At the noise of Kaminski's hammer, his neighbour, still in his nightshirt, rushed out into the unpaved street.

"Did they come yet?" he cried.

Kaminski shook his head.

"Precautions," he said, through a mouthful of nails.

His neighbour stared at his own window. It was full of blouses.

"I could lose my entire stock," he muttered. "It's been a bad winter."

Kaminski spat out his last nail and banged it home.

"It makes a difference?" he said.

"With blouses," replied his neighbour, "it makes a *big* difference."

"How come?"

"The whores don't go home," replied his neighbour. "That's how come. They stay in the barracks maybe six months. The normal rate is a blouse a month. Figure for yourself."

"With furs," said Kaminski, "it's different. I got a class trade. Officers only. For their wives."

"Could be a nice little business," said his neighbour. "If they paid."

"If they paid," said Kaminski, "it could be a terrific business. I could be a chain by now. Mail order, even."

"Don't joke," said his neighbour.

Kaminski sighed, and went back into his shop, and took the best coats down to the cellar. Then he came back, slowly, up the cellar steps, put on his black homburg with the reinforced steel lining, and waited for the Cossacks.

It was nearly noon before the first hoofbeats shook the shuttered town. Kaminski cocked a practised ear, assessing his personal timetable: they would stop at the butcher's for a little rape, the way they did every spring, then they would burn down the school, say fifteen minutes, after that they would probably—he tensed, gasped! His heart lurched, missed, lurched irregularly on: they were *not* stopping! The thunder of hooves grew louder, shaking the wooden walls, then suddenly died in a jangle of tack and a rasp of dismounting boots, outside his very door!

Fists banged upon it.

"We're out of stock!" cried the furrier. "We're awaiting deliveries! Could be a month, but I can't promise, maybe a—"

The door flew from its hinges.

"All right!" shouted Kaminski, leaping up. "Okay! I lied, I admit it, I got a nice musquash stole, mink it isn't, but in a good light —"

He stopped.

The figure in the doorway was very small, for a Cossack. The uniform was unfamiliar. The hat was most peculiar. And the perfume, in particular, was very expensive. Most Cossacks wore wolfdung.

Kaminski took an uncertain step towards the doorway.

"Yes?" he said.

The short figure drilled Kaminski with two glittering eyes.

"I am Napoleon," it announced, "Emperor of Europe!"

Kaminski reeled, and clutched for support at the cutting-table.

"So!," he cried. "You have invaded at last! You are looking for Moscow! Okay, so you turn left at the—"

"Yes," said Napoleon, holding up a beautiful little hand, "and no. Yes, I have invaded, and no, I am not looking for Moscow. What I am looking for is something in sable, full-length, with a raglan sleeve. Chic, but not ostentatious."

As Kaminski gaped, and mopped his face, a tall and iron-jawed man strode into the little shop, and bowed stiffly.

"May I urge Your Imperial Highness to make haste?" he said.

"No," said Napoleon. "You don't rush sable, Ney. Am I right, Mr, er —"

"Kaminski," said the furrier. "Absolutely, Your Imperial Highness! I can see Your Imperial Highness is an Imperial Highness of terrific taste. With sable, artistry is what you have to have, also skill, also the experience of a lifetime, never mind a—by the way, Your Imperial Highness, what is this raglan sleeve business? We at Kaminski Bespoke Furs like to think of ourselves as being in the forefront of—"

Napoleon smiled, not without smugness. His kiss-curl bobbed.

"It could be a whole new fashion," he said.

"French, naturally," said Kaminski, nodding, "such taste, your people, such what shall I say, such—"

"As a matter of fact," said Napoleon, "no. You may recall the storming of Badajoz during the Peninsular War?"

"I read about it in the *Fur Trade Gazette,*" nodded Kaminski. "A terrible business. Persian lamb prices shot right down."

Napoleon glared at him.

"At Badajoz," he said, his voice rising to a not unfetching soprano, "there was this absolutely *ravishing* English officer, wasn't there, Ney?"

The marshal looked out of the doorway, and sucked his gilt chinstrap.

"Anyway," continued Napoleon, "he was wearing this wonderful frogged jacket, sort of half off-the-shoulder, with a very full—"

"You could sketch it, maybe?" suggested Kaminski.

"Your Imperial Highness," said Ney, as

"Ebsworth, you're a man of the world—what's my wife's telephone number?"

"This one frankly admits it's overpriced."

Bonaparte licked his crayon, rolling his eyes and tutting creatively by turns, "we have 435,000 men of the Grande Armée awaiting Your Imperial Highness's orders to advance, and while we have the brief meteorological advantage afforded us in this God-forsaken spot, we—"

"Leave us, Ney!" snapped Napoleon. After his marshal had stamped furiously out, he drew Kaminski confidentially into a dark corner of the shop.

"You don't think I'm a little, er, short for a full-length coat? I should hate to look squat."

"Take off the topcoat," said Kaminski. He took the coat, hung it up, turned, closed one eye, considering. "Your Imperial Highness has a terrific figure," he said finally.

"But not a little, er, *full,*" giggled Napoleon, "here?"

Kaminski tutted professionally.

"Since when was a big bust a disadvantage? Be grateful. It gives you presence. Also, you have nice slim legs. What we call a pocket Venus in the fur trade, you should pardon my familiarity. In sable you'll be a knockout, believe me. Would I lie?"

Napoleon smiled, and squeezed Kaminski's arm.

"Measure me," he breathed.

The Grande Armée bivouacked on the banks of the Niemen, confused, disgruntled, while their Emperor waited for his first fitting. Ney began to drink heavily. Most nights, Napoleon waited up for him, and the camp rang to his subsequent screaming complaints. During the day, they argued about the coat.

A week later, Napoleon returned to Kaminski Bespoke Furs.

"It fits you," said the furrier, "like the paper on the wall! You and that coat were made for each other."

Napoleon minced back and forth in front of the triple-mirror.

"It makes me look hippy," he said at last.

"Let me take it in a bit at the back," offered Kaminski.

On the banks of the Niemen, two divisions of Prussian infantry deserted.

By early August (having been sent back twice, to have white ermine cuffs added, and to have a matching hat made up), the coat was ready. Kaminski sent a messenger out to the camp, who returned with Napoleon, and a hollow-eyed muttering Ney.

"Elegant," said Napoleon. "I'll take it."

"Thank God!" croaked Marshal Ney. "Can we go to Moscow now?"

"Shall I wrap it?" asked Kaminski. "I'll find a smart box."

"I'll wear it," said Napoleon. "If you've got it, flaunt it!"

Kaminski's neighbour came out, along with the rest of Plotz, to watch the Grande Armée pull out.

"Did he pay, at least?" enquired the neighbour.

Kaminski showed him the cheque.

"Cash it quick," said the neighbour. "I understand the Tsar managed to get a big army together."

Three weeks later, in the middle of the night, a stone crashed through Kaminski's window. He sprang up, poised for Cossacks, and glanced outside.

"My spurs keep catching in the lining," shouted Napoleon, from the head of his army, who stretched, bleary-eyed, from Kaminski Bespoke Furs to the moonlit horizon.

"I'll come down," said Kaminski.

He lit a few candles, and examined the coat.

"I didn't notice at first," said Napoleon. "I got involved in my new hair-style. I couldn't think of anything else. You know how it happens."

"One ringlet is very fashionable," said Kaminski. "Where did you get the gloves?"

"Szolov," replied the Emperor. "They made me up eighty pairs."

"It took two weeks," said Ney.

"I'll have to shorten the coat a little," sai Kaminski.

"Moscow," said Ney, and fell on hi bottle.

Two days later, with autumn chill already i the September air, Napoleon strutted up an down outside Kaminski's, testing the nev length. Kaminski and his neighbour watche him, respectfully, from the shop.

"A pity he keeps the hand inside the coa all the time," murmured Kaminski. "It' ruining the shape."

"He's a Frenchman," said his neighbour grinning. "Maybe he likes to keep his han on his winkle."

"What winkle?" said Kaminski.

The Emperor came back inside the shop.

"Perfect," he said, and was about to leav when his eye rested on Kaminski's rack *"What's that?"* he shrilled.

"Chinchilla," replied Kaminski. "Th best."

"I'll take it!" shrieked Napoleon.

"It's not Your Imperial Highness's size," said Kaminski.

Napoleon waved his hand impatiently.

"Then make me one up!"

"With chinchilla," said Kaminski, "i could take three weeks minimum."

"I'll wait," said Napoleon firmly.

"But Moscow!" cried Kaminski. "No that I couldn't do with the business, bu didn't you already waste enough time?"

Napoleon stamped his pretty foot furiously.

"Moscow, Moscow, Moscow!" he screamed. "Why is everybody in such a *rush* to get to Moscow?"

And even as he spoke, in the little stree beyond the shop, the first pale snowflak floated down and settled on Ney's sleeve.

*"Mind you, if it **isn't** a mirage we could be in big trouble."*

MIDLAND BANK announced a £150,000 pilot project yesterday which could result in its being the first of the big four UK clearers to offer customers banking at home.

Financial Times

DONEGAN CHEQUE POINT CHARLIE

". . . and will your home banking terminal cry for you, sigh for you? When there are grey skies, won't it mind the grey skies? Will it hold your hand, will it understand . . . ?"

"Sorry, Derek and Enid, that wasn't ***your*** *balance, that was Leo and Dorothy's at number twelve."*

"Good morning, Mr Boyle! It's precisely seven-thirty, the sun is peeping coyly over the rooftops, and you're bankrupt. Have a nice day."

E. S. TURNER presents his 1982 Christmas Pantomime:

CINDERELLA

Assisted by many illustrious hands, namely (in order of performance) Mr Dryden, Mr Kipling, Mr Housman, Mr Wordsworth, Mr Coleridge, Miss Austen, Mr Burns, Mr Brooke, Lord Byron, Mr Shakespeare, Mr Poe, Mr Milton, Lord Tennyson, Mr Longfellow, Mr Shaw, Mr Dowson, Mr Masefield, Mr Chesterton and Mr Gray.

Act One

Prologue (read by a man in a stuffed shirt)

In pious times, when maidenheads were prized,
When single parents went uncanonised,
When whores were larruped, when suburban lives
Were unbedevilled by exchange of wives,
Ere vengeful Herpes felt constrained to strike
Impartially at catamite and dyke,
Ere foul Lubricity usurped clean Wit,
When intercourse meant talk—

Audience: Get on with it!

—When vernal innocence enclosed the land,
Lived Cinderella.

Buttons: Give her a big hand!

Enter Cinderella, singing:

Cinderella! The name's O'Grady,
And I'm as good as the Colonel's lady.
A rag and a bone and a hank of hair—
They call me that and it's just not fair.

Chorus:

By the livin' Gawd, she is not all there.

Buttons:

No name have I but Buttons,
All buttoned up am I.
I'll swing at one-and-twenty,
Or know the reason why.
O ne'er a rose-lipt maiden
Would wish to share my cup.
For lads ablaze with buttons
Are sure to be strung up.

As Cinderella and Buttons console each other, enter an Old Gaffer, reciting:

Three sisters were there. Two were overweight,
Like sacks of dripping in a knacker's cart,
The more they gorged the more their ankles swelled,
Which made them grow worse-tempered every day.
They went about "like mutton dressed as lamb",
But how unlike those lambkins of my youth
That frivolled on Helvellyn's beetling slope,
Distracting simple Ordnance Survey men
Like Colonel Grimes, whose man sold ginger wine
In Hopton Vale—

The Old Gaffer is hauled off with a long-handled hook. Enter the Two Ugly Sisters, singing:
Our ways are rude, our looks are lewd,
And furiously we scold!
Two vampires hot from Hell are we.
Damn Cinders and her housemaid's knee!
She'll do what she is told.
We'll keep her stark in cellar dark,
Where, every time it rains,
A thousand thousand slimy things
Start coming up the drains.

Instead, up from the drain, comes a Good Fairy. She announces:
It is a truth universally acknowledged that a downtrodden step-sister, if secure in her virtue, must eventually espouse a prince with eighty thousand a year. What ails you, child?

Cinderella: I want to go to the ball.

Good Fairy: Then to the ball you shall go. For at a fashionable assembly are to be heard the liveliest effusions of wit and sapience, expressed in the utmost felicity of language, hardly to be surpassed in the pages of a female novelist. But young ladies are delicate plants and ill befalls the incautious maid who does not leave by midnight.

Cinderella, delighted, turns to Buttons and sings:
One fond kiss, and then we sever.
There's nae future for us twa.
Rin aboot the braes, guid laddie,
All is tapsalteerie, ha!

Re-enter first Ugly Sister, shrieking:
This flaming clock says ten to three,
Where is the honey for my tea?

Act Two

A grand ball in a Trust House. Prince Charming soliloquises:
Hark to the sound of revelry by night!
Dear God, we have the sweepings of Debrett.
All England's birth and chivalry, half-tight.
Sights that would freeze a succubus. And yet
Surely I spy a saucy midinette,
A minx who might be worth the follow-through,
And leave a glow that one would not regret.
With any luck 'twill help to cure my 'flu.
She'll smell of bread-and-scrape. But, hell, she'll have to do.

Enter a hunchbacked clown, cackling:
Marry, here's a fine pickle, good cuckolds! If wishes were jock-straps, then might twelve philosophers sit in Adam's navel. By the beard of Quinapulus, I am the Great Worm of Lambton.

Children in audience: Oh no, you're not!

The clown replies "Oh yes, I am." This continues for ten minutes. Then the Prince approaches Cinderella, singing:
Cindy, thy beauty is to me
Like those Nicean barks of yore
That softly, o'er a perfumed sea—

Cinderella:
I do love Poe! Pray say some more.

Enter a Messenger from the Good Fairy, announcing:
From womb of Midnight torn,
Succeeds the infant Morn,
Warmed by the glint of Phoebus's axle-rod—

Cinderella:
Midnight, he says. It's midnight. Oh, my God!

Cinderella flees, leaving a crystal slipper. The Prince picks it up and soliloquises again:
Ring out, wild bells, across the snow.
Ring out the happy midnight chime.
The girl is fleeing—let her go.
I'll track her down some other time.

Act Three

A community centre packed with shrieking females. A member of the unemployed recites:
From the shores of Gitche Gumee,
From the Third World's reeking swamp-lands,
From the bestial inner cities,
From unhallowed conurbations,
Come the Koos and the Samanthas,
Come Miss World and Miss Mail Order,
All the anorexic scarecrows,
All the slags and topless bar-girls,
Mostly on suspended sentence,
And the terrible Sloane Rangers,
Here to try the crystal slipper.
And, of course, the Ugly Sisters,
Wriggling their toes in frenzy.
Will it fit?

A bearded Irish wit:
Not bloody likely.

Enter Cinderella's old Auntie, crooning:
Cinderella, wake beloved!
Try your luck, you potty ha'porth.
Do not keep Prince Charming waiting.
There you are, you see, it fits you!
Now we can go off to Harrods.
Lawks-a-mercy, what a pother!
Still, I warrant it was worth it.

Cinderella (to Prince):
My maiden heart beats with a deathless passion.

Prince:
I shall be faithful, Cinders, in my fashion.

Cinderella:
No longer shall I have to waste my days
Midst firewood, iron-ware and cheap tin trays.

Chorus:
Hurrah for England, Queen and Cinderella!
We always knew that she would get her fella.

Enter two geriatrics, quavering:
We are the old-age pensioners. We may be weak and wet,
But we are the people of England and we have not spoken yet.

Children in audience:
Oh yes, you have!

Geriatrics:
Oh no, we haven't *(And so on.)*

Epilogue
(read by another man in a stuffed shirt)

Now, as you homeward plod your weary way,
Lapped in the gloom our artless tale begets,
To dumb forgetfulness be not a prey—
Make sure you leave no smouldering cigarettes.

Large was your bounty, your applause sincere.
God bless you all, though rude and undevout.
If strong Emotion bids you shed a tear,
Pray do not slash the seats as you go out.

Robert Morley

The Yule Catalogue

It's several years now since I gave ants' nests for Christmas. "I hope," I used to remark, "that you haven't got one of these already—but if so you can cross-breed." As usual, I had no very clear idea of what reason prompted. I certainly never bought one for myself. The ants lived under glass in wooden boxes. I am not sure what they fed on, goldfish spawn perhaps?

Christmas is back with its customary vengeance, but this year for me it's different. At last I have made the catalogues (well, only one) but it's a start, surely? In August they took the photographs. I was on the sofa at home, wrapping books, biting through ribbon, and in the background were a balloon and a monster cracker. I haven't seen the finished catalogue in which I feature, but I feel pretty confident it's floating around.

Of course I've been asked to be Father Christmas a few times. Once it was for the Beatles when they were young and, I hoped, foolish enough to reward me with something really startling after the party. I had read somewhere that they gave motor-cars to their staff—people used to write a lot of nonsense about the boys in those days. I wasn't on the staff, just loaned, along with the ballroom of the Lancaster Gardens Hotel, for the evening. When I looked into the sack I was to carry, it was filled with Mars bars and Smarties and there were a few left over for the reindeer at the end.

Then again, I started my theatrical career as Santa, when I was about seven, at the Folkestone Metropole Hotel—plenty of cotton wool and a wish that Father Christmas would never be forgot. I was only an amateur in those days but this year I turned professional, for a cheque and some of the prestige books in the catalogue which couldn't find a coffee table. It's only a start, as I said, but I live in hopes.

Looking around at my distinguished contemporaries who have made the more prestigious catalogues, I think the palm must go to Larry Adler who rates a full page in Selfridges' magazine. He seems to have achieved the sort of Christmas I have sometimes dreamed of, alone at a table for one, with a selection of cold cuts and a glass of claret (Château Romanée-St Vincent Conti, 1976, Ground Floor). He makes no secret of his wardrobe—white dinner jacket £109 (from a selection, First Floor), white silk handkerchief £2.50, black velvet bow, onyx cuff links, etc, etc. I trust he had the sense to keep them and also to carry off the Sheffield silver knife and fork (£7.50 Basement).

His is a hard act to follow, for although apparently alone this Christmas, he lists the guests who might as a rule help to make a party go. A good many of them, alas, like Judy Garland and Hoagy Carmichael, are no longer with him, or us for that matter. He is eternally grateful, he says, to Leonore (Gershwin) who, when she invited Larry and his wife over, never came up with the dreaded line—"And you will bring your mouth organ, won't you?" I am inclined to think he did, however.

Larry Adler advocates good wine (we've been into that) and no hard liquor, before dinner or afterwards. "It's the whisky and soda that makes the drunks," he insists and then adds a final word of advice: always write a note of thanks. Don't phone, that can be a distraction. If the occasion warrants it, though, you might send flowers to the hostess. Better perhaps be on the safe side (fresh flowers, Ground Floor).

Selfridges' catalogue pays homage to their founding father and part of his story is told and illustrated with pictures of his great love, the Dolly Sisters, who regularly looted the premises. There's a mention of the bargain basement maintained by Mr Selfridge so that "even the less affluent felt at home, and were able to afford something, however small."

Still, austerity is not allowed to predominate for much longer, and there is a happy spread of two lively modern Dollies in Canadian lynx and natural lynx at £79,950 and £59,950 (Second Floor). For some reason they have removed shoes and stockings—and possibly everything else—and are pouring Laurent Perrier Champagne, at £11.75 the bottle over their feet. The Orgy Department floor is not listed.

Hamleys, I find, have devoted a page of their catalogue to feature a tiny portion of stars of stage, screen and sport who regularly visit them to meet the children. Rolf Harris is seen talking to Jean Rook and her son Gresby. There are snapshots of Richard Meade holding on to a pantomime horse and of Angela Smith meeting her fans in the squash world. There is mention, too, of the authors who have honoured the store—such as the late and much-loved Jack Warner and the very much alive Patrick Moore, while Geoffrey Boycott has apparently always been a regular visitor and has helped many a customer by freely giving advice and tuition. Surprisingly, the only cricket bat to be found is included in Hamleys Beach Set, one of the non-oil varieties along with four stumps, a bail and a special rubber ball, all for £6.50.

Even Harrods, it turns out, are not above quoting from satisfied customers. They feature a touching letter from the widow of Lord Douglas of Barloch (Scottish Department) recalling a grim morning for the ex-Governor of Malta. He, since 1912, had, it seems, insisted that every slice of bread he ate must bear a Harrods label, which he presumably spat out. One morning, however, his Lordship discovered a fault in the 100 per cent wholemeal mix and wrote off immediately, accusing Harrods of contravening the Foods and Drugs Act. Harrods' analyst was on the phone in no time, sounding slightly hysterical and admitting the error. By an extraordinary sleight of hand, the analyst had two replacement loaves whisked on to a special delivery van forthwith. The next morning Lord Douglas was munching happily again, the catalogue reports proudly, and he continued to do so until the day of his death at the age of 91.

Turning the pages we find Jo Wright sending a big thank you for the disposable lighter which saved the lives of his friends in a game reserve. With it they managed to light a bonfire, despite being bogged down in the

"He's terribly proud of his new dentures."

ain forest, thus warding off the savage beasts while they slept. I note also that Harrods are offering, for personal shoppers only, exclusive Russian broadtail coats with deep sable cuffs, in sizes 8–12, and costing £16,200. Those in search of cheaper gifts might care for the Supreme Luxury Hamper at only £1,000. They don't tell you what's in it, but there is sure to be something like Bahlsen Afrika Wafers, Marina crab salad or even a decorated vase filled with Earl Grey tea-bags.

Fortnums are no less proud of their history and their current ability in these lean times to fill laundry baskets (non-returnable) to the brim with Sir Nigel's vintage marmalade, Cornish crab soup and tins of giant cashew nuts. To me there always seems an element of patronage in the gift hamper. On the other hand, I, for one, can easily swallow my pride along with the Baxter's whole pheasant and the half-dozen bottles of Dom Perignon. Just what the doctor ordered for me, or no doubt will before long. Why not keep the old thing happy? Champagne can't hurt him these days.

Fortnums claim to have gone great guns at Scutari. Queen Victoria herself paid for the beef extract forwarded c/o Miss Nightingale, though it seems a modest order alongside *The Wiltshire* (double Devonshire fudge, tin Culrose ham, black cherry preserve) or *The Lincolnshire* (smoked barbecue baste Negroni Parma ham, all-butter Dovedale biscuits) or *The Yorkshire* (Consiglia peaches in Grand Marnier, F. M. apron, F. M. shopping bag). I am disappointed that there is not as yet *The Falklands* (Boudoir sponge fingers, Epicure

rock lobster tails, beehive pottery jar . . . ?)

Years and years ago, when I toured Britain and spent Sundays on interminable train journeys, I had a friend who, as we halted in the dusk at wayside stations en route, was wont to summon some bemused official and, handing him a few pennies, would announce that they were for the poor of the neighbourhood. The joke, like many other good jokes, was in doubtful taste, yet never failed to amuse.

I was then young and uncaring and poor myself up to a point. The phrase has stuck in my mind until now I am old and no longer poor, but still in the main uncaring.

There is little point, I tell myself, in sending a hamper to the Underground station at Charing Cross, even supposing Fortnums deliver at night. Besides, the caviare, the Maldon salt, the Pâté Maison with truffles, even the kiwi fruit in syrup might only serve to remind those sleeping fitfully in cardboard boxes of the better times some of them may once have enjoyed.

I am thinking particularly of the ex-headmistress of a fashionable girls' school who suffered the terror of a gang rape and, drifting into madness, ceaselessly patrols the Embankment, dossing down when night falls behind the coffee bar and only occasionally suffering the indignity of a water cannon splash at the hands of a caring Westminster Council.

I know there are among us those who, especially on Christmas Day, boil soup and roast turkeys for such as her. But I am a family man. I shall be eating my turkey and pulling the crackers with the grandchildren. Come to think of it I had better get on with the shopping.

This year I'm determined not to fall into the trap of leaving it too late.

Not every child will wake up on Christmas morning with a toy in their stocking, but, as they say in the catalogues, for those lucky enough to have a little boy or girl to buy for, and who have just become proud parents, grandparents, or aunts or uncles, it is a magical time. For all of us, Young Hamleys has been specially created this year. I cannot imagine that they sell ants' nests.

"Why can't we have what we had last year—leg?"

Jack Trevor Story

Cold Meat

As a dark and handsome young man with Brylcreemed hair and pointed patent-leather shoes, waiting to become a dance-band leader, I was lucky enough to work in cold meats. The manager of the shop asked me what I wanted to be and I told him frankly that I wanted to be a dance-band leader. I did not want him to think that cold meats were the limit of my ambition.

"This is the very place to start then," he said. "We can teach you your counterpoint." When I asked him what I had to do—his name was Marlow—he said that I had to wear a white coat and apron and when customers came in I was to point at the counter.

"Haslet, saveloy, chitterlings, tripe, breakfast sausage, Black Pudding, poloni, ham, York ham, corned beef, pressed beef, roast beef, roast pork, jellied veal, tongue, potted meat, faggots, veal-ham-and-egg pie, pork pie, sausage rolls, steak-and-kidney pies, milk cheese, cream cheese, red cheese and white cheese, St Ivel, treacle tart, don't forget the bacon—"

He then sucked in a great Norman Wisdom mouth-organ note and continued, "Streaky bacon, back bacon, collar bacon, flank bacon, gammon bacon, shoulder bacon, forehocks and hocks. Green bacon, smoked bacon, Danish bacon, English bacon, rabbits, chickens and three kinds of dripping. Who's your favourite band-leader?"

"Roy Fox."

"What's your instrument?"

"Guitar."

"Well, take your geetar and geetartovere!"

You've guessed it; I had fallen amongst a comedian.

On Thursday afternoons he had two painted women down in the brine cellar on sacks of sawdust. I had to go out for cream buns and take care of the counter trade. Thursday afternoon is early closing except in the cold meat business. Monday afternoon was early closing for Marlow but work in the slaughterhouse for me. The animals were electrocuted, stabbed, shot and bled; I had only dance-band sort of jobs but they included balancing two buckets of blood on my carrier bike all the way back to the factory for the puddings.

Workhouses were rather more obvious then than now—these days they are euphemistic with social workers; the tramps sit around hand-out offices but then they were more colourful and shuffled into our shop as they left town for the ditches. Marlow prepared what he called lucky dips for them at a penny and tuppence each. These were surviving scraps of mildewed edibles—we had no refrigerators. Maggoty pieces actually *moving* with new life he saved for blind tramps.

Nothing was wasted. One of my continuing tasks was turning bits of fat into dripping; I had a big pork-dripping tin on a gas ring, all day long. The little cinders were carefully screwed into bits of greaseproof paper for tramps and undergrads—it was a twin-poverty trade in Cambridge.

"Don't give the gowns any mildew." That was one of my instructions after somebody had got a report on a roast jowl of pork from the Pathology lab. Gradually I got to know the grumblers—Alastair Cooke, Michael Redgrave, Hugh Foot, the Earl of Birkenhead, Arthur Marshall and Gilbert Harding and one or two blacks—Gandar-Dower. Selwyn Lloyd got some maggots and we had to give him a poloni free of charge. He ate it in the shop.

"If it stinks pour formalin on it. You're a dance-band leader, I shouldn't have to keep telling you." Marlow again.

It became so that he was making fun of my style. Style has always been one of my things. Walking.

"Have you got a bad foot?" my daughter-in-law asked me yesterday. I limp to break the monotony. Without a dance-band at present, I conduct myself. Rubbing olive oil over mildewed bacon and black pudding or melting mouse-prints off dripping is not stylish. I had to cycle from the eggmart with six or seven score of eggs without breaking one. If I broke one I had to swallow eleven raw, otherwise it would be noticed.

Brawn I was good at. You can't get brawn now. I bought some recently and it was rubbish. The jelly was artificial. Jelly is the whole secret of brawn. Anyone can chop up a pig's head and sprinkle the whiskers in.

One day I got back to the shop and found Queen Mary sitting in Mr Marlow's accounts chair fanning herself with a butter pat. She used to come to Cambridge out of season to buy cheap antiques and she had seen a terrible accident at East Road Corner—or so she thought.

"There's a dead boy on Donkey's Common and the gutters are running with blood," Mr Marlow told me, quietly.

"That's pigs' blood!" I cried. I had got knocked off my bike and into a bus and the Black Pudding buckets had gone flying. I was unconscious for ten minutes and then allowed to walk back to the shop.

"Don't go to a doctor," Marlow said. He was afraid of getting the shop into trouble under the Act. I was taken home to Green End Road (107, still there) in the Royal Roller. For the record, I met Queen Mary once more when I took a banned turning (late Forties) at London University, not noticing the signs in Gower Street, and found my Austin Seven radiator halted by that formidable mobile throne. Though that's not, strictly speaking, shops. I am, however, on these occasions, cold meat.

"My home computer thinks I'm at a conference in Southport."

". . . and now, ladies and gentlemen, we are entering the very heart of Mount Rushmore."
mike williams.

"Jet lag! Who, me?"
DONEGAN

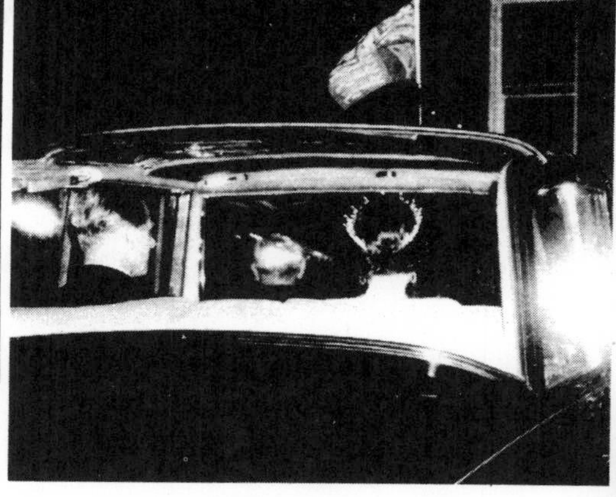

ROYAL RUMOUR DENIALS–LATEST

A handy cut-out-and-keep checklist to this week's scandalous stories now being strenuously denied by outraged Buckingham Palace spokesmen

HER MAJESTY THE QUEEN

1 Has not, as a gesture, consented to being positively vetted
2 Does not plan to give serious thought to abdication if, over Her Majesty's dead body, His Royal Highness The Prince Andrew has the brass neck to expect to be entertained for Christmas luncheon with yet another chorus-girl in tow
3 Is not prepared to comment on whether or not the Royal Yacht *Britannia* was carrying nuclear weapons during the recent official visit to the South Pacific
4 Is not hopping mad as a result of not being able at Balmoral to get a decent picture on Channel 4
5 Is not suffering from any appalling psychological torment or hushed-up baldness which is baffling Her Majesty's personal physicians and which in the opinion of His Royal Highness the Duke of Edinburgh, has like as not been brought on through not having slept a wink for fear that Fleet Street's Men Who Really Know The Royals might at any time walk into Her Majesty's private chambers without formal introduction
6 Will not be entertaining Mr Yuri Andropov to tea at Windsor as part of any hush-hush approach at top-level détente

HIS ROYAL HIGHNESS THE DUKE OF EDINBURGH

1 Is not secretly worried sick at the possible ill-effects which over-zealous adherence to the F-plan Diet may be having upon members of the royal family
2 Has not been secretly approached to read the news on breakfast television
3 Has not recently in so many words described any members of the working class as a bunch of bloody-minded, back-sliding selfish layabouts who might benefit from being ruled by a former head of the KGB in order to determine how they might, or might not, like any such onions
4 Is not expecting a baby
5 Is not, so help His Royal Highness, about ready to tell in no uncertain terms the Editor of the *Sun* where he, the Editor of the *Sun*, can stick his so-called newspaper in the event that any of that newspaper's ferret-faced, beer-swilling, muck-raking court bloody correspondents so much as dare set foot within ten miles of EITHER Sandringham OR Balmoral
6 Is not to make any attempt at the world land speed record for a four-in-hand

HIS ROYAL HIGHNESS THE PRINCE OF WALES

1 Is not seriously concerned and visibly shaken by the fact that his only son, His Royal Highness The Prince William, has on a number of recent occasions refused to contemplate another rusk
2 Has not privately threatened to take up transatlantic hang-gliding or roller-skate down Everest if just one more time His Royal Highness is obliged to sit through another lecture on the alleged risks which might attach to the occasional game of polo
3 Has not commissioned an intimate biography from Miss Angela Rippon or, for that matter, anyone else
4 Has never seriously been urged to consider a toupée
5 Does not intend to propose his brother, The Prince Andrew, as Governor-General of the Falklands or anywhere else that is several thousand miles from either Fleet Street or London's more notorious nightspots
6 Is not anxiously maintaining a round-the-clock bedside vigil at his wife's side for fear she might at any moment fall victim to whooping cough or Legionnaire's Disease

HER ROYAL HIGHNESS THE PRINCESS OF WALES

1 Is not to be rushed to a secret sanatorium for urgent treatment for chronic over-exposure
2 Is not suffering from Nappy-Changer's Elbow
3 Has neither agreed nor declined to enter the competition for Miss World
4 Is not to enter the competition for Slimmer of the Year
5 Has no secret ambition to open a health food, tap, aerobics and work-out studio in Mustique or anywhere else
6 Has not been privately urged to produce twins in time for the next General Election

OTHER ROYAL RUMOURS IN BRIEF

1 It is flatly denied by Buckingham Palace that there are whispers from the Government's think-tank concerning any feasibility study of privatising the monarchy or putting BritRoyal shares out to tender
2 Their Royal Highnesses The Princess Anne and Captain Mark Phillips are not prepared to consider any suggestion that they be hived off into separate units as part of a cost-cutting exercise
3 Her Royal Highness The Princess Margaret has no reservation on any British Airways Caribbean Poundstretcher at this time under her own or any other name
4 None of the mentally twisted or sexually deviant subversives who may, or may not, presently be remaining in service with the Royal Household is thought to be in any position to put the lives of British Intelligence agents overseas at risk or to threaten the Atlantic Alliance
5 It is denied that Miss Koo Stark has applied for a position as barmaid at The Bag O' Nails public house
6 So far as can be ascertained, none of the royal corgis has, or has ever been suspected of having, rabies

Oxford Revisited

I was standing in the mock-baronial gentlemen's lavatory (built, no doubt, by mock-baronial gentlemen architects) in the Oxford Union Society when a rather stately, plump young buck-man came in wearing a cashmere coat, a dinner jacket and a most uneasy smile. He stood squarely in front of the mirror and as I joined him—or rather took possession of the adjacent basin—he pulled out a lipstick with all the aggression of those two-ton pub maestros who spear darts into treble twenty.

"Better tart myself up a bit," he said; to himself, I presumed, and on went the lipstick—a rather unbecoming deep purple, but each to his/her taste. I washed my hands rather more slowly. The young man sucked and smacked his unskilfully smeared lips and then, with some panting at the exertion involved, heaved a hand between his plump frame and his inside pocket to haul up a pad, or wad, or tin, or whatever the container is called, of mascara. This he applied lavishly—daubed might be the word—while I dried my hands in slow motion.

He gave himself a final rather desperate glance. Glance? Stare. "I know you," he said. "Met you. You talked at my school." Neither of us offered to shake hands. Clearly he was now finally prepared for his evening strategies. "*Rocky Horror Show* party," he said. "Thought I'd tart up a bit." Ah, so. Grimly he left the room.

And up and down the stairs in the place which has seen the ascent and descent of so many prospective prime ministers, so many political pundits, charlatans, successes, men of honour, was the Oxford response to the *Rocky Horror Show*. Good taste outrage: all in moderation—although I have to admit I did not enter the room where the film was showing; who could imagine the excesses there? But I think it would have been much the same—a little coy Berlin, a little toy sex. If Oxford is any pointer to the way in which the future establishments, including the cultural establishment, sees itself, then even a licensed time for sensation will not get out of hand. Conservatism (small c) has struck back.

There is a tendency to be embarrassed by the inclination of those who have gone to Oxford or Cambridge to dig up their university past or pore over their university days. It seems too near gloating. And who wants to be seen doing this when much of the prevailing wisdom sees the place epitomised and characterised in the single word of the Oxford film now given an unusually widespread release, *Privileged*? "I suppose you'll find it interesting if you've been to Oxford," said several undergraduates who spoke about it: none admitted having liked it.

It was exactly twenty-five years ago th I went up to Oxford. During the pa weeks I've been back there a few times to ta to various literary and arts societies. Th undergraduates have always been keenly i terested to know what I think about Oxfo now: about them, I suppose. My answer h been that I didn't know enough to offer a useful comment. Over the last few day though, I've been thinking over what w said at those meetings and how it was sai what the temper of the place was lik whether there could be any pointers to th future.

After all, twenty-five years ago, the prese editors of *Punch*, *The Guardian*, *Private E* and the *New Statesman* were all "up": so w the new Director of Programmes, BBC Tel vision; as was the Chairman of TV AM, th Minister of Technology, the Shadow Mini ter for the Arts and Education, innumerab other MPs, journalists, writers, televisio presenters, producers, film directors, don jokers, who, one way and another, have p footprints on the sands of our time. Foo prints which might be no more permane than sandcastles, but footprints nonetheles The profile of a substantial part of our e panding communications establishment ca be constructed from the generation that pa ded through the autumn streets of Oxfo twenty-five years ago.

What of this latest generation? Many mo women, of course; cleaner buildings; mo self-awareness, I think, of themselves as "a Oxford generation"—even though some them mourned the "fact" (as sanctified b Martin Amis) that there were no longer "ge erations" at Oxford. It is quite a shock discover that the lot you belong to (lot 1958/61) is regarded as a tightly knit clust of enviable achievers. If only they knew Still, there is a self-consciousness about bein at Oxford which I am sure we did not have anything approaching the same degree. Or we felt it we kept it dark. Twenty-five yea on, they flush it out. Admirable, in its wa Heightened no doubt, by the *Brideshead* spi over and the fairly recent exposé of juvenil aristo goings-on among the over-monied se

Scarcely anyone I met was at all happy wit the tuition being given. They felt their tuto were either lazy, incompetent or too bus furthering their careers on the metropolita market to give them a fair innings. Onc again, I think they are more inclined to ha sher judgements than we were: twenty-fiv years ago, lazy, incompetent and self-servin dons were regarded as cuddly character Now it appears they are seen as obstructiv and conceited bores. Quite a lot of wel considered feeling on this one.

A hardening all round, it seems. I was tol that the university mags had adopted some the nastier habits of Grub Street and peddle gossip, malice and vendettas for all the worl like their skilled models on the Street Shame.

If there is this lack of fudging, this eye o

"If it's only another book club offer, why are you eating it?"

the world's chance, this impatience with cosy things like generations, then it is understandable. For the vast difference, possibly the chief difference, between our two generations is that *we* all slept safe in the all but certain expectation of a job at the other side of the degree. Some sort of job. Often enough we were careless about what sort of job. But there were jobs.

Not now. Even in their second year, the present undergraduates are sifting the possibilities of the job market. They are worried and confess it. The awareness of the black holes on the other side of the university surely influence them more than any mere changes of fashion. It seems to be driving them towards a rather subdued conservatism; a Titanic jollity; questions centred not so much on what you do but on how they can get to do what you do.

And yet, in Pembroke College at a pleasantly rowdy meeting of the Johnson Literary Society, the questions asked about contemporary fiction were thoughtful and funny; in the ante-room to ultimately fashionable *Rocky Horror* at the Union, an audience was prepared to be engaged about the arts and television; there was the young man who is troubled at the fictional preoccupation with sex, the young woman who is going to be a writer, the undergraduate photographer with his flowing coat and elaborate poses, the two young men well advanced with a funny and possibly commercial book about Oxford. The book seems to draw an awful lot on that awful lot who were there twenty-five years ago: otherwise it could be—well, the focus which will eventually be seen to define *this* generation as yet another Oxford generation which, twenty-five years on . . .

Paul Jennings

Even Higher Criticism

Faultline, by Sheila Ortiz Taylor. **"Faultline is faultless . . . an earthquake of a book"—Rita Mae Brown. A new, outrageously funny novel featuring Arden Benbow, lesbian mother with six children, 300 rabbits and a very relaxed attitude. Surreal adventures, sustained comic writing with real depth.**

Women's Press Bookclub handout

Arden Benbow is the pen-name chosen by Rosalind "Jim" Flint, lesbian mother of six, who is writing a novel about lesbian Celia Gunn and her ambivalent sexual relationship with Ben Jacques, the father of her sixth child, Sir Oliver Silver. Ben has discovered that the other five—freaky seventeen-year-old Audrey Pugh, in love with a rabbit, fifteen-year-old chess genius and pop singer Blind Touchstone, twelve-year-old millionaire hermaphrodite model in the plush Sculptors' Mile district of Sacramento, Long Rosalind Hawkins, and the curious time-obsessed ten-year-old homosexual twin clocksmiths Israel Martext and Benjamin Disraeli—were fathered by his previous lover, Phoebe Bones, before her sex-change operation. This had been necessary because Phoebe, as Orlando Pugh, had realised that he/she had no chance of selling his/her novel about the homosexual novelist, Captain "Audrey" Flint, father of 300 rabbits, unless he became a woman.

In this amazingly surrealist story, set in downtown Oakland and neighbouring uptown San Francisco, astride the famous Californian faultline, the counterpoint between "real" and "imagined real" and "really imagined" is brilliantly maintained by a simple device. The births of "Arden Benbow's" children—Touchstone Livesey, teller of tales, Corin Martext, pornographer and harpist in whom "innocence" and "sin" are perfectly fused, Jacques Arden, who achieves the Perfect Thing by inventing invisible paint, the hermaphrodite twins Blind Rosalind and Long John Amiens, and the mysterious footballer Forest of Dean—are graphically and physically described. They take place in the "real" but messy world. But "Celia Gunn" is attempting to discover, or at any rate "create", a perfectly "really imagined" world in which all novels owe their birth to a lesbian and all homosexuals are fathers of rabbits *but are not rabbits themselves*.

Since all the novels are about novelists, *Sir Oliver Silver, Audrey Pugh* and the other four are, whenever they appear in italics, not the children of "Celia Gunn" but the titles of novels—by, of course, Arden Benbow. And just as no reader of a novel ever sees the typescript, or hears the novelist's cries of rage on discovering that a sheet of carbon has been put in the wrong way round so that instead of a carbon copy he/she has a top-copy, a mirror-image on the reverse side of it, and a sheet

"No, mate—this is Purgatory. That's Eternity over there."

of "virgin" paper, one of the unpredictable lacunae of "life", or knows about the eighteen months' delay between handing over the typescript and printing, because a publishing takeover meant arguing with some totally new editor, but simply opens and starts reading, so are Celia Gunn's children encountered complete (or "written into life"). We do not see their gestation. They just *are*, in downland Oaktown, uptown Oakland, crosstown SF (which of course means "Science Fiction" when the locality of a novel, but "San Francisco" when the locality of one of Arden Benbow's children).

It is crucial to the comic "surrealism" of this novel that with the appearance of each child (or novel), this locality is fundamentally changed; and although no earthquake is actually described, we know that each birth is mysteriously synchronised with an earthquake, after which the whole locality/landscape is a different one. Sometimes upland Oaktown is a swamp, sometimes a huge rain forest, sometimes a decaying inner city. Significantly, it is in downtown Arden that Jacques is painting his invisible picture of Israel Martext and Benjamin Disraeli (often spelt "Disreali" or actually spoken "you're disreal, man") when the clocksmith twins fall into a chasm, left by a previous earthquake, which instantly closes up and it is as if they had never been. "Time has disappeared into the earth," Jacques says philosophically as he packs up his easel and goes off to sleep with Audrey Pugh and test his homosexuality.

In all this instant, "responsive", human decision-making and change it is the rabbits who provide a not altogether comforting constant. William Shakespeare, the father of Arden Benbow's sixth and last child (the mysterious footballer Forest of Dean) is persuaded by her to change sex and become Roberta Lousie Stevenson, partly because her typewriter dictates this to her in a dream, partly because she wants a full lesbian relationship before possibly herself changing sex and being the *father* of any future children of Roberta's—but most of all because of the rabbits.

William (later, of course, Roberta), an Assistant Sperm Bank Manager at the Californian Institute for Useless Experiments, is obsessed with his dream of a world, totally peaceful, in which there are no men at all, only women and rabbits. Arden is not so sure, since then to be lesbian would be "normal" ("and who wants to be normal, let alone write about it?"); this is why Celia Gunn's children, paradoxically, are conceived in the "normal" way.

With William's sex-change, however, his desires undergo an extraordinary change also, and "Roberta" finds herself totally committed to working for a world in which there are no *women* at all, only homosexual men and rabbits (whom they can, with the hitherto suppressed feminine side of their natures, love as surrogate children). He selects himself for injection before his sex-change, however, and it is one of the characteristic ambivalences of this "innovlement" (Celia Gunn's word for what her wayward typewriter describes as the end-of-the-road art-form of a dying or at least static culture, the "novel within a novle") that we do not know whether it is the injection or the seventh (magic number!) and last earthquake that causes her to become the mother of 300 rabbits.

It is part of the real depth of this book that "Arden Benbow" succeeds, I think, in finding, via Celia Gunn, adequate symbols for the equation bad-change-generation-sex-children-time-hetero-men opposed to good-timeless-end-peace-death-changeless-homosexual-women-rabbits-women-hooray women. Arden finishes her novel triumphantly with Ben Jacques's sex-change int herself, and receives an advance large enoug to enable her to retire from writing and star an enormously profitable rabbit farm as fa away from the fault-line as it is possible to ge and still *be* in America—in up-countr Maine. No wonder Jim Flint has a relaxe attitude.

"Sid, this place may not be as tough as we thought."

"No, I'm sorry—if I let ***you*** *keep your underpants on, I'd have to let* ***everyone*** *keep their underpants on."*

IT'S A FAST-MOVING, FUN-FILLED FEAST OF ENTERTAINMENT AND EXCITEMENT WITH DRAMA, LIVE ACTION AND ADVENTURE PLUS IN-DEPTH NEWS ANALYSIS AS TV'S ALL-NEW AUTUMN SCHEDULES ARE UNVEILED . . .

A NEW DIMENSION FOR YOUR VIEWING TONIGHT

• An exciting new look for the ever-popular test card

NEW FROM BBC1

6.00 BIM-BAM BONKETY-BOING
TERRY WOGAN, NOEL EDMONDS and JASPER CARROTT are your genial hosts for a laugh-packed hour of side-splitting entertainment in which educationally sub-normal families are asked to name their favourite cat for a jackpot prize of appearing next week on *Game For A Giggle*.

7.00 THE LATE-LATE WHACKY BREAKFAST SEASIDE SPECIAL
HOT GOSSIP do a number in suspenders based on a round-up of the latest world news before we go live to TERRY WOGAN with EMU aboard the orbiting Salyut IX for a phone-in discussion across space with NOEL EDMONDS in Beirut and PAMELA STEPHENSON in Pebble Mill.

8.15 SHERLOCK HOLMES MEETS TENKO, THE JAPANESE DETECTIVE
JASPER CARROTT plays the great detective and TERRY WOGAN is the faithful Doctor Watson for this first episode of a 13-part series set in Pearl Harbour. Tonight's Special Guest Star: ESTHER RANTZEN as the Hound of the Baskervilles. Also starring NOEL EDMONDS as Moriarty and CYRIL FLETCHER in a walk-on part as Mycroft Holmes.

9.00 SIERRA ECHO X-RAY YANKEE
PAMELA STEPHENSON stars as the soft-hearted Bolton WPc who is called in to assist when ALAN WHICKER is found wandering on the lonely moors, recalling his first ten years in television at a time before *Plinkety-Plonk* went to Number One.

10.00 BIG NITE BLOCKBUSTER MOVIETIME SPECTACULAR SHOWCASE HOLLYWOOD FILM SPECIAL '83
A made-for-TV special based on the best of Bim-Bam-Bonkety-Boing: *CARRY ON UP THE RATINGS*.

NEW FROM BBC2

6.00 PRO-CELEBRITY WHIST
Mrs Gwendoline Pilchart and her husband, Rupert, four times champions of The Rat & Ferret Alhambra Rooms in Runcorn, take on celebrities TERRY WOGAN and JAN LEEMING for the best of five rubbers in The Alan Weeks Challenge Cup.

11.15 PRO-CELEBRITY SHOVE HA'PENNY
The semi-finals of the Terry Wogan Cup from the popular Lytham St Anne's venue finds ALAN WEEKS battling it out with NOEL EDMONDS and a couple from Staines.

12.55 SWAZILAND CINEMA SHOWCASE
An 8mm epic story centred around the opposition Ngwane National Liberation Congress of 1952, introduced by DILYS POWELL, the late ALFRED HITCHCOCK and JASPER CARROTT.

NEW FROM ITV

6.00 STONE ME FOR A CORKER!
MIKE YARWOOD, SHEENA EASTON and wrestler BIG DADDY are your genial hosts for a laugh-packed hour of side-splitting entertainment in which educationally sub-normal families are asked to name their favourite dog for a jackpot prize of appearing next week on *So You Think You're A Nitwit*.

7.00 YOUR BIG NITE OUT AT THE MOVIES SPECTACULAR
Morecambe and Wise star in THE AIRPORT EAGLE THAT LANDED ON A LADY SINGING THE BLUES IN THE DEEP II with special guest stars BODIE and DOYLE and TINNY TIM the whacky wonder robot who wants to be Sherlock Holmes!

9.00 CHARLIE ROMEO ALPHA PAPA
JACKIE COLLINS plays the soft-hearted Hartlepool WPc who is called in to assist when ALAN WHICKER is found wandering in the Dales recalling his second ten years in television during the days before *Oops Ker-Plunk* went to Number One.

10.00 AGATHA CHRISTIE'S NEWS AT TEN
Mystery surrounds tonight's world headlines when ALASTAIR BURNET is found wandering about in a haunted mansion looking for the door to Channel 4. Meanwhile, aboard the orbiting Solyiz VIII, SELINA SCOTT and MIKE YARWOOD have an open line to TERRY WOGAN in Beirut and NOEL EDMUNDS in the Tyne-Tees studio to discuss the latest play in the BOB HOPE PRO-CELEBRITY CURLING CHAMPIONSHIPS at Troon.

NEW FROM CHANNEL 4

6.00 LIVE THIS VERY NITE FROM THE TOXTETH ROOMS
TREVOR MACDONALD and SARAH HOGG chair a 6-hour studio discussion about last night's Channel 4 soap opera concerning problems among Rastafarian rock musicians who refuse to watch sport on Saturdays or religion on Sundays with the Irish.

12.00 FILM ON FOUR
First showing on the new channel of the Best of Buster Keaton. (repeat)

Alexander Frater

Two Weeks Before the Mast

I first heard about cruising during a childhood spent mostly in the South Pacific where the only way of getting about was by boat. Our waterborn equivalent of the family car was a tiny antique launch called *England Expects*. Only two people understood her foibles and eccentricities. One was my father and the other his sailor, a small, bent man named Hovis who had a scuttling gait, moist, lidless eyes and an oddly furtive look. Hovis was an expert at traditional Polynesian navigation, which involved jumping into the sea and floating motionless to get the measure of the currents and the steepness of the waves.

Over the years bits of him kept getting nibbled off by passing predators, and I recall him sitting there with only half a heel, chin resting on the good knuckle of his left hand and sniggering with disbelief as my father explained the principles of the compass and sextant.

The launch had been bought from a firm of sea-slug exporters on the mainland; the clerks had used it for taking documents and manifests out to the freighters moored in the harbour. The firm, many years earlier, had purchased the launch from a wild-eyed, London-born planter named Clench, and it was he who had given the craft its absurd name. It had a two-stroke engine, probably stolen from someone's Riley, which, even when running sweetly, laid down a smokescreen of such density that the flying fish whizzing in and out of the gloom landed in our swirling scuppers with eyes watering, while the patrolling hammerheads were racked by terrible barking coughs if they ventured too near. The hull, clinker-built, leaked steadily and from Hovis I learnt the art of fast two-handed bailing with coconut shells.

There were hard rainwood seats which could also be pressed into service as paddles and an awning that had once sheltered the entrance of the El Tropicano nightclub. Though torn and badly weathered, the phrase " . . . iptease by 12 Dusky Luvli . . . " was still just discernible over the bows. In the bows also was a small storage locker which Hovis had turned into a tiny stateroom with sleeping mat, pillow and candle.

Despite all that, she wasn't a bad sea boat and we had some pleasant times in her. When we landed at a new place my parents and I sought accommodation ashore, but Hovis preferred to sleep in his locker, usually rendered legless beforehand by a two-gallon bucket of palm toddy. My own duties included assisting him tidy up after a day at sea, coiling ropes, stowing cushions and so forth, and in the course of these hours together we grew quite close.

I still remember the island—Yip—and the circumstances attending his sudden confession that, more than anything else in life, he wanted to work as a ship's steward. At the time we were scrubbing the hull with giant sponges, removing evidence of a protest made apparently by disaffected bushmen upset by the policies then being pursued by Chamberlain and the British government. "No Apeezmunt!" said the phrase scrawled across our blistered paintwork in teak ash and honey, a mixture that was virtually indelible. "A *what*?" I said.

"Steward blong big boat," said Hovis. The westering sun glinted briefly on his bald head, reminding me that it had the shape and texture of a giant light bulb. "Blong ocean liner, actually. But not one 'im blong North Atlantic run, allsame so-called Blew Ribbun boat, masta. They just trouble—big seas, big storms, night cold allsame buggery, brass monkey nights as they say."

"Oh," I said.

A lumbering, cod-like creature suddenly hauled itself from the water and lunged at a hovering mosquito, a young anopheles dozing on the wing; badly shaken, it took off in the direction of Australia, travelling so fast that it seemed to leave a tiny sonic boom behind it, no louder than the sound of a wavelet falling on shingle.

"What I really want," said Hovis, "is to go cruising." A young nun walked along the beach collecting driftwood and he leered at her. "Blessings blong bigfella Jissus be upon you, missus," he called.

"And the same to you with knobs on, sport," said the Little Sister of Mercy in the accents of South Sydney. Perhaps she had not heard him properly.

"*Cruising*?" I said.

"Yis. One friend blong me, old Po'ongo, work as steward on French Line cruise ship

lavis Lotti in charge of deck quoits. He say noney good, hours short and women all over im. He say sea air make them allsame lesperate, roaring for nooky nooky behind umber two smoke-stack every bleeding hour f day and night." He stood back and, with ead tipped to one side, considered the lanks he had been scrubbing. "Po'ongo say vomen trip you up and beat you to the round, dropping faster than marines hitting lirt when flak fly. And they tip good."

I thought about this for a moment, assuming that Po'ongo's ladies kept throwing hemselves to the deck because of rough seas. The lure of big money and short hours, hough, I quite understood, and I knew also hat these French cruise liners were very nice nside, their bulkheads lined with exotic voods like angelim, avodire, tiger oak, satinvood, sycamore and synara. The dining saoons were three decks high and longer than he Hall of Mirrors at Versailles, which they vere supposed to resemble. There were Olympic-sized swimming-pools made from narble and, every morning at 11 sharp, tewards brought trays of ices around. Hovis confirmed that this was indeed so, and added hat cold gin could be had for just threepence glass.

I went off to join my parents for dinner, eaving him to his palm wine and stewed eel, with mangoes for afters. The months went by. War was declared and Hovis joined the nerchant marine, working as a trainee stoker aboard a dumpy little coaster that did the general cargo run up to Wao.

Then came the news of Pearl Harbour and, amidst persistent rumours of invasion by the Japanese imperial fleet, arrangements were made to evacuate expatriate women and children to Australia. We were told to ready ourselves. On a certain day a steamer would call.

It turned out to be the French cruise liner *Calais*, 27,500 tons, a notably sybaritic ship with public rooms the size of skating rinks and walls of crystal. The sumptuous furnishings and fittings helped heal the hurt of parting from my father. We sailed and that evening, before dinner, heard a sudden shout. I looked around and there, approaching in a spotless white uniform, was Hovis. He beamed at us.

"Well, well, missus, bugger me, fancy this," he said, seizing my mother's hand and shaking it warmly. I was delighted to see him and capered about a bit. There were gleaming epaulettes on his shoulders. He looked as grand as an admiral.

"What exactly do you do?" I asked him.

"I is chief bouillon steward," he said, importantly. "*Fust cluss.*"

"Oh, smashing," I said. "Can I have an extra cup tomorrow?"

"You not fust cluss, masta. You evacuee, special cheap fare, no fancy treatment, *no bouillon*."

He was as good as his word. For the duration of the voyage he remained friendly but firm. Our roles had been reversed. He was now in charge and when I approached him for a chat I did so with a certain deference. I learnt that Hawaii and Florida were the best destinations for the cruise boats which, on those runs, carried legions of big tippers who were not overfond of bouillon and, consequently, made few demands on his time.

"Except for the women," he said, darkly.

"Yes?"

"They can't keep their hands off me," he said. "Some days I so utterly exhausted that I got to have a lie-down. But you still too young to know much about this matter. Probly you still think babies come along in big birds blong Dutch fellas called allsame, um, corks."

"Storks," I said. His missing bits, I noted, had grown back again and he looked more or less complete.

"Okay. But I tell you this. Movie stars are worst. You know my limp? No? Well, I got to hobble about because all this famous international beauties kip sneaking up when I is unwrapping the Knorr cubes and kicking my feet from under me."

I last saw him on the morning that we steamed into Sydney harbour. As we stood at the rail he approached with a jar of Beluga caviar and a pair of plucked geese that he had stolen from the ship's deep freeze. These he handed to my mother.

"For you, missus," he said. "No good food in Australia." My mother demurred, but he was insistent. "Souvenir of your first cruise," he said, returning to his little kitchen behind the bridge.

What became of him later is not clear. According to one report he remained with the ship for ten or twelve years and then left abruptly after an incident at Divine Service one Sunday morning. My informant—who was not aboard—says Hovis threw his hymnbook at an edible noddy bird as it flapped across the deck and brought it down, squawking, within inches of the portable pulpit in which the captain was preaching a sermon that took, as its text, the words, "If Jesus had been on the *Titanic*, would he have gone down with the ship or walked away from it?"

WORLD SERVICE
THE TWO POUND PUKE BURGER
£1·60p
HAPPY M
I WORK HERE BECAUSE I WANT TO BRING AN END TO SOCIETY AS WE KNOW IT
I KEEP FIT BY EATING OUT
DONT FORGET — NO NUTRIMENT!!
I DON'T CARE IF THEY DON'T HAVE ANY TASTE — NEITHER HAVE I
I DON'T KNOW WHY I GO FOR FAST FOOD — I'VE GOT NOTHING TO DO ALL DAY
THE PACKAGING TASTES EVEN BETTER
WELL, YOU DONT HAVE TO EAT IT!
I'VE BEEN TOLD THEY USE KANGAROO
EAT YOUR HEART OUT EGON RONAY
IT'S JUST LIKE MOTHER GETS OUT THE DEEPFREEZE

THE QUEEZY 75p
QUEEZLY
MR QUEEZY
THE LYMESWOLD BIG ONE £1.5op O.N.O
ERGENCY ETCHUP SPRAY
UNDERTAKER
POT OF TEA R TWO YOU EASE
THAT'S WHAT I CALL FAST FOOD!!
WHAT DO THEY KNOW ABOUT TAKE-AWAYS!
I WANNA CHANGE IT! IT TASTES OF REAL MEAT!
YOU HAVE JUST RUINED MY PACKAGE HOLIDAY
KEEP MOVING!
LITTE
HEATH

AUTUMN *on Sunday*

The seasonally aware MAGAZINE-WITHIN-A-MAGAZINE CONCEPT that builds up, week by week, into a month of Sundays—a treasure-house of autumn knowledge you will want to keep beside you, and your children, in the comfort of your o home—to admire again during the long winter evenings.

FEATURING—the excitingly different **WOW! SEPTEMBER!** pages and, beginning soon, our **CRIKEY! IT'S OCTOBER!** section.

PLUS . . . a new look to the **UP THIS AUTUMN EYE-OPENING LIFEBEL** pull-out home tapestry, car-maintenance and family tax-saving guide, commemorating in vivid colour the once-in-a-lifetime expedition by cuisine escoffier steam enthusiasts to the rugged s slopes of The Oktoberhorn.

AN AUTUMN OF MY OWN

Interviews by Angelina Crookstone. Photographed by Ben Nevis.

Lady Emilia Urquhart-Betjeman of Rumsey

FROM the conservatory at Droppings, Lady Urquhart-Betjeman's ancestral home in Hampstead's Trevor Grove, the autumn tints of the great Beech, the under-gardener whom Her Ladyship dresses in old sacks, are in arresting contrast to the rich vermilion velvets of the curtains shading the Droppings orchid collection from the autumn sun. Beside an exquisitely-crafted escritoire, ordered by the Urquhart-Betjeman family from the Scott Harvey Collection featured in last week's magazine, a quarts-digita long-case clock, powered by just two U-2 batteries availabl from any hardware store, keeps watch over the rolling acres

(continued on p. 88

THROUGH AUTUMN BY STOPPING MULE

The world's last-surviving donkey-drawn commuter train snakes between the Andean passes from Texaco to Coppaketl. ALEXANDER KINGTON BRUNEL went to write up the colour of the surrounding rain forest.

EVERY morning between 02 September and 29 October (excepting Thurs., Saints' Days and Market Day in Cucuracha), Manuel-José Goering picks up his stick and carrot and walks the 4,301 miles from his stone cottage overlooking Peru to the marshalling yards at

(continued on p. 61)

Exquisitely Fashioned in Finest Dishwasher-Proof Porcelain—TREASURES OF THE AUTUMN GLADES—THE COLCHICUM, OR AUTUMN CROCUS

Picture for a moment a handsomely-crafted egg-cup, upon its obverse a two-colour depiction of the Colchicum autumnale, *a perennial plant of the family Liliaceae, found in moist meadowlands about this time of year, whilst on the reverse a haunting image of the young corm which grows to roughly the size of an apricot.*

Just imagine it—all the myth and majesty of nature depicted before you on these misty mornings. Treasure your friends' faces when you tell them the amazing history of the Colchicum which comes with every dozen (12) egg-cups ordered . . . of how the alkaloid, Colchicine, can cause violent sneezing, enteritis, or death from collapse!

Now you can subscribe to the Treasures of the Autumn Glades Dishwasher-Proof Egg-Cup Collection—once a month, for a whole year, you will receive another egg-cup at the attractive price of £19.99 (eggs not included). To acquire this magnificent heirloom, simply *(continued on p. 52)*

INTRODUCING A NEW 52-PART WEEKLY PULL-OUT SECTION:

THE RAISING OF THE AUTUMN ROSE

September was drawing to a close when Henry VIII's most illustrious old boat went down in an equinoctial gale of England's autumn coastline. Thousands were to perish of boredom as years later they read and re-read of the epic struggle to bring this unique piece of history to the surface so that she could be sold off as bits of timber to lend grace and spellbinding charm to any mantelpiece *(cont. on p. 101)*

Autumn Chop-Smackers

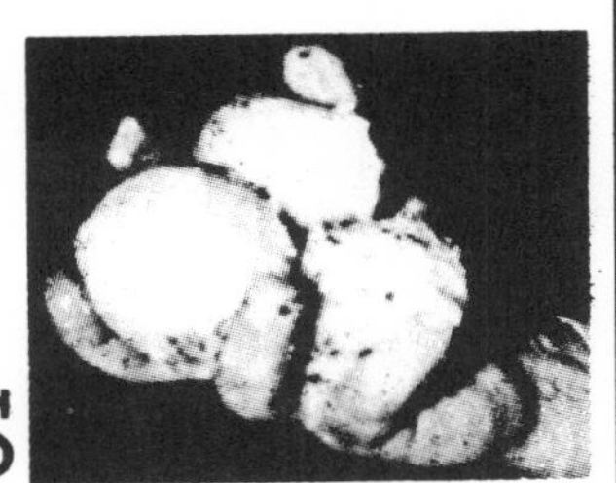

MAKING MORE USE OF LITTLE-KNOWN AUTUMN-SPAWNING DEEP-SEA MONKFISH

by Pru Massingberd-Lavoisier

FOR the walnut-skinned, aromatic goat-herds who for centuries have laboured at the vines beneath the pellucid skies of Montelimar, autumn wouldn't be autumn without the succulent delight of *BLANCHED SCROTUM OF PERIGORD TRUFFLING HOG,* a traditional September brioche-filler that's given misty piquancy from its filling of Porquerolles sea-urchin paste, nougat and pulverised salsify stalks. Decorated with almonds and marinated figs *(continued on p. 22)*

AUTUMN ON SUNDAY READERS' OFFER

AN UNFORGETTABLE OPPORTUNITY TO ACQUIRE FOR JUST £99.99 A RICHLY LEAF-COLOURED BLOUSON TOP FOR AUTUMN—INDIVIDUALLY SIGNED BY ARTHUR GUINNESS

Smart enough for those autumn evenings at the opera. Yet tough enough for those seasonal chores of sweeping up leaves, rodding out gutters, worming the tortoise etc etc. You'll not find these exclusive autumn blouson tops in the shops this autumn—why wait until they're remaindered in the January Sales when they could be YOURS now for the incredible price of just £99.99 including a Summer bath-mat, a Royal Wedding toothbrush-holder and a unique pet's litter bowl, commemorating the Pope's visit to the World Cup—ABSOLUTELY FREE! when you order one dozen or more. Just fill in the requisite details on page *(continued overleaf)*

★TRANSATLANTIC★CABLES★

Deer Diary

Weekends of late, sidewalks all over America have been glutted with dazed and disoriented men, driven from their natural habitats in front of television sets by the pernicious football strike. Everywhere, that is, except in the Great Northwest, where Real Men with big guns spend weekends of every waning year thirstily pursuing a different game.

The first autumnal nip in the air finds the men of Oregon and Washington state banding together in small macho knots, planning hunting trips together. During these preparatory sessions, exaggerated tales of past kills are exchanged over countless cans of beer, as each virile Narcissus tenderly caresses his powerful rifle and anoints its beloved barrel with costly oils.

When the hunting season finally arrives, these stalwart sportsmen tend to fall naturally into three major categories. The first is the Camouflage Hunter. These come in matched sets of four, identically attired in the baggy, bunched-up garb of army surplus mottled greens and browns. Their weapons are similarly bundled in little colour-coordinated guerilla suits, and their exposed epidermis is daubed in primitive blotches of drab warpaint. For finishers, to ensure their absolute invisibility, they roll about in the dirt to blend their earthy tones, then douse themselves in some secret stench painstakingly formulated to drive love-sick bucks crazy with desire.

Then, dressed to kill, they all leap inconspicuously into their unmuffled green and brown mottled Jeep, two facing forward and two facing back, and roar imperceptibly off into the forest. Thus camouflaged, and further obscured by the cloud of choking exhaust fumes and road dust, these invisible quartets easily convince both deer and other hunters that they are not really there at all.

The next category of hunter is the Tracker. He can be identified by his red plaid shirt, tan lace-up boots, florescent orange hat, and concentrated efforts at all times to resemble a stalking panther. He prowls solitarily through the forest, hunch-backed and beetle-browed, with his trusty rifle clutched alertly in a ready position at his side. Slung from one rugged, denim-clad hip is a Colt .45 in a Marshall Dillon holster, and from the other, a buck knife of a design and dimension to disturb even Jim Bowie's tranquillity.

The Tracker typically stops abruptly and freezes into the position of a first-rate bird dog. Then, he either staightens bolt upright and cocks his head quizzically to determine the size, weight, age, sex and colour of the savage beast that just trod on yonder pine needle; or squats suddenly and scoops up a handful of fresh spoor which he rolls about thoughtfully in his palm to ascertain the height, width, dietary preferences, relative intelligence and astrological sun sign of its depositor.

Trackers spend a great deal of time posed picturesquely on ridges, peering through the magnifying lenses of their high-powered rifle scopes. Although the untutored eye, sweeping its gaze in the same direction, sees nothing but the vast floral glory of God's untouched handiwork, it can only be assumed that the Tracker either sees much, much more, or that he is rehearsing for an audition as a Clint Eastwood understudy.

The third type is the Blind Hunter. This class, in our context, anyway, is the one who hunts from a blind, which is an adult treehouse, the location of which is fanatically guarded from man and beast alike.

The Blind Hunter scours the woods for weeks prior to opening day, looking for his

"Of course, Gordon can only go in search of the Holy Grail at weekends."

"spot". Once located, an invisible platform must be constructed high up in the branches of a nearby tree. This involves packing in lumber, nails, tools, paint, and a tall ladder, with the rabidly paranoid carpenter simultaneously dragging a ragged limb of manzanita brush behind him to wipe out his give-away tracks. Great efforts are then expended in attempting to construct the tree house without betraying one's whereabouts through such revelatory sounds as handsaw rasping through wood or hammer coming into abrupt conjunction with nail head.

Then, inconspicuous painting completed and access ladder carefully concealed in dense underbrush, the Blind Hunter covers the tell-tale sawdust with dirt clods and dead leaves. Finally, bent nails and lumber chips are stuffed into various vacant pockets to wreak subsequent manly havoc on the little missus's Maytag, while the hunter smirks smugly at his own smooth-moving stealth.

This is the most fun the Blind Hunter has. Although groping through pitch-black forest to the blind to await dawn immobilely while one's extremities turn blue from frostbite is undeniably delightful, it is, nevertheless, somewhat anti-climactic.

All of these hunters, whether they stalk solitarily or in packs, invariably rejoin their comrades in arms around the evening campfire to play Man together. Playing Man involves not only the actual hunt, but the subsequent ingestion of vast quantities of whisky drunk directly out of a half-gallon jug. (A hunter who is found to have packed a razor, a pillow, pyjamas, after-shave lotion, deodorant, cookies, or light beer, however, is not accorded recognition as a legitimate participant in Man.) Rules require that the lip of both bottle and mouth be wiped with the selfsame sleeve one uses for one's nose, after which the Man grasps the jug by the finger ring, supports it on his shoulder, pours the whisky in a gurgling amber cascade directly down his throat, and passes to the left.

Points are deducted for sipping, mixing, grimacing, and shuddering. Audibly gasping results in immediate disqualification. This goes on until the Loser heaves face downward into the campfire, and simply heaves; at which point the Men are free to lurch off to their respective bedrolls and collapse inertly. Additional penalties are attached to anyone betraying the emasculating signs of a hangover the next morning.

If someone actually shoots something, the carcass is transported to the butcher as flagrantly as possible, where a few steaks are cut off and conspicuously labelled for freezer display. The rest is ground up and liberally infused with beef, pork and suet, thus quadrupling the total amount of "venison" tendered to the fearless stalker's hungry wife and babes.

But bagging one's deer is by no means the end of the Northwest hunter's fun. After that comes elk season, and then bear season. And after that, the Real Man moves delightedly into duck season, where he is able to wriggle on his belly like a reptile in freezing puddles through knife-edged marsh grass in the icy pre-dawns of the dead of winter. With amusements like that still in store, what man of mettle cares if there's a Super Bowl or not?

UNREPEATABLE PUNCHCLUB CHRISTMAS GIFT OFFER!

DIGITAL AFTERSHAVE SLIPPERS

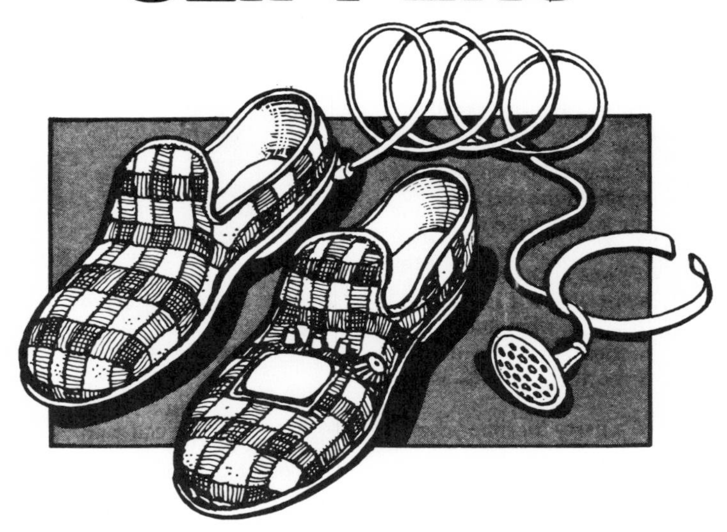

Yes, it's true! Through an astounding breakthrough in South Korean marketing technology, we are able to offer regular readers of this magazine the opportunity of solving all their seasonal gift problems at a single stroke!

These handsome plaid slippers in non-stick dishwasherproof Seoulene, a direct spin-off of the remarkable Korean space programme, are not just an example of elegant head-turning footwear at its economic best. The left slipper has been micro-circuited and digitalised to play up to 700 different electronic games through the handy mini-screen neatly built into its instep and activated by the great toe, while the right slipper contains nearly two litres of smart Old Phoo Yong Machomusk aftershave in its virtually imperceptible built-up heel.* A slim tube connects to the specially designed and fashionable neckband, so that when the heel is brought down sharply, the face is automatically sprayed. Eyes should be kept shut to avoid damage.

THESE ITEMS ARE A GIFT AT ONLY £39.95 PER PAIR! ORDER BEFORE DECEMBER 8, AND RECEIVE A SMART SOLUBLE BATHCUBE MUFFLER AND MILK CHOCOLATE 1983 PERSONAL POCKET DIARY ABSOLUTELY FREE!

Available ONLY from Punchclub Tatcade Promotions, 23 Tudor Street, London EC4.

* *Caution:* a slight limp is inevitable. Punch Publications Ltd is not responsible for any accidents or social embarrassment deriving therefrom.

Alan Brien

Writers Tramp

"There is a mighty increase of dirty wenches in straw hats since I knew London," noted Jonathan Swift during one of his walks through Chelsea. Well, it's reassuring to know some traditions never change in the changing metropolis.

I lift the quote from David Piper's *Companion Guide*, one of the most companionable of London guides, and ever-ready with an apt observation from a well-stocked memory of the city's literary residents. It was flicking through Piper's list of "Houses of Great Men" that I hit upon a theme—a tour of the capital, dropping in to leave my card on some of the vanished celebrities whose homes here still remain preserved more or less as they were when their owners still lived in them.

Over the years, I have made the provincial's pilgrimage to several of these. No one who has grubbed a career in Fleet Street can resist a call on Dr Johnson's place in Gough Square, just a totter up a rolling alley from the Cheshire Cheese, nearby Johnson's Court where he also lived for a further eleven years, though it bore the name of another Johnson long before he arrived there.

I recall this as a rather cramped, shadowy lair for such a bulky, bear-like lodger, built around a fortunately solid and well reinforced staircase, a suite of scholar's rooms for a perpetual mature student with space for little else but work. It is difficult to seek entry here without feeling somewhat nervous of the reception his ghost might provide if summoned from that attic where, incredibly, he laboured long past his deadline on the famous dictionary with six assistants, as you rehearse your famous first words. Dare one have asked him why he clung so inextricably, among all Britain's literary men, to that Doctorate which most of us have forgotten was in fact an honorary degree?

Dickens House, in Doughty Street off Grays Inn Road, the novelist's only surviving London residence, did not become a memorial until 1924 and so lacks that intimate sense of presence, the aroma and possibly even the fingerprints, of the resident. Nevertheless, it is full of relics which summon up his life in almost overwhelming detail, though now all that sticks in my mind is the slightly Disneyish reproduction of the kitchen at Dingley Dell which has been installed in the basement.

Another on my list, when I first came to London, also had the spoor of its most famous inhabitant overlaid by many subsequent owners before returning to adopt his name. This is Keats House, in Hampstead's Keats Grove, formerly Wentworth Place, which was bought by public subscription in 1925, mainly through contributions from American admirers of the poet. Here he lived for two of his short, blossomingly creative years, filling every rift with ore, sharing half a house with a friend. Fanny Brawne, his brief life's love, was not just the girl next door—her family was in tantalising proximity in the other half. Here, though more of a museum than a home, there are also many of his possessions that fall just short of being marked with his blood spots, including the manuscript of his last poem, *Bright Star*, written on a blank page of a copy c Shakespeare. Oddly, the part of the premise that it is easiest to fancy still bears a recollec tion of his touch is the charmingly seques tered garden, even if we are not entirel convinced that it was under this very mulber ry tree that he heard and immortalised th nightingale.

"I think my wife's becoming suspicious, Miss Dobson."

I was looking forward to refreshing m now faded images of these stops on the touris trail and also perhaps including some I ha never visited, off the beaten track, such a William Morris's House in Walthamstow Wesley's House off the City Road, and th Wellington Museum in Apsley House, "No 1, London", at Hyde Park Corner. But decided to begin with Carlyle's House i Cheyne Row, where the "Sage of Chelsea" stuck it out for longer than any of the othe great Londoners from 1834 to 188 ("Chelsea abounds in omnibi, and they tak you to Coventry Street for sixpence").

This, above all the others I know, gives th impression of the old dyspeptic egoist, the D Pessimist Anticant of Trollope's *The Warden* half prophet, half mountebank as his wif complained, having just popped out for th moment, possibly on a jaunt to Coventry Street. The whole place reverberates with hi personality, from the jerry-rigged, Heatl Robinson cold shower to the clothes and walking canes on the hall stand.

On the doorstep, though every guide and reference work on my shelves insisted i would be open every day except Tuesday Carlyle's House turned out to be closed ex cept between April and September. My scheme, as so often with my attempts to encapsulate a cross-section of London according to a rational plan, had foundered on one missing link.

Still, serendipity, as ever, came to my aid Walking back to Fleet Street along Roya Hospital Road, I considered a visit to the Royal Hospital itself, always a fruitful source of anecdotal reportage for the London essayist. Some of the pensioners, as befits an establishment set up more out of pragmatism than altruism to prevent discharged or invalided soldiers roaming the city as robber and rioters, have been more interviewed than Peter Ustinov. Though few can match the tall, but (almost) true, tales of some of their predecessors. I have always been affected by the legend of William Hiesland, who served in the Army for most of the eighteenth century—eighty years—then married at the age of a hundred, only to find he had to spend the next twelve years separated each night from his wife who was forbidden by the Hospital rules to sleep within its walls.

And I cannot help admiring the perverse and mistaken obstinancy of Harriet Snell, who managed to get buried there, after joining the Army disguised as a man, despite having deserted following a sentence of five hundred lashes and remustering as a Marine.

Next door, however, I came across a rather stylish modern building I had never noticed before housing the National Army Museum. Moved from Sandhurst in 1971, it is, surprisingly, a registered charity, and the first phase cost a million pounds raised entirely by donations. At the moment, it tells the history of the British Army from the reign of Henry VII, with galleries of paintings, weapons, uniforms, battle plans, photographs and documents, ending rather abruptly at 1914. A second phase is now in progress to continue the story up to the present day.

The most extraordinary exhibit, rearing up ahead of the visitor to chilling effect, is a huge glass case containing a wired assembly of weathered bones like a display of giant's dentures. On closer inspection, it turns out to be the skeleton of a horse, and I thought for a moment it was an incongruous and unexpected deviation into symbolism, possibly representing the Fourth Horse of the Apocalypse. The reality is almost as peculiar—it is the fleshless remains of Napoleon's charger, Marengo, named after his famous victory, and ridden by him at the scene of his most famous defeat, Waterloo.

The National Army Museum, openly dedicated to the celebration of militarism, and the unspoken assumption that war is the continuation of honourable politics by a noble means, nevertheless provides a wealth of evidence for those who wish to mount the opposition case. Most of us tend to remember only the long, and familiar, massed clashes between European powers of the Napoleonic Wars and Great War, with the Crimea a rare interruption to a century and a half of peace.

But for the professional soldier, through whose eyes we are shown the apparently endless roll of battle honours, it is clear that there has scarcely been a single year when his comrades in arms were not fighting some enemy somewhere. Even in the decade and a half following Waterloo, the Army was used in the role of gun-carrying police to impose law and order on seditious, rebellious mobs at home, though the soldiers themselves were often disaffected and mutinous—"half their pay deducted for food, and accommodation worse than that provided for convicts".

From then onwards, each now half-forgotten campaign is given its display cabinet. The First Afghan War of 1838 to 1842 when a British force, retreating from Kabul over snow-bound passes through hostile tribes, lost every single one of its 16,000 troops, the sole survivor a non-combatant Dr Brydon. The skirmishes on the North-West Frontier alone lasted from 1849 to 1914. There were the Sikh Wars, the Second Afghan War (1878–80), the First, Second and Third Burma Wars, the First, Second and Third China Wars, the invasion of Tibet in 1904, the West African Wars from 1867 to 1871, the Zulu Wars, the Abyssinian War of 1864 to 1868, war in Aden and the Sudan, the Boer War. There were also truly forgotten campaigns like those against the Maoris in New Zealand or separatists in Canada.

In the accompanying text, the enemy tend to be represented as at best wrong-headed and unwise to oppose the British might, even when they won. A Mullah who rallies his people against the British occupation force is naturally "mad" and the opposition of natives with spears against invading Europeans

"Well, I've been in three or four documentaries, two feature films and loads of commercials, of course. Mostly as a dog."

with machine guns is usually "fanatical". But even here, the admission has often to be made that the British justification for fighting on other people's soil is no more than a "pretext". It is enough to "suspect Russian influence" to start the troops marching to their death in disputes which are routinely settled a year or two later by negotiation and diplomacy. It is impossible to find any coherent thread of moral argument—sometimes the Army is dispatched to help the legitimate ruler put down a rebel rival, at others to aid a rebel rival dispossess a legitimate ruler.

There is no nonsense about democracy, and only a little about the rights of small nations. The balance of power is as near as the Government which is dispatching the gun-boats and the troop ships comes to a war aim, and this boils down mainly to fighting European opponents on the territory of other peoples as far away from Europe as can be arranged. The results in international politics are almost invariably inconclusive and fleeting. What matters is that the Army has been in action to the excitement of the newspapers, the plaudits of parliamentarians, and the satisfaction of the taxpayer in getting some distant rumble of cannon-fire, and reports of gallantry and heroism under appalling conditions, for his money.

Even before a temperance organisation, the United Kingdom Alliance, complained last week to the Advertising Standards Authority that the current massive promotion for Guinness was a breach of the ASA guidelines, it seemed to me that the new central slogan had several basic flaws just as a commercial, selling proposition.

First of all, negatives, even double negatives, always register not unexpectedly in the mind of the idly-glancing public with antipathetic effect. A quick poll among friends who had driven past a London hoarding announcing "Guinless isn't good for you" established that two out of three automatically read the initial word as "Guinness". And David Langdon's cartoon in this paper last week makes the same point—a bill-poster looking up at his street-corner bill from which a runaway vandal has just excised the intrusive "l" and remarking: "Seven million quid of advertising campaign ruined at a stroke."

Secondly, the statement as it stands is irritatingly ungrammatical, and obscure without a context. The subject of the sentence is an adjective not a noun.

Even then, "Guinless" cannot mean anything, on the analogy of "legless", since there is no such thing as a "Guinn." To create a workable substantive, the word should be "Guinnesslessness."

Thirdly, and perhaps most importantly, there is some evidence, at least around where I drink, that what has turned a new generation off stout—Guinness sales have halved in the last ten years—is just that slogan, imprinted on us all since the Thirties, that the new one is seeking to re-activate at one remove. "Guinness is good for you" may have been an attractive appeal in the years of pre-war Depression and wartime Austerity. All beers are seen by most Britishers as a kind of more palatable and potent variant of soup which is why, I believe, we were so long accustomed to happily drinking it tepid. And of foods masquerading as drinks, Guinness was reputed the most filling, and healthy. My teetotal grandfather used to down two a day with many a shudder on doctor's orders.

The average modern drinker is then conditioned to believe that Guinness is something you drink when you're run-down and missing a meal. He believes it is good for him but he doesn't want a drink that is good for him.

"Guinless", a word almost impossible to say for another thing, seems to me a non-starter. The brewers may stand a better chance of luring back the now weight-conscious, pub-food-eating drinker with Langdon's invention—"Guinness isn't good for you."

DONEGAN

Blackboard Jungle

GREATER protection for teachers from classroom assaults by pupils and adults was demanded yesterday by the 90,000-strong Assistant Masters and Mistresses Association.

Daily Telegraph

"I can't take any more—I'm joining the SAS."

"Stop bothering your Dad, Lenny. You're old enough now to go and belt the Housemaster one yourself."

"O'Reilly has an intriguing theory that the dinosaurs were wiped out by their young."

"They make an odd couple. She pushes glue and he runs the White Slave Trade."

*)h well, little
ings please
tle minds."*

"Couldn't you have a word with me in here, lads? It's freezing outside."

"Ah, Mr Panopoulis! Just give me a moment to remove my contact lenses."

"It's nothing, Miss Radley—just a touch of the old migraine."

"The Games Master? Well, it's break time, so he'll be hiding in one of the dustbins round the back."

"Martial it may be, Mr Grimley, but is it Art?"

Arthur's Seat

Following objections in the press that he was always critical but never constructive, Mr Arthur Scargill graciously offered Punch an exclusive Press conference on his future plans. The following is the merest digest.

DEFENCE

Outraged at the Government's "insane refusal" either to consult the NUM before embarking on its Falklands campaign, which might well have had disastrous effects upon anthracite sales had a prolonged war forced people to tighten their belts, or to ship miners to the South Atlantic aboard the QE2, thereby depriving them of both overseas allowances and healthy sea air, Mr Scargill vowed that this would not happen again. He had every reason to believe that if the opinions of miners were not canvassed prior to any future war, then the rank and file of the armed forces would refuse to fight. British soldiers would not cross picket lines.

He also maintained that the majority of the working people of this country stood four-square behind the NUM on the need to develop a coke-fired missile system.

THE MONARCHY

Contrary to what he called scurrilous lies manufactured by the running dogs of Fleet Street's baronial mafia, the NUM, averred its president, had no immediate plans to abolish the monarchy. Though stung by the Queen's failure to submit Lady Diana Spencer for scrutiny and secret ballot prior to her engagement, the miners did not bear grudges. They would, however, not stand idly by if Prince William were not sent down the pit.

The conversion of Buckingham Palace, Sandringham, Balmoral, Highgrove and Gatcombe Park to solid fuel would, of course, have to be expedited within the deadline given, if a national strike was to be averted.

THE MEDIA

NUM plans for the media are extensive, since, according to Mr Scargill, "the media is a running canker flying in the face of democracy." Members were enraged that Channel Four had not been given over to mining; they were now, however, being realistic and asking only for "a reasonable presence" on existing networks. Major sitcoms such as *To the Coalface Born* and *It Ain't Half Dark, Mum!* were already being scripted, prime-time quiz shows like *Mastermine* and *Quadruple Your Money!* were well past the casting stage, and some three hundred hours of the blockbusting epic *Pithead Revisited* were already in the can.

That these would soon be appearing on our TV screens, Mr Scargill had little doubt. NATTKE and ACTT would be solidly with the NUM on that issue, if they didn't want to end up supporting the roof in Bolsover No. 7.

Similarly, there would soon be great changes in Fleet Street and its treatment of the coal industry. It was a well-known fact that all that NGA, SOGAT, NATSOPA and the NUJ wanted in this life was a fair deal for miners.

BRITISH LEYLAND

If the NUM was committed to anything, Mr Scargill said, it was to the continued subsidy of British Leyland. Loose talk to the effect that the NUM would rather see the hundreds of millions that were poured into shoring up BL given instead to the mining industry were just foul canards designed to split working class solidarity. The NUM wholeheartedly supported the British carworker, and always would. Indeed, as soon as the ashtrays in his NUM Jaguar were full, Mr Scargill himself fully intended getting a NUM Rolls Royce.

SPORT

Mining, affirmed Mr Scargill, would definitely be included in the 1984 Olympic Games. The international working-class brotherhood would see to that. A glowing Welsh nut would be carried from Mount Olympus to Los Angeles, which he was sure the Olympics Committee would prefer to a mass boycott of the Games by the thousands of athletics workers world-wide who were, he knew, deeply concerned by the threat of pit closures in the Yorkshire coalfield.

As far as the forthcoming Australian tour was concerned, he had spoken to the MCC about the disadvantages to the country of a Month of Action in support of healthworkers, and they had welcomed the opportunity of holding the First Test at Grimethorpe. He would be going it at number four.

LITERATURE

Due to the inexplicable absence in the short-list of any novels about redundancies threatening Scottish face-workers, the Booker Prize will not be awarded this year.

South of the Border

Jeeves was always going to something called "subscription dances" in Camberwell. That was between the wars. Much earlier than that, in the 1880s, George Bernard Shaw, for some extraordinary reason, got quite cross when someone suggested that Camberwell was in the suburbs. This was not true at all, the great man said. Camberwell was, he said, Bloomsbury transported across the river. Not the suburbs but "a genteel slum", said GBS.

I often think of Jeeves and GBS as I pick my way across Camberwell Green, carefully stepping over the chaps who seem to gather there each day of fine weather for sherry parties. But most of the time I think of the Editor of *The Guardian* who is a neighbour of mine and who suggested, when I moved down to London from Liverpool four years ago, that I set up in Camberwell. Misery, I have often thought since then, truly does love company.

But Shaw was right. Camberwell is both genteel and a slum. But should a man who managed to spend twenty years in Liverpool complain about South London? Well, just as folk in the metropolis do not understand the provinces, we of the Smoky North do not understand London. For most of my years in Liverpool I lived in a house that had been built as a bishop's palace, set in the middle of a park where hardly ever a word of Scouse was heard and where, even though we shared an MP with Toxteth, one could go for months without setting eyes upon the angry lumpenproletariat, white or dusky.

I had no idea that nowhere in South London is free from blight. Step from the unequalled charm of South London's Cleaver Square and there it is, all around you, hideous, appalling, crumbling houses and stunted people; a crime against architecture and a sin against humanity. You remember how it was when you first came up or down to London, looking for a place to live, staggering about in a daze, the compass broken, with no bearings, how easily you were seduced by the pleasant street full of trees or the one house, like the one good tooth in a mouth full of decay. You see the one good house and turn a blind eye to the rest; like the husband of a loved but wayward wife.

The house I bought belonged to no less a grand and beautiful couple than Albert Finney and Diana Quick, Lady Julia out of *Brideshead Revisited*. Neville Chamberlain once lived in the street. Boris Karloff was born there, in 1887, as William Pratt. We have something called the Camberwell Society which sells Christmas cards and postcards of scenic old Camberwell, which we send to one another. So far I haven't been to a subscription dance, but Christ knows how many times I've been to the police station. Five break-ins last year alone.

The last one was a real beauty, a real Camberwell Beauty. The car wasn't in its usual place so my friendly neighbourhood burglars thought I was out when I was upstairs in bed, turning into a pacifist as I read a book about the horrors of nuclear war. But allow me to set the scene.

I was in bed wearing my major-general's greatcoat, an American Civil War Union Army greatcoat which has been in the family ever since great-great-grandad, for some reason best known to himself, went out and freed the slaves—and which I use as a dressing-gown. Suddenly I heard footsteps on the stairs. Thinking this was merely my baby coming home to me, I continued reading the pacifist tract. Then I heard what sounded like more footsteps. But I thought it was merely my baby coming in on all fours, again. Then I counted them. There was no way my baby had six feet.

How quickly one acts in a situation like that! They had come in before. God knows how many times. But I was never in. You wonder what you'd do if they came when you were there. I heard of a man who opened his wardrobe door to find a six-foot-three-inch West Indian standing there. Quick as a flash the man asked, "Would you like a cup of tea?" "No, man," the West Indian said, "I gotta be runnin' a-long."

I like to think that I shouted "Charge!" or maybe even "Banzai!" I rather suspect it came out more as "Arrggggh!" as I grabbed the baseball bat and had at them, chasing them down the stairs, thinking all the time, "This is why you left America all those years ago! This is the reason you are not living in New York!"

And the bandits? What fear a military figure like mine must have struck into them! They thought it was hilarious. They turned to see how close I was in pursuit, saw the major-general's greatcoat and they started to laugh. Not even laugh. They were giggling, all the way into the garage, which is built into the house, and where I had them trapped while I dialed 999.

Of course I didn't have them trapped at all. That was the way they had come in. They managed to break right through a steel garage door.

"They'll get through anything, sir," one of the coppers said as we all stood round in the cold, looking at the smashed door. At least *I* was looking at the door. The cops were looking at me, in the general's coat, with these ridiculous pyjama-legs coming out of it, and out of the pyjama-bottoms my ridiculous, big, white bare feet. The police were giggling, too. "Hey, Bill," I heard one of them say in a stage whisper, "come on in and see this."

They were black that night but they could have just as easily been white. Ever since I moved to Camberwell I've been swotting up on the social history of South London and it has always been a den of thieves. In Victorian times it was even worse than now. Lambeth was particularly bad, full of slums and gangs and prostitution. Lambeth has been cleaned up; we go to Lambeth to wine bars and restaurants, and soon we'll be going to the Old Vic again.

Brixton, just round the corner from my place in Camberwell, has that jolly market along Electric Avenue—famous now in a pop song—and we go there because it has the best fishmonger in South London and a lot of local

"What the hell is 'I heart NY' supposed to mean? I see it everywhere."

colour and good times, really, unless something sudden happens or it gets dark.

You cannot walk the streets of Brixton from, say 10 p.m. to 3 a.m. without getting mugged. It doesn't matter what colour you are, you'll get mugged. Lambeth has been restored to civilised life. But Brixton, once full of music halls, a place of lovely, tucked away, little squares with prim Victorian houses, where theatricals loved to live in order to be close to the West End and on the road to Brighton, is lost to civilisation once the street lights go on.

No place in South London is safe from burglars or the muggers suddenly leaping out at you. The poor, innocent Camberwell Society fought an heroic but, thank God, vain battle recently to have Southwark council put replica Victorian lamplights in my street. How much light would they have shed on the muggers?

And what of those beautiful trees that line the street and which first won my heart over to it that snowy day in February, just four years ago this week, on Valentine's Day, in fact, when I first set eyes upon the Grove and fell in love at first sight, thinking, "How like a Christmas card it looks!" and "Won't it be lovely in the spring?"

In a horrible vision of a future South London I see these trees being cut down because of the hiding place they offer the muggers, waiting to spring on you as they did on a dear old lady neighbour of mine, who might possibly walk out of the house again, some day.

One fine day, in the height of summer, I came home from work to find they had been in again. But nothing was taken. Then I went to close the back door and the door was gone. Obviously someone had smashed their own door and they needed another. They eke out a modest living in South London robbing each other. A girl I know in Brixton, who says she has been broken into so many times she could not possibly add them all up, came home and saw they had got in once more but they hadn't taken anything. Then she went to put a record on the hi-fi and nothing happened. They had come to get a new needle.

Another girl was walking home alone at night in South London when three of them were suddenly surrounding her. She was a *Guardian* woman. "Why don't you piss off and join the police where you belong?" she said. They stood there, sort of puzzled, and let her past. Which leads me to the police. They never seem to catch any of the burglars, but they always manage to seem interested when they come round after a bit of banditry. What I'm more worried about are my neighbours. When you've been done enough times you realise they know your every move. You realise that the neighbours do not dial 999 when the bandits are breaking into your house in broad daylight because it is the neighbours who are breaking in.

This fact would seem to undermine any hopes for the Home Secretary's new neighbourhood police-support scheme in South London. The neighbourhood scheme, announced in Parliament two weeks ago, is not, Sir Kenneth Newman, the Metropolitan Police Commissioner, is quick to say, the setting up of vigilantes. What he and the Home Secretary have in mind is a neighbourhood committee composed of a local copper, a councillor, traders and simple ratepayers to "help in the fight against rising crime".

"It's from 'The Observer', they want me tc talk about my room."

Just how they would do this nobody has said. Somehow I don't see them getting my door back. And the sort of committee you'd get out of my street is rather terrifying to imagine. My local, which I suppose gives you the best idea of what a neighbourhood is like, is composed in equal parts of the National Front and loud, jovial South Londoners with their mouths full of Cockney, who suddenly get all quiet and confidential and attempt to sell you all sorts of things which have just fallen off the backs of lorries.

"Stan, you're in the writing lark, Stan," one of them said to me the other Sunday lunchtime. "How'd you be interested in four new electric typewriters, golf ball style? £150 each." Sunday lunchtime is the day for such bargains. (Fellow in there the other day selling a back door.) The only thing I ever bought in the pub was a dozen bottles of Thousand Island Salad Dressing. £1.50 the dozen. Off the back of a lorry. They had absolute cases of the stuff going that day.

Oddly enough, the Home Secretary's neighbourhood committees did not actually spring from people being worried about the robbers. It comes, we are told, in answer to "the demands of some Left-wing groups for more control of the Metropolitan Police". So the whole thing is a notion to watch the cops rather than the robbers.

In the end, what the South London householder does is barricade himself in with all manner of special locks and alarms. The drain-pipes at my place in Camberwell are covered in grease and the downstairs windows are barred. None of this enhances the beauty of a house when you are attempting to sell it. Neither does the presence of the locksmith and chippy when, after the house had been more than a year on the market, a live one finally came to call the other day.

There is something highly distracting about a man hammering and chiselling away, putting in a special lock and attempting to shore up the garage door, while you are showing the prospective home-buye around.

"There," the locksmith and carpente said, "that ought to keep the bastards out."

"For Gawd's sake," I thought. "How am supposed ever to sell this place?" When all a once the man who came to see the hous laughed.

"Do you have break-ins?" he asked.

No, I said to myself, I'm a crazy man, I'n trying to lock myself in. It's a harmless eccen tricity.

"Well, you know how it is," I said, "it' something you have to put up with every where in the world today, the way the worl is today, what the world is coming to today don't know. Have you seen the box room You know, that could easily be used a another bedroom. Why, the people who live here before did. There was a girl living i there, six foot four, twenty stone if she were day. Said she loved it."

"I'm in electronics," the prospectiv buyer said. "I won't bother with locks. I' electrify the place. That'll give them shock." Then *he* giggled, a dirty, evil sort o giggle like a crocodile deciding he'd lie ver still and pretend to be a log.

I sold the house. I am turning back th clock, moving back to the original gentee slum of Bloomsbury. Found a wonderfu little place.

"Get many break-ins?" I asked as he wen through the motions of unlocking a fron door which had so many locks and chains on it that it could have doubled for Marley's Ghost.

"No," he said, "I honestly don't know why I bother. I just happened to get these cheap. From a fellow at the local. Apparently they fell off the back of a lorry. You in the literary game? Well, sometimes Virginia Woolf's ghost manages to break in but . . ."

Actually I did check with the cops at Theobalds Road station. In Bloomsbury the villains don't bother with petty stuff like the Literary Editor of *Punch*'s pathetic little flat upstairs, they're busy dynamiting the safe in the jeweller's shop on the ground floor. I can hardly wait.

Larry's Plumbers

Richard Gordon

Long-range Cricket

With winter comes a recurrent attack of *insomnia Australiensis,* to which I have been a martyr since childhood.

Four-thirty a.m., click, and there is Henry Blofeld babbling of green fields 10,000 miles away. Snuggled under blankets and eider-down, in a blank, silent, freezing English bedroom, I lie till breakfast, breathing gently and visualising our white hopes battling in the sunshine with the resolution of the Commandos and the grace of the *corps de ballet*.

A Jules Verne imagination is unnecessary for us compulsive cricket voyeurs. We know exactly what they look like when Bob Willis bowls and Greg Chappell strikes, when Rod Marsh takes a catch from his slips' toecaps, Ian Botham believes he was really not out, Derek Randall fidgets and Dennis Lillee dismisses a batsman who has just hit him for six. Their idiosyncrasies are printed on our minds like the faces of our loved ones. We can even picture the drinks being brought out.

My imagination failed only that Saturday afternoon in Perth. The mugging of Terry Alderman was a scene beyond conception. I could but stare wide-eyed from my pillow and sip the froth of Blower's indignation.

I clap the wickets and boundaries under the bedclothes, which wakes my wife and tends to annoy her. I silence her with the reminder that I was in bed with the Test commentary long before I was with her. Our honeymoon competed with India v. England at Bombay, a draw, we made 456 and 55 for 2, Tom Graveney got 175.

My affair began in the 1930s when I was still a Gugnunc (password *Ik ik pa boo,* reply *Goo goo pa nunc*, it was run by the *Daily Mirror*). The listener then really knew that the BBC was bringing it all the way from Australia—"Whoooosh whoooom Larwood running to the wicket eeeepppp wowowowowow Bradman's turned him to long krkrkrkrk good wowowow, sir!"

Family breakfast tables on dim icy mornings listened silently over their Grapenuts to those crackling broadcasts from a far-away country of which they knew nothing except that it was hot and inhabited mainly by Aborigines and kangaroos, often confused. "Down Under" had a ring of pioneering remoteness lost in our world of boring accessibility.

With Australia further than a Poundstretcher away, we had to construct a mental picture of the Hill at Sydney, the Swan river and seagulls at the Waca, the Gabba at Brisbane. When I could afford the fare forty years later I found them disappointing, and the Christmas weather in Sydney typhonic, with people risking frostbite on the Nudie Beach.

We learned by ear that the Australians wore green gorblimey working-men's caps, for extras said sundries, for close of play stumps, and for a batting collapse a debarkle. We discovered that barracking could be for or against, and I suspected that Australian crowds were one-sided after overhearing "Leave our flies alone!" shouted to Jardine in his Harlequin cap swatting them in the outfield. Contact was lost when you went to work. The radio was a luxury in a car comparable with a cocktail cabinet, and a portable wireless was the size of a mobile commode.

Cricket in the Thirties was as stark as th transmission. There was no cosy Geoffs Robins, Chrisses and Mikes. English cricketers were divided ruthlessly into gentleme and players (a distinction in Australia o course impossible). The gents bore initials o the scorecard, the players were all unbaptise heathens. When it was embarrassingly necessary to distinguish between two ungentlemanly brothers in the same side, they wer tagged with a letter like police-court exhibits—as Compton D and Compton L.

Cricketers took the field through separat gates, and a gentleman would be as shocke at familiarity from a player as from a servan in his other clubs. Appeals were made *sott voce*, flannels were made of flannel, and a bo was an object as unmentionable as the po No one ran on to the pitch, even with thei clothes on. Only straying dogs disturbed th single policeman dozing on his seat by th sightscreen and convulsed the crowd. Ho ward Marshall was believed to keep a terrie in the commentary box for release when pla grew dull.

To see the Australian Tests before the wa you had to wait six weeks for Britis Movietone News to arrive by P & O. When rose from a Gugnunc to an Ovaltiney, the cut the suspense by flying the flag with Imperial Airways to the grassy runways Croydon (Heathrow was a view from the A and you went to Gatwick for the races).

Even with the Comet, we had agonisin days before setting our eyes on the excitement. Now Richie Benaud arrives withi hours, though BBC2 sometimes inconsiderately keeps him in the wings until midnight. wait up with beer and sandwiches, comple ing the atmosphere by the dying fireside b

"This is the bit I like best—flaunting their rabies laws."

"Here's looking at you, kid."

wearing my MCC boater, but four hours' sleep is barely enough for us accustomed to doze in pavillons for afternoons on end.

The TV screen this Test series has become as self-indulgently over-complicated as James Joyce's prose. Watching simultaneously ball speeding to boundary and batsmen speeding between wickets induces a nasty case of strabismus. The opening music should be sold to horror films, and that dreadful little duck to a Pekinese restaurant.

The Highlights, like Hamlet's players, are the abstract and brief chronicles of the time, but spare us hours of watching a ball in a wicketkeeper's glove wondering when it is going to stop raining at Old Trafford. They also spare the infuriation of Saturdays, with jolly Frank Bough suddenly appearing to announce, "It's all very exciting at Lord's, but now it's time for the underwater slow bicycling racing from Scunthorpe Baths."

The action replay changed cricket-watching as the telescope astronomy. Were I a neurosurgeon, I should die happy after perfecting an operation on the brain's visual cortex to permit it naturally, like the green orb when you close your eyes against the glaring sun. My guinea-pigs would be umpires. I must content myself with inventing a way to watch Test matches while writing novels, an occupation otherwise as tedious as oakum-picking in solitary confinement.

The man of letters needs know only the easily acquired run-up times of all international bowlers. He sits facing the TV with the sound off, on a table just beyond his developing opus. He writes, *All happy families are alike* and looks up to see the ball delivered. If the fielders leap all over the screen, the novelist turns up the sound to discover why. Otherwise, he watches the ball pushed into the covers and continues *but an unhappy family is unhappy after its own* next ball *fashion.* The quickies allow the author to weave sentences of Jamesian complexity. With the spinners, he comes out like Ernest Hemingway. I shall never get the Booker Prize, or even be on the Frank Delaney show, but I shall sit happily in this sunlit niche in English literature.

"Just think, three weeks ago you were only a telephone number among the graffiti."

L'Acquisition d'un Arbre de Noel

ACTE I. Le 23 decembre

Monsieur: Excusez-moi. Mon nom est Tuckerton.
Shopman: Enchanté. Mon nom est J. Smith Limité, Fruits et Veg.
Monsieur: Non, vous ne comprenez pas. Je suis M. Tuckerton et j'ai reservé un arbre de Noel.
Shopman: Ah. C'est différent. Reg! L'arbre pour M. Tinkerton!
Reg: (*off-scene*) Y en a plus!
Shopman: Je regrette, squire. All gone. Les arbres sont tous dans une sold-out situation. Un petit slip-up. Sorry, et tout ça. Look, j'ai un petit arbre ici. Je peux vous l'offrir pour £1.
Monsieur: Un petit arbre? C'est un grand button-hole!
Shopman: Oui, well, c'est un peu diminutif.
Monsieur: Dites-moi, at least, la source de supply de vos arbres de Noel.
Shopman: Volontiers. Vous prenez le M1, vous prenez l'Exit 14, vous allez trois milles, vous voyez à la gauche un spinney de conifères, vous voyez le signe, *Les Trespasseurs Seront Prosecutés*, vous allez dans le spinney . . .

ACTE II. Le 25 decembre

Garçon: Maman, pourquoi notre arbre de Noel est si diminutif?
Maman: Parce que quand votre Papa est arrivé au spinney après Exit 14 du M1, le spinney avait été totalement vandalisé par les marchands d'arbres de Noel. C'était le last remaining.
Garçon: Pourquoi est Papa dans le lit?
Maman: Il a une dose de flu après son flit de minuit à Exit 14 du M1.
Garçon: Maman, pourquoi . . . ?
Maman: Pourquoi vous posez tant de questions? Allez lire votre nouveau livre, "Mille (1,000) Interessants Facts pour les Garçons".

ACTE III. Le 27 decembre

Garçon: Saviez-vous que Sarah Bernhardt, avec un wooden leg, a joué Long John Silver en pantomime a Nuddersfield? Saviez-vous que satsuma, en Japonais, signifie "tomato"? Saviez-vous . . . ?
Papa: Saviez-vous que si tu ne fermes pas ta bouche, je vais jeter "Mille (1,000) Intéressants Facts" dans le dust-bin? Voici un fact intéressant. Saviez-vous que même un petit arbre de Noel deposite 19,000 needles sur l'average carpet? Les arbres de Noel sont un wash-out. En 1983 nous achetons un arbre artificiel en aluminium, OK?
Garçon: Saviez-vous que l'aluminium, en Borneo, est adoré comme un precieux metal? Saviez-vous . . . ?
Papa: . . . que je vais au pub! (*Slam de porte. 5,000 needles tombent sur le carpet dans le draught.*)

Jonathan Sale

Selling a Dummy

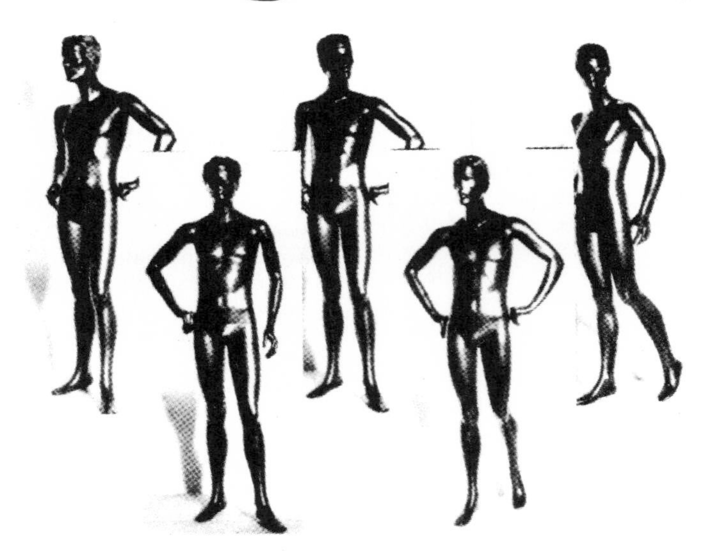

"I'm calling about the dummy," I explained.

"*Dummy!*" she yelled. "How dare you use that word?"

"No, not you," I said, "the one in the shop window."

"Never say that," she snapped, "*especially* about the one in the window. It's a terrible word, only used by people who are not part of what's going on."

Yes, I do admit to being without the slightest share in what's going on, anywhere, but I now know that if referring to a rubber teat on a feeding-bottle, a dopey person or a feint in football, I am perfectly entitled to say d***y. For an assemblage of sticks, with several resemblances to human beings, upon which clothes are hung, one says "model". But for the humanoid object seen in shop windows, it is "mannequin" or nothing.

To the January locusts currently swamping the stores, a mannequin is merely something that holds up marked-down garments for ease of grabbing. But to a shop like Harvey Nichols it represents £300 worth of "Lazy Lizzie", one of eighty that make up the capital investment of some £24,000. It has a five-year span, getting to see different parts of the store on a frequent crop rotation, with a fresh coat of make-up and a new wig on an annual basis. Then it is pensioned off to a more tolerant boutique where they present its best profile and turn the lights down a bit.

Mannequin-makers keep their production figures pretty close to their chests. (They also keep their chests pretty close to their chests; their creations' glass-fibre breasts would be eclipsed if, say, Barbara Windsor stood in front of a shop window display and turned sideways.) But the top three companies produce up to 25,000 a year, with, in the case of Gemini in Bayswater, 50 per cent of their cloned creations finally gracing foreign shops.

Since fashion, which is at the fringes of our lives, is taken by its practitioners with all the seriousness of a Pershing missile installed at the bottom of their gardens, you might expect the mannequins, which are on the fringes of fashion, to be taken even more seriously. And you would be right, to judge by the manufacturer who bit my tongue off for using the word "dummy" without due authority to do so.

And to judge by the existence of a massive volume entitled *Mannequins* by one Nicole Parrot. You can buy this now at a bargain £25 but hurry, hurry while stocks last. At least, the stocks will still be there on February 28th but the price won't be, as Academy Editions hoik it up, in a reversal of the principle of spring sales, to £29.95.

The work may have suffered in translation (certainly some of the spelling has) but maybe not. It is possible that a sentence of which the publishers are particularly proud, "As soon as the curtain rises on the Fashion Theatre, men will dream of them, and their flesh and blood sisters will be jealous of them," sounded better in the original French, but it is equally possible that it did not.

It is possible that if you donned a beret and a string of onions, and, stretching out the arms a little with the palms uppermost in so far as that was compatible with balancing on an elderly push-bike, uttered the first sentence of the book, "What is there to say about a civilisation that at no time in its history ever dreamed of leaving a legacy of corpses?" it might seem more helpful. Or it might not. Either way, the reader is more likely to pass on to something more interesting, such as the picture on page 22 of which the caption is "Eroded sexual organs, English mannequins, 1970."

Still, I would not like to differ with my colleagues on French magazines whose fulsome quotes decorate the dust-jacket: "A book of immense oneiric power", *Express*; "A jewel of sophistication", *Libération*; "Chic, well designed . . . it's beautiful," *Chasseur d'images*. Beside all that, "Merde alors—*Punch*" would not look too good. We have to take mannequins seriously, if only because there are people who believe a book about them is worth all of £25, £29.95 after February 28th.

They—the glass-fibre dummies, not the

"Just sell the tortoise Jenkins."

uman versions—certainly outshine in hysical terms any humans of my acquaint-nce. Gemini do a "Young and Fun" range at comes "in four different moods—youth nd vitality, poise and sophistication," at 255 complete with wig and make-up. They re a sort of life-size Lego and take to bits to ary the poses, a three-dimensional version f those sliced children's books in which a ook's head is superimposed on a police-an's stomach.

Yet my favourite remains "Olga", at £275. here was a time when "Olga" meant a eautiful Russian spy, but now "OLGA pitomizes the woman of the 80's—the ightly tempestuous look that reflects the ood of today's fashions—determined and ynamic in her fashion choices". She comes poses numbers one to six; please state if ms required behind head, by sides, on ps. Her optional extras include "Dogs and heetahs" with a starting price of £185, and, om £275, what are described as "Black-moors".

Her friends include "Monty", not so much homage to the victor of El Alamein as "A lassic Man's Accessory Head for ties, arves, sweaters etc." If he has a fault as a annequin about the house, it is that he is bsolutely legless and indeed armless, so lga had better settle for "Jean-Paul", com-lete with eroded sexual organ, at £255, or New Tall Abstract Man in any gloss or matt nish" at £295, metallic finish extra, please ate if blackamoor required.

Gemini, I have to say, represent the cceptable face and limbs of mannequins. I ave to say that partly because no one wants damage their export drive and partly be-ause they lack the pretentiousness of some f their colleagues (it was not a Gemini execu-ve who made me wash my mouth out after e "dummy" episode). They have a long ay to go before they disappear down the lughole in which swirls the prose of Mlle arrot.

"It's electronic—it goes up and down without you doing anything."

Mannequins, according to *Mannequins*, have several advantages over man. "The lack of hair, sweat and smell," "the perfection of the face", for example. "Not only does a mannequin not wear panties; she also has no varicose veins," goes the argument, if that's what it is, Parrot-fashion. How true. Talking-point of the week. Discuss.

Where we have to disagree with the thesis is in the statement that "In every period in history, women of all ages have searched the mannequin's body in vain for the stigma of the thousand flaws and scars etched on their own bodies by heredity and time." Female readers may do just that when window-shopping outside C&A Modes today, but "every period in history" is pushing it. That translator has got to go. The first mannequin is placed, a few pages later, in sixteenth-century Venice, which leaves several thousand years of recorded history without mannequins and hence without women searching glass-fibre torsos for stigma etcetera.

It was one Ascension Day, on the Grand Canal, that the latest French fashions were presented by the first recorded dummy, the Missing Link between a coat-hanger and today's Olga with Cheetah. Only one chronicler jotted it down in his notebook and all the masked marchionesses said was, "Doesn't say a lot, does she?"

It was a long haul to New Tall Abstract Man. In the eighteenth century, the rag trade came up with a wickerwork scarecrow, but this seems to have lacked a head and anything that you could call tempestuous, even slightly tempestuous. Halfway through the next century came, yes, a British export to Paris in the shape of 7000 pieces of articulated wire: Action Woman upon which you could hang your coat.

The next technological development was wax; to this were added eyes, and teeth, boxes of which, sorted into colour and size respectively, were man-handled into the workshops of the manufacturers every week like the delivery bay of a spare-part surgery clinic. Later, plaster was used and assistants arranging them in the windows found hernias to be the occupational hazard. Some weighed up to 250 lbs and came to bits for transportation in coffin-like containers.

The Golden Age of the mannequin, for my money, was in the early Thirties, when they mirrored not what shoppers wanted to look like but what they actually looked like; skinny, bald, possessing pot-bellies—and that was just the females. There were dummies of chinless aristocrats that were dead ringers for the originals, except that their conversation was possibly more interesting.

Alas, those designs soon reached the knacker's yard and now it is only the finest folk that are good enough for the full treatment. That treatment includes stepping into a sort of jelly bath, like a living, all-over death mask, from which the mould is taken. Then the warts are ironed out.

There is talk of mannequins that will talk. They will hail passers-by and discuss the merits of the garments. They will be transistorised and equipped with artificial intelligences. And if we call them dummies, they will set the cheetah on us.

"Bad news, Spenlow—we're in it up to here!"

"I suppose you're another of those dirty bastards who urinate in the water?"

"I've got to tell someone, I killed the dinosaurs."

CABLE STITCHING

The Hunt Report has told you what you can get w cable TV comes in. We tell you what you *will* get.

In **THE FORMERLY GEORGE HOLMES HOUR,** neo-Spanish soubrette Dorita Holmesa sings songs to the electronic fan. Topping Channel 38's *Saturday Nite Out* extravaganza, Dorita, who was once the foremost spot-welder in Birkenhead, comes to you live from downtown Algeciras with an elegant and fashionable repertoire of Flamenco favourites and novelty juggling, assisted by Moldo the Human Marionette and his Elastic Dog.

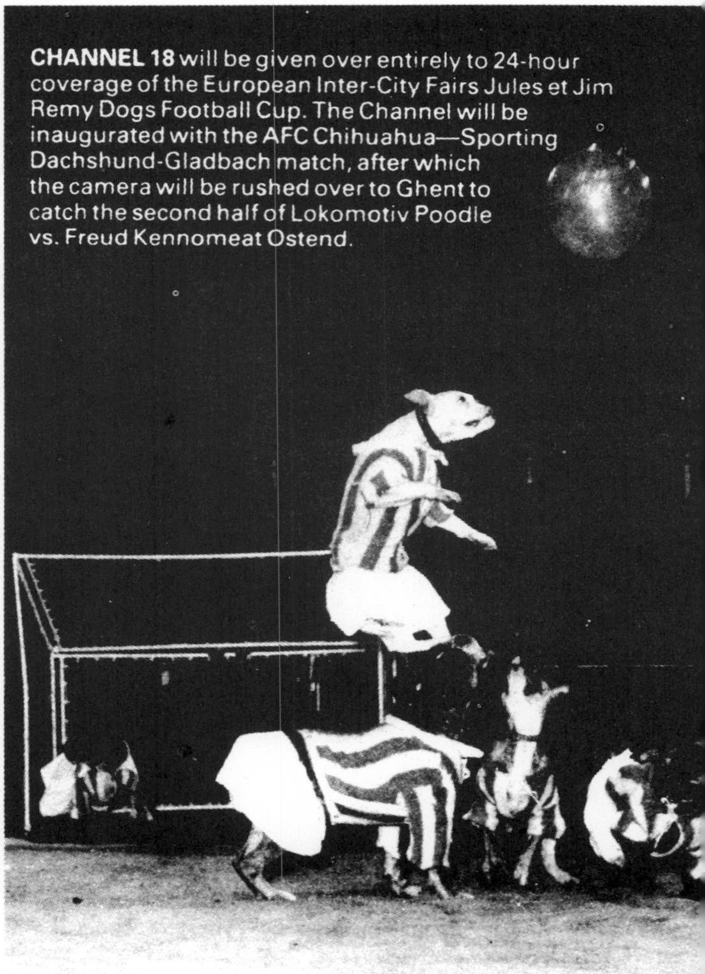

CHANNEL 18 will be given over entirely to 24-hour coverage of the European Inter-City Fairs Jules et Jim Remy Dogs Football Cup. The Channel will be inaugurated with the AFC Chihuahua—Sporting Dachshund-Gladbach match, after which the camera will be rushed over to Ghent to catch the second half of Lokomotiv Poodle vs. Freud Kennomeat Ostend.

INTERNATIONAL PRO-AM CELEBRITY DRAUGHTS DIRECT AND LIVE FROM HANGCHOW, Channel 17's main nightly offering, has inter-round commentaries from Mycroft Wogan in Praed Street Gents Studio, and will be followed each evening by an hour of Frank Sinatra's all-time greats, played by the NUM string quartet.

For sophisticated thrills, most viewers will want to lock into Channel 13's heartstopping series **INDONESIAN NOVELTY GOODS SALESMAN.** Bought by 13 from WBFTV Jakarta after it unaccountably failed to make the Dutch East Indian Top 90, **INGS** stars Nyoko Suharbo as the man trying to track down an egg-timer in the shape of a miniature hog which his competitors have filled with poisoned sand in an attempt to discredit him.

DIFFERENT SIZED PEOPLE, the astonishing new weekly documentary series for Channel 22, brings big and little members of the public together to discuss clothing problems. "A major breakthrough in minority broadcasting," explained an excited programme director for 22. "Some weeks, hats, the next week it could be, oh, I don't know, mittens, morning-suits, you name it. When you break through into hitherto unknown territory, who can say where you'll end up? Quite frankly, we're feeling our way."

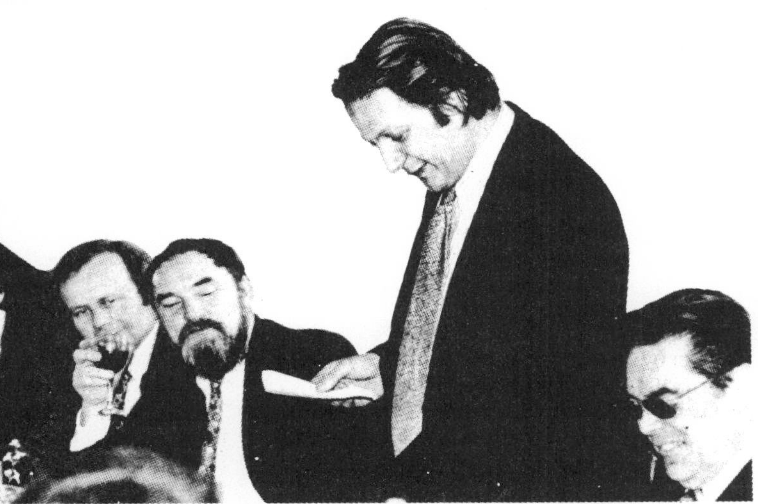

CATCH MY DRIFT! is the fantastic new talent-spotting programme vanguarding Channel 27. They are looking for the man who will be Best Non-professional After-Dinner Speaker to Luton and District Quantity Surveyors' Associations 1983. The winner will get his own show and a £3.00 Robert Dyas gift voucher.

NOT FAR FROM DALLAS, the new blockbusting 94-part 8mm serial for Channel 32, shot entirely on location and using local people who thought they were having their passport photographs taken, has so far cost almost £78.40, a record for the network. It traces the compelling story of the Doings and their struggles to find their shoes in the morning, work out bus routes, get the fence fixed, and discover why the cat has ringworm. The repeat has already been sold to Channel 46 for a two-figure sum.

albert · **Pavement Artistes**

Harassed buskers seek quiet life abroad—*The Tim*

"Fifteen years and that's the first time I've recognised a tune."

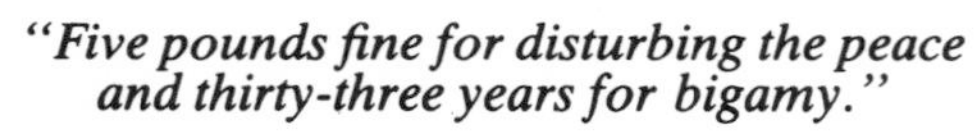

"Five pounds fine for disturbing the peace and thirty-three years for bigamy."

"Retained for a further week by public demand."

"Someone must know the Red Flag!"

"I like Sweden but the monkey fancied Borneo."

Lewis Burke Frumkes

The Chic of Araby

SHEIK ACHMET EL MAMOUN

Before his promotion to Sheik, Achmet El Mamoun, which means "Son of ranch fossil" in Arabic, was chief flog for the South Yemen police department where he developed the now popular middle-eastern technique of whipping miscreants publicly to the tunes of *Get Along Little Doggie*, *Moon Over Miami*, and *On Wisconsin*. *On Wisconsin* was his particular favourite.

An early devotee of bizarre S & M, Sheik Mamoun came close to losing his life in the spring of 1974 when a camel he was beating turned on him and bit off his fishnet stockings and most of his garter belt.

SHEIK YAMANI TURKI IBN WORKING ON THE RAILROAD

In the world of the lesser sheiks, no one is considered lesser of a sheik than Yamani Turki Ibn Working On the Railroad, whose main claim to fame is his 2% interest in the old turban works at Abu Kemal. Sheik "Ibn Working" as he is called by his friends, believes strongly that head coverings are coming back and recently spent a week in Texas trying to sell the Dallas Cowboys on the idea of using turbans instead of helmets. Catching onto the concept quickly, and impressed by all he was trying to do for them, the cowboys used "Ibn Working" as a tackling dummy in five successive workouts. Microsurgeons from Baylor University Hospital and a special team from London have spent the last three weeks trying to piece the sheik back together again.

If the surgery is successful it is thought the sheik will most closely resemble an old shoe in the years ahead. Sheik "Ibn Working" thanks Allah that he didn't try to sell turbans to the Steelers.

SHEIK MURRY COHEN

Sheik Murry Cohen of Abi Gezind, a settlement on the West Bank, is not exactly a sheik in the strict sense of the word, though he does drive a Seville and hand out five dollar tips to the barber, manicurist, and shoe-shine boy at Mohammed's hair styling emporium every Tuesday.

What he really is, is "chic" says his wife Muriel who thinks he looks stunning in his new navy and white leisure suit which she gave to him on the occasion of his 59th birthday last July. God knows he has enough ties and cuff links.

SHEIK SAAD SAAD SAAD

There are sheiks and there are sheiks, but this one is Saad, Saad, Saad. No matter where he goes people say, "That is Saad, Saad, Saad," and wag their heads from side to side as if to say, "Saad, Saad, Saad." In final analysis, there is not much to say of Sheik Saad, Saad, Saad, other than that he Saad, Saad, Saad, and leave it at that.

SHEIK FAHD EL DOONEY

Small and inconsequential, Fahd El Dooney of Oman made a life decision early on to renounce the trappings of decadent western society, the oil fields, jets, fast car and wild women, and to become a servant the people. Because of his self-sacrificing philosophy and ascetic ways, El Dooney is looked upon with great respect by his fello sheiks who call upon him frequently to tak out the garbage. Uncertain as to whether c not he made the right decision, Sheik El Dooney can often be found kissing the toe the other sheiks and begging to be beaten used as a doormat. He is in treatment thirty-five times a week with a strict Freud analyst.

SHEIK ABDUL EL FAZIZ Y COCOBLANCAS

By far the richest of the lesser sheiks, Abdul El Faziz y Cocoblancas of Kuwait a Hallendale, Florida, has a daily oil income twice the gross national product of Mars nc including outside investments in real estat and securities or royalties from his best-selling book, "Abdul's Complete Boo Of Sand".

Sheik Faziz y Cocoblancas is known to b brave: invariably he eats his mother-in-law cooking; and handsome, he bears a strong resemblance to Nanook Of The North. However he is not much of an athlete and prefers spending his time at home, hanging around the seraglio with his favourite odalisque, Herpes.

As Good as a Feast

We are now well into the season of public dinners which began at the end of eptember and continues into Lent: office arties tend to occupy early and mid-)ecember but annual beanos, company re-eptions, anniversary celebrations, profes-ional get-togethers, and especially wintry ıt Homes, are still sending out their distress ignals in the form of heavy white cards ub-scribed *RSVP*.

What they have in common is a real or nagined belief on the part of the host that he hould provide or return hospitality for more uests than make sense.

Now we all know that you can cater hand-omely for a dozen people at a time; up to orty guests are manageable, if you take care vith the menu, but after that number the ems that you cannot serve become too umerous to list and to date no one has listed nem—though heaven knows, those of us ho tread a heavy fantastic club-foot from allroom to banqueting suite would need a rge foolscap sheet were we to make a start.

If I were insane enough to feel that I must ıvite two hundred guests to a drinks party I hould begin by providing an abundance of ecent wines at the right temperatures; also a ufficiency of attractive glasses and a few orkscrews.

This would make a welcome change from ne norm of too many waiters pouring too ttle wine into glasses chosen for the sole eason that they are inexpensive to replace hen they are broken or nicked.

I would then designate the far corners of he room for food—and I mean real food, like moked salmon with brown bread and but-er, lemon and peppermills in one corner; armhouse Bries and Hovis biscuits and adishes in another; pieces of crisply fried eking duck with Chinese pancakes and Hoi in sauce as the *chef d'oeuvres*, to be brought ı when people are looking and the most gregious gourmands have satiated their reed on butties. What I get, give or take a andful of Japanese rice crackers, are: dips, hips, olives, biscuits, peanuts, pretzels, elery stalks, pineapple cubes, Cheddar vedges, tomato quarters, egg-halves, ucumber hunks, canapés, and all manner of ried nasties on cocktail sticks.

If they gave you a whole succulent, steam-ng, aromatic York Ham and a chef with a ast knife (and French bread and butter and ood mustard) there would be communal ontentment, though a school of thought has t that the consumer might feel the host had not *cared* if there is no choice. Consequently, we get what banqueting managers are encouraged to plug as "a selection of delicious appetisers". The good old battle-cry of "You can't please them; therefore confuse them," beloved of the catering trade, has actually been adopted in private households; party guests could be given saucers of hot pheasant kedgeree or bowls of Italian salad—made of strips of underdone roast beef, a julienne of celery and apple and thinly sliced onion rings dressed in a creamy mayonnaise.

Instead we get dates into which busy fingers have injected Philadelphia cream cheese while the family genius has covered the whole dish in a thin film of gelatine which he now calls aspic.

Hotels and professional caterers do their little numbers to justify high asking prices. I mean, people know that a huge ham, enough for fifty people to hack at, cannot cost more than £20 to buy and they would baulk at having to pay more than £45, even with accompanying French bread and butter; but *sixteen* different dishes of small nasty/spicy/stodgy/salty titbits, some hot, others luke-warm, most at room temperature, are not as easy to price and look as if someone had made a huge effort; they are therefore paid for ("Shall we say £3 a head for this terrific selection?") without protest.

From the point of view of the caterer, the greater the selection, the more important it is that no one should say, "Those round peppery brown things were great but they ran out"; so caterers ensure nothing is terrific, which means that no one will complain. The

One person at this party is a hypochondriac. To find out who it is, switch off the light.

criterion is that no item shall be so good that you will want more and everything must look so appetising that you will try it—once.

But it is the sit-down dinners for large numbers that are the real ball-breakers, if you will pardon the expression.

Big and successful companies employ experts to advise them on office equipment; teams of lawyers monitor their contracts; accountants oversee their financial deals; high-powered consultants devise pension schemes; surveyors, insurers, maintenance men and cleaning companies all provide their own brands of technical know-how for the greater glory and efficiency of the corporation—but when it comes to the annual dinner, the managing director's secretary (she who eats fish-paste sandwiches in her office at lunchtime), is sent to the local hostelry to organise the function.

They do not know (how should they?) that mass caterers find it very convenient to produce tomato soup, roast chicken, and ice cream and sliced peaches; nor that they could get a clear oxtail soup with puff pastry Marmite straws, boiled leg of lamb with caper sauce, and peeled orange segments with Curaçao—if you threaten to take your trade elsewhere—just as the experts who do other things for the company take trade elsewhere if the estimates or specifications for typewriters and stationery and floor coverings and pension plans are not to their liking.

And if caterers tell you, "I am afraid *that* menu would cost rather more," explain that the ingredients are the same price—and if it is manpower that they are concerned about, why not have fewer waiters wresting wine bottles out of your hand as you start to pour? In fact, let's have the wine open, on the tables; that will release a few men. Then let us dispense with those who ask us if everything is all right—after the food has gone and it is too late to do anything about it. By way of further economies, ask for napkins to be laid by the side of the plate instead of having them folded to look like pregnant albatrosses, and in a spirit of total helpfulness towards reducing staff costs, demand to have cream and sugar placed on the table so that guests can pour their own coffee and speakers can speak without having to shout over the pervasive chorus of "Black or white, do you take sugar?"

I do feel that if restaurants must do things so very differently from the way nice people do things at home, the difference could be manifested by richer, better, more caringly produced food rather than extra pretentiousness and grovel.

"Bit of luck, that—landing a cushy summer job."

"To hell with natural selection—let's just eat the nice fat young ones."

BBC INTERNAL MEMORANDUM NO 193,484(b)

M: ConMemRad (Controller of Memos, Radio 4)

ALL DEPARTMENTS

u will perhaps have gathered from recent llines in the press and a brief paragraph in *The ener* just under *Life With Marghanita Laski Part 14* ; it has finally been decided to award Mr Norman ter, architect, the contract for the designing of New adcasting House on the site of The Langham in rtland Place.

This will necessitate certain other changes in order to ing BBC Radio into line for a dynamic new oadcasting concept to be known as Radio in the 1990s r, if certain builders' merchants are behaving true to orm, Radio in the year 2028. Kindly therefore take note of the following, which is not to be leaked in any form to he *Standard* diary.

1/The bar in The Langham will have to be vacated at least fifteen minutes prior to demolition of the present structure. All foreign correspondents and contributors to *Gardeners' Question Time* should then be awoken, asked to return the teaspoons and politely evicted onto the pavements where they will be collected for *Pick of the Week*.

2/Close inspection of preliminary drawings for New Broadcasting House indicates that certain of its potential inhabitants will also have to be drastically restructured in order to blend into the new technology. Mr John Timpson has, for example, been left untended for far too long due to internal budgetary restrictions. There are distinct signs of dry rot here, and a major rebuilding programme may be necessary on his upper sections where rising damp is also now evident.

3/It has also been brought to our attention that the new building will almost certainly have studios at ground level and possibly above. It has in the past always been BBC policy to locate all radio studios underground, to avoid the danger of members of the licence-paying public coming into sudden unexpected physical contact with Mr Roy Plomley. Now however there is a very real chance that radio broadcasters could be seen by unsuspecting passers-by, and it might therefore be advisable for the relevant producer to have a discreet word with Mr Robert Robinson's tailor and barber at the earliest possible opportunity.

4/It is also now considered likely that daylight could filter into certain studios with disastrous consequences. Mr Brian Matthew and Mr Tony Blackburn are for instance believed not to have seen daylight since early in 1951, and the last thing Controller Radio 2 wants is a lot of ageing disc jockeys reduced to dust as per *Lost Horizon*.

5/It is also entirely possible that the new building may contain lifts with fully-functioning doors. Contributors to *Woman's Hour* and *Kaleidoscope* should therefore be discouraged from clambering out through the hole above the chandelier when they have reached the required level as per current Broadcasting House practice. They are further advised that several of the new studio microphones may in fact be functioning when those studios are technically "on the air". The BBC will therefore no longer be paying a stamp supplement so that contributors to *Stop The Week* may write to both listeners telling them what they were planning to say.

6/There is every likelihood that the new building will be at least partly sound-proofed, on lower levels. Listeners accustomed to checking their watches by the 8.05am Central Line tube from Oxford Circus to Bond Street as it rumbles through the *Today* studio are therefore advised that it might be safer to set all timepieces by the booming of Sir Robin Day as he interrupts Foreign Secretaries on *The World at One*.

7/It has been decided that the new building shall contain only three canteens and one licensed bar per floor. This, it is fully realised, does not come up to normal BBC specifications, but it is hoped that broadcasters may care to avail themselves of the subsidised canteen round the corner at ITN, thereby further improving the chances of an ITV economic crisis.

8/The ceremonial withdrawing-room for Mr Terry Wogan will be on floor five of the new building, and allowing for rest periods and time spent in lifts it is estimated that he may well be off the air for anything up to twenty minutes in any 24-hour period. It should however still be possible to hear Mr Richard Baker at almost any hour of day or night.

9/During the move from old Broadcasting House (which will eventually become the Kenneth Robinson Museum of Radio Artefacts) to New Broadcasting House it may prove necessary to suspend for a week both *Any Answers* and the letters section of *PM*. As this is liable to lead to a sharp fall in the pound and a lowering of British morale, it has been agreed to declare a period of national emergency during which loony Right-wing floggers will be entitled to have their correspondence read aloud from the stage of the National Theatre by Mr Nicholas Parsons and Mrs Barbara Woodhouse in front of an invited audience.

10/To celebrate the opening of New Broadcasting House, Mr Terry Wogan and Mr Alistair Cooke (if not previously ennobled) have agreed to give readings from Lord Reith's Last Will and Testament with especial reference to the bit about how the Light and Third Programmes and the Home Service were not to be allowed to degenerate into a load of self-serving old rubbish numbered from one to four.

Fat Lady Shops

Now there's a blow for freedom struck already, in the very title. Not *Sixteen Plus* or *Big Beauty* or any such coy euphemism; not even the once tactful *Outsize Outfitters*. I speak of shops which cater, let us bravely face it, for the fatter female form. You may set it all down to glands, or cellulite, or Negative Role-Model Conditioning, or ten children, that your figure has swollen to the likeness of a World War II concrete blockhouse on legs; however pat the excuse, you must still find something to swathe your Rubenesque perimeter. And you will not find it easily, down the High Street.

"Well," says Debbie of Evans (used to be Evans Outsize, only people wouldn't be seen going in, used to lurk behind bus shelters till the pavement cleared) "it's the manufacturers. They do a design and they can scale it up to 14 on the same pattern-block, but after that," she paused, inhibited by a lifetime of instinctive tact, "the, well, proportions change. The armholes get bigger, for one thing." Quite. So the High Street caters blithely for stick insects and walking ribcages with pimple boobs, and the more majestic of us must slink to the Outsizeries.

For those unacquainted, thanks to the merciful miracle of radio, with my own qualifications, I should admit that I hover on the brink between High Street Woman and Woman-Plus. When I wish to feel elfin, I float through Evans and Dee Dawson and Big Lady, gleefully pushing aside rails of elephantwear and rolling the magic syllables of *Haven't you got it in a smaller size?* round my tongue like vintage port. When I wish to send blouse buttons pinging merrily across great communal changing-caverns, with luck striking a stick insect painfully in the eye, I ruffle the standard boutique rails like anyone else. But I have watched the frankly fat shops closely over the years, and from their front line now I bring most heartening news.

It is no longer necessary to look like something the Ministry of Defence forgot to remove from a Norfolk beach in 1945. You can now, at size 24, 26, nay, 30 and 32, abandon the concrete-fortification look and opt to resemble a gigantic Serbian peasant wench, an enormous Red Admiral butterfly, or a Frog Footman by Tenniel.

"Yes, we *did* do knickerbockers," says Debbie. "We were a bit scared at first, put the big ones out in Birmingham or somewhere on trial, but seven pairs walked out the first day."

The rails of huge grey and beige cylinders, the great square tweed skirts, the floral smocks that balloon dartless from neck to dimpled knee, are all still there; the hippo-legs of the grey cord slacks, the tactful navy suits for Matron's day off and the spotted tie-bows that perch dizzily above her shelving bust; but they are pushed into the darker corners near the hydraulic girdles and iron megabras. Thanks partly to aggressive, overfed, feminist America, the fat lady shops have gone sassy. Our own dear Evans (founded Clapham, 1936) has taken a deep breath, thrown off its stays, and gone all dirndled and upbeat, all flaunt-it, velvet-britches happy. And the customers wallow.

"They used, you see, to be frightened even of pink," says Debbie. "Now, they aren't exactly proud to be big, no one ever is, but they're getting so much *braver*." Oho, we are, we are. The Birmingham Seven, knickerbocker glorious, should be immortalised in stone. Lots of it. Every huge lady in a cloud of peroxide hair, a plunge-neck Mexican see-through blouse and circular floral skirt and bangles and beads, is a monument to human progress.

"There is nothing we wouldn't sell, if it would sell. Nothing." Nothing? Oh come now. The mind bogg- "Well, now I think of it, ra-ra skirts. Those American drum-majorette things that stop at the thigh, with pleats. I don't see us quite . . ."

I would not be too sure. I saw a size bikini, the other day, on open sale and p voking no scenes of public disorder. F inches round. Boring old good taste is on run, sisters; if you got it, flash it at th Power to the paunch.

But then the dream dissolves and the inhibitions return, clinging and sour as smell of sweaty Crimplene. (Why do the n heat-prone of the populace get sold so m synthetic fibre, eh? Answer me that.) T the changing-rooms—only one fat sho know has a communal one.

"Size 30s would feel self-conscious. L dignity." So they hide in the hutches. Or t the assistants; in Utopia they would bil and smile and use up yards of extrovert o all material, keeping the textile industry work and the customers in cosy complic As it is, most of them are still stick insect modest 16s. And the shop window mod once upon a time they were hewn from living plastic like Henry Moores, and dra with the appropriate ruffled smocking fo to see.

"But they were a bit blocky to look Enquiries indicated that people do not w to be reminded quite so publicly what t look like, and Evans descended to figuri of size 14, which is what your wife is w she says size 12. With the rest of the H Street exhibiting mannequins with la post waists and golfball breasts, the dif ence will be apparent enough, they say. not enough to shout "Vive!" about. Not The day of the kandy-coloured tanger flake streamline whale will come. I shal ready.

"I understand that if it's a success they plan to close down the whole chain."

On Your Skid Marks

"Every motorist is likely to have to use his car during the winter," says the *AA Book of Driving*, and what I say is that you can't beat the experts for getting these things into perspective, "and so preparation for adverse weather conditions should be regarded as a matter of routine." Absolutely. Second nature, in fact.

"The first priority," according to Consultant Editor Marcus Jacobson, MSc, FIMechE, MSAE, MIProdE, FIMI, the AA's Chief Engineer, "is to ensure that the car is in first-class condition and is well serviced." He's on the button, this man. "A car that is well maintained and regularly serviced should have no problems with winter driving," he re-asserts.

"Certain aspects of the car need special attention, however," I read on. For example: "*Air intake*: Some air cleaner inlets have summer and winter positions, and, if so, they should be adjusted for the winter." Similarly, "*Brakes*: Always keep the brakes in good order; any which work unevenly are especially dangerous on wet or icy roads." Then again, "*Exhaust system*: Any leaks from the exhaust could result in poisonous carbon monoxide fumes seeping into the car," which is certainly something I'd want to avoid in winter conditions. "*Windows*: Clean windows are essential for safe driving and they will need cleaning more often than usual in winter. It is also as well to check that there are no leaks which could let in water or exhaust fumes."

Now of course much of the inconvenience brought about by severe weather can, as the AA rightly points out, be minimised by careful forethought and by keeping a few simple items in the car. Cloths, for instance. Or shoes: "The heavier footwear appropriate for walking in snow or rain is not always ideal for driving." Skis, I imagine, could easily foul the window-winders, causing exhaust fumes to be drawn into the car. And "A useful precaution against getting wet or cold during an unexpected stop is to carry an anorak in the car."

Incidentally, whilst we are double-checking our in-car winter kit: "Problems of getting stuck in the snow or on ice can often be overcome by driving over some sacking (and now for the crucial tip) *placed under the wheels*." Could easily have been there till dusk, innocently putting the sacking *over* the wheels, in which case it pays to remember "*Torch*: It is always useful to keep a torch (in working order) in the car, not merely during the winter."

Right-ho, now that the car is in tip-top shape with its anorak, sacking and torch all properly maintained and in first-class condition, it's time to "*Prepare yourself*: It is wise to start to think about your journey further in advance than usual." No mention from Mr Jacobson here of *how much* further in advance, though I imagine that "in good time" would be about right. "In foggy and swirling snow conditions," you should be starting to think as you plan your journey in advance, "try to avoid right turns". Surely also it must pay to practise your winter-driving technique for going round in anti-clockwise circles in adverse, swirling conditions.

Of course, conditions in winter can vary. "Although bright sunlight is generally welcome," the AA points out, "it can bring problems of visibility." For example: "Staring directly at the sun for any length of time can permanently damage the retina and cause a partial or total blindness".

Nor does the horror end here. "The switch from bright light to relative darkness on entering a tunnel causes a potentially dangerous situation. If you wear sunglasses when entering a tunnel you will be unable to see for the first few yards. The best solution is to remove any sunglasses before entering the tunnel."

Yes, it's easy when you know how. "If you have been swept out into really deep water, it will be necessary to abandon the car . . . keep the heads of all occupants above the level of the water as it rises inside the car . . . wind down the windows to allow water pressure to equalise inside the car and out . . . push the doors open wide and step out. Form a human chain and swim or float to the surface."

Now, after a change of clothes and a change of car, let us consider one of the commonest hazards facing the motorist in winter, cold. "The first thing to remember on a cold day," urges the AA, "is that although your car may feel warm inside, the temperature outside could be at freezing point or below." In which case, of course, certain tell-tale signs of danger, even for a well-maintained car being driven by a man in a sturdy anorak, or sacking, will need to be watched out for. "Where there is a danger of falling rocks, there can also be the possibility of ice on the road in winter, because rocks are often dislodged by water. Your ears will also tell you when you are driving on ice. Unlike the swishing sound made by the tyres as they roll through water, on ice there will be much less noise and no swishing sound."

It can be pretty eerie, too, in fog. "One of the less-commonly realised effects of fog," the AA has discovered, "is that it can change the colours which lights appear. Those at the red, amber and yellow part of the spectrum can pass through fog, although with some changes. Those at the blue and green end do not, however, and sometimes cannot be seen at all. So, in a dense fog, a red light may appear to be amber; an amber light might seem white; a white light almost green but a green light may not be seen at all." Incidentally, the law requires that fog lights fitted to cars registered before 31 December 1970 must be separated by 13.8 inches. On cars registered on or after 1 January 1971, there must be 15.75 inches maximum distance between the outer edge of the light and the edge of the vehicle." In neither case, presumably, should the lights be invisible green. "Meadows, rivers, lakes, gravel pits and some woodlands," by the way, "can all give rise to fog. The moisture from freshly-tilled fields, however, can aggravate the situation still further."

OK, just a couple of tiny items left to check. "*Oil*: If a summer grade oil has been used, it should be replaced with winter-grade. *Heater*: The heater will be subjected to extra use during the winter. See that the vents are not blocked with paper, dirt or rubbish. *Lights*: Dirty road conditions will mean that they all need cleaning more often than usual. Keep enough cloths in the car for this purpose. *Shovel*: Digging away the snow down to the road surface may be the best way of getting going on a difficult surface."

Until the problems of spring which affect every motorist likely to use a car during the early part of the year, mind how you go.

Arnold Roth

Hail to the Chip

ARNOLD ROTH programmes into America's craze for personal home computers

THE CONCERTO VERY GROSSO FOR SYNTHESIZERS AND ALTERNATING CURRENTS.

DON QUIXOTE TONY HAYGARTH *as Sancho Panza* PAUL SCOFIELD *as Don Quixote de la Mancha*

Hewison/THEATRE

MAN AND SUPERMAN PETER O'TOOLE *as John Tanner* LISA HARROW *as Ann Whitefield*

THE RIVALS
GERALDINE McEWAN *as Mrs Malaprop*
MICHAEL HORDERN *as Sir Anthony Absolute*
TIM CURRY *as Bob Acres*

BERLIN BERLIN
RAYMOND SAWYER *as Max*
SUSAN COLVERD *as Lena*
CHRIS BARNES *as Moosebrugger*
JACK ELLIS *as Ulrich*

Laid Back

One of the more endearing eccentricities of America's folkloric tradition is that of townships bestowing upon themselves the most curious honorary titles. It's not unusual to drive through the heartland of the Mid-West to find yourself entering the precincts of, say, "Zilchville, Ohio. Pop 2345. Elastic Bandage Capital of America."

Or "Little Vacuum, Missouri. Pop 3456. Home of the Turkey Boot."

Be it bandage or boot the good citizens are rightly proud of their community's contribution to the Great American Way. If you've got it flaunt it, say I.

Were I a member of San Francisco's ruling Board of Supervisors I would issue an edict declaring that all such signs of welcome to the City by the Bay should bear the legend, "If you can't get laid here you can't get laid *anywhere*."

Forget the Golden Gate Bridge, which is painted a severe rust-red in any case. Banish from your mind the cable cars, just as they themselves have been banished from the streets for two years while the entire network is dug up and re-sown.

San Francisco's gift to the nation is sex.

Whatever shape or form your particular sin of the flesh runs to, it's up for grabs, or gropes. Be you hetero-, homo-, or just a plain old-fashioned bi-sexual made for two you'll find yourself accommodated. Not just the sleazoid celluloid offerings in the Tenderloin where you can thrill (or not) to *Wanda Whips Wall Street,* which may be responsible for the sudden mania that has gripped the Stock Market recently. Nor the specialised "phone services", whereby the obscene phone call has turned out to be profitable for those young women who sit at one end of the line whispering sweet everythings to clients at the other.

No, this is the real thing. Tactile.

In the Fifties it was the Beats who made their cultural mark on the city. In the Sixties it was the hippy influx. The Seventies and early Eighties have seen the homosexual community as the latest nomadic tribe to establish their presence.

Just as the Hispanics occupy the Mission district, the blacks the Fillmore and surrounding streets, so there are clearly-defined homosexual areas in town, most notably Castro, Polk Street and the more affluent parts of Haight Street, the former hippy stronghold.

The mass gay migration to San Francisco has had significant repercussions. Homosexuals make up an estimated 25% of the city's population, so they are not without influence. Woe betide the up-for-election candidate who fails to court the gay vote.

The last major disturbance i the city came in 1979 when a ga Supervisor received a very lenien sentence after shooting and kill ing the mayor, George Moscone The residents of Castro swarme into the city centre attacking th City Hall and burning ten polic cars.

Needless to say the predictabl police reaction that night has le to strained relations between th two groups ever since. An interesting side note to the affair is that the accused Super visor's defence pleaded that their client wa suffering severe mental stress at the time precipitated by eating too many Twinkies, favourite American confectionery. A leg first and, I hope, last.

Without doubt San Francisco is "Single City USA", a fact confirmed by the jus released census that shows that over 53% the population (678,974 at the time of coun ing) live in what are classified as "nor family" households.

The rest of the country (Johnny Carso laughs at San Francisco and the gay facto nightly perpetuating the "fruit and nuts myth of the city, with such biting lampoo as "How many SF straights does it take change a lightbulb? Both of them—ho, ho.

A London colleague of the "persuasion" convinced I've leapt from my closet as I' now enjoying my seventh visit in four year Well, as long as the popular image is mai tained, I for one am not complaining. doesn't need the brain of Mycroft Holmes fathom that if there's a preponderance of ga in the town it cuts down the heterosexu competition to the point where even an o sexual cynic like myself can have a fair successful run of luck without having to p himself out too much.

The best advice any financial guru cou have offered five years ago would have bee "Take up thy ferns, take up thy Tiffa lamps and walk . . . to San Francisco a there open a singles bar."

Night after night the single persons a personettes gather in the electric glow Henry's Africa, with more vegetation th the average rain forest, Paoli's, the Holdi Company (most apt) in the financial distric and, probably the definitive joint in town, t Pierce Street Annexe (no relation, sexual otherwise).

If, like me, you have every faith in t maxim that sex is the cruellest form of sla stick comedy, there is a wealth of material be had treating oneself to a "night on t pull".

It is not without its hazards, or its difficu ties. The first thing you must do is rid you self of any misgivings that what you're doi is sexist. It swings both ways, and there every possibility you'll find *yourself* on t defensive, under siege from some arde

*"I wish **I'd** said that."*

oung thing. The role reversal can set you ack in surprise, and it's a good lesson for any oung buck who thinks he's God's gift to the XX chromosome.

The next hurdle to overcome is that *you* now you're hetero, despite the attempts of ay friends to convince you that inside each ıan is another man trying to come out, but oes she?

Assuming there are two of you out on the pree there's no reason for the brace of love-es to your left to assume you're not gay, specially if you tend to adopt an English ıode of dress. Being a martyr to last year's ashion, I'm prohibited from cladding myself ı the plaids and sports coats, the "sensible" hoes, that are the hallmark of middle-merican man. Neither is my hair subjected ɔ the statutary blow-dried waves. The Pierce udding bowl has been handed down ırough generations and I've no intention of idding myself of the moptop merely for the ake of sexual gratification. Not just once ave I and my companion been asked by ɔme svelte thing, "You guys faggots?"

"English," always comes the reply, which an often do more harm than good, many merican girls being unable to decide which the least suspect.

Assuming that you've hooked the victim's ıterest, now comes the strenuous task of etaining it. Her motives for being there are oubtless the same as yours. You may think ou're the best thing in black suede shoes to valk into her life but you're just another Joe.)r Mike. Or Duane. Or Scott. Now must ome the crunch tactic. The Big Lie. It's an xpected and integral part of the courtship itual.

OK, so you're a visiting journalist, cover-ıg the rock scene, trying to put down roots ı the city. Yawn. She's heard it a thousand imes. You've told it as many, if not more. Comedian Steve Martin reckons the line best uited to any situation when chatting up an merican girl is to amble over to her and vithout introduction say, "I make a lot of noney." He's not far wrong. Comics are the est gaugers of the contemporary scene. They make sociologists redundant.

My particular favourite is that I'm check-ıg out the town for the forthcoming tour by he Stones/Paul McCartney/Roxy Music/ Anyone Big Who She's Probably Heard Of.

My imagination can really let fly. Rock nusic is still deified on the West Coast, so any onnection, however tenuous, however abricated, will invariably fall on listening ars.

The routine has become so polished that I m confident that I could offer my services to ny band who might wish to employ a recon-naissance man in the area.

The tale of mystery and imagination is ccasionally gilded by the presence of Dave, ny flatmate, who bears a vague resemblance o Pete Townshend of The Who (vague is bout as far as you'd want), and I have passed im off as the celebrity on a couple of occa-ions. Strangely enough we ended the even-ng empty-handed both times.

A lesson I learned early on is not to ply our sparring partner with what you think asses for scintillating English *salon* wit. She'll greet each *bon mot* with "Sorry I don't understand," wondering just how she'll rid herself of the inane fool giggling to himself. Worse still, her pupils will distend and with almost Zionist zeal she will exclaim, "Oh, I just *love* Marnty Pyth'n!"

Sophistication is not the order of the day on the singles scene. Keep the lie big but keep it simple, is the golden rule.

Not even the contagion-level of the dread Herpes (god of sexually transmitted diseases) can quell the enthusiasm of singles devotees.

Real men not only refrain from quiche but they don't let irritating factors like Herpes overly concern them. It's become such a norm that one New York publisher has produced a monthly magazine for sufferers.

And it's in the Big Apple that the singles culture has reached a new state of the art in "scrufting", whereby you run through the entire proceedings, from A to Zee without learning your partner's name. Bonus points if you get breakfast and your cab fare home the next morning.

If the singles game, and it's little more than that, seems calculated, a sexual exchange for lonely, sometimes insecure people, that's what it is, with the hope lingering that Mr or Ms Right might be the one leaning over the bar clutching his/her Rusty Nail or Whisky Over. Strings remain firmly unattached 99% of the time, however.

While hardly the most cerebral of exercises it is not without its romance, its intellectual appeal. Once, wishing to impress with my knowledge of the cinematic canon of Woody Allen, I leant across her semi-slumbering body and whispered the closing line from *Sleeper*: "The only difference between sex and death is that you don't feel nauseous after death."

The bruises on my ribs should clear up within a few days.

"Of course, I shan't be cutting him down before Twelfth Night."

PUNCH MAGAZINE AND THE ADOLF HITLER ARCHIVE

A Statement by Punch Publications Limited

This week is a very unique one in the century-and-a-half which *Punch* has been in business in. It is quite possibly the most unique week we have ever had. It could definitely change the course of history, this week could. No question. We have taken the precaution of getting opinions off of many top historians, and they all said the same thing: this week is a real winner, they would stake their reputations on it.

Due to this, we have departed from normal procedure, e.g. in other words, the Editor will not be writing his piece here as per usual. Instead, we publish an interview with the Editor carried out by a famous authority, household word would not be putting it too strong, in which the Editor explains how he came by the amazing material and so forth now revealed for the first time. The authority naturally prefers to remain anonymous due to where it could cause embarrassment up his university on account of him getting large sums off of us, you know what they can be like, universities.

For and on behalf of
PUNCH PUBLICATIONS LTD

AN INTERVIEW WITH THE EDITOR OF PUNCH

Famous Authority: Mr Coren, I have studied the truly astonishing photographs contained in MEIN SNAP ALBUM which you are publishing this week (*see overleaf*), and my first question must obviously be: how on earth did you come by this amazing find?

Alan Coren: Yes, a number of people have asked me that. Well, a few weeks ago, a man came into my office carrying a badly battered and clearly very old biscuit-tin.

FA: You say "clearly very old". What do you mean, exactly?

AC: Well, you could just make out the remains of the picture on the lid. It was of King George VI and Queen Elizabeth at their Coronation. It had had Huntley & Palmer Oval Osborne Fingers in it.

FA: A range no longer current, I believe?

AC: Exactly. We sought a recognised authority on the subject, the proprietor of The Little Gem Corner Shop, Willesden, and he signed a statement testifying to the fact that he had had no call for them since before the war. We had also discovered from meticulous research in *The Big Boy's Book* [cut off] *Dates* that the coronation depicted h[cut off] taken place in 1937. Things were beginni[cut off] to come together, and make sense. We we[cut off] then prepared to direct our expert inves[cut off] gators towards the question of the writi[cut off] scratched on the side of the tin.

FA: Which said?

AC: Which said: *Dieses Tin gehört Ad*[cut off] *Hitler*. We took it to James Gelbard [cut off] Birmingham University, and he imme[cut off] ately translated it as *This tin belongs* [cut off]

Adolf Hitler. We naturally became very excited!

FA: Naturally. Mr Gelbard is presumably the Professor of German Studies?

AC: No, Mr Gelbard helps out with the car park, but he has a CSE in German, and there was no point chucking money about at this stage.

FA: I quite understand. You were then prepared to open the tin?

AC: Certainly, but the owner refused to allow it until we had signed an interim contract to examine the contents against a large advance, nearly fourteen pounds in all, including his fare money. I'm afraid that the days when Fleet Street could put one over on gullible members of the public are long gone!

FA: So you naturally asked him to first give you some indication of how the tin had come into his possession?

AC: Of course. I was not born yesterday. The Editor of a great national paper has to be a pretty shrewd cookie! Mind you, I have to confess that I *was* very favourably impressed with him from the outset. Not only did he have a firm dry handshake, he also looked you straight in the eye when he was talking.

FA: I see. So how *did* he come by the tin?

AC: It fell through his greenhouse on the night of June 5, 1943, during a German raid on Sheffield. It had clearly fallen from an enemy bomber.

FA: And have your own experts visited the house in Sheffield?

AC: What house in Sheffield? The man was living in Ilford. We have, it goes without saying, visited the house in Ilford, and he certainly lives there, and has done since 1936, according to both the man himself and his wife. We have their sworn affidavits.

FA: So you believe the German pilot mistook Ilford for Sheffield?

AC: Certainly all the evidence points that way. For example, the tin fell through a greenhouse in Ilford. Not in Sheffield.

FA: But as targets, are these two locations not strikingly dissimilar?

AC: They are today. No-one is saying they are not dissimilar *today*, but the matter must be seen in its historical perspective. We have spoken to a number of experts, all of whom were unanimous in pointing out that, in 1943, there were blackout regulations, something a layman can forget. During a blackout, and from twenty thousand feet up, there is no difference at all between Sheffield and Ilford, especially to a German.

FA: But did any bombs fall on Ilford that night?

AC: Apparently not. I do, of course, follow your drift, but the hard evidence all points to the fact that the Germans realised their mistake almost immediately, and changed course for Sheffield. That hard evidence is that it was Sheffield that they ended up bombing, which they could not have done if they had not realised they had made a mistake about Ilford. What clearly happened was that one of the Germans, to make doubly sure they were over Sheffield—and we know for a fact that they are a meticulous race, expert opinion is unanimous on this one—opened a window to have a clearer look down, and inadvertently knocked the biscuit tin off a shelf near the window. It is easily done.

FA: Yes, I see that, it all holds water, but did you not ask yourself what a British biscuit tin was doing on a shelf near the window of a German bomber?

AC: Not once we knew it belonged to Hitler. If it had belonged to, say, Churchill, then, all right, yes. By 1943, the top Nazis were shipping stuff out all over, they could see the writing on the wall, crateloads of paintings, sculpture, antique clocks, you name it, were filling up hangars all over the Fatherland, waiting to be flown to South America etcetera. The box containing MEIN SNAP ALBUM was obviously picked up by mistake, stuck in a bomb-bay, and when the crew realised what had happened, they took it out and put it on a shelf for safe keeping.

FA: Have you managed to trace any surviving members of that crew?

AC: It is easy to tell you are not an expert on the Third Reich. Have you any idea what would have happened to that crew when they got back off the raid and were summoned to Berlin to be asked by the Führer himself: *"Wo ist mein Snap Album?"* We wouldn't be trying to trace a crew, we would be looking for a set of paperweights.

FA: Nevertheless, the biscuit tin was *originally* British. How did it come into Hitler's possession?

AC: Millions of those tins were exported for the Coronation, especially to Germany, where they had been unable to crack the secret of the Oval Osborne Finger, as any expert will tell you. To this day, you cannot pick up anything of that order on the European mainland. Also, Hitler was an Anglophile, he fully expected a neutrality pact with Britain, it is all in the documents if you look, does it not naturally follow that he would have been partial to an English biscuit? Particularly as so many of the photographs in MEIN SNAP ALBUM show a hitherto unknown side of the Führer; for example, leading his horse in at Ascot, having a day out at Clacton, bowling his tricky inswingers at the Oval, and so forth. I should think that that biscuit tin was very close to his heart. Why else would he have kept his favourite photographs in it, answer me that?

FA: Yes, I agree, that aspect of the matter hangs together perfectly, but can I be alone in wondering why your contact from Ilford should have waited—what?—forty years before getting in touch with anyone? Did he not realise he was sitting on a goldmine?

AC: Since you ask, he thought he was sitting on a landmine. Once again, I'm afraid, you have failed to see the situation with the perspective of history: had *you* gone out into the garden on the morning of June 6, 1943, seen your demolished greenhouse, and noticed a dented biscuit-tin with Adolf Hitler's name on it sticking out of a hole in the ground, would *your* first reaction have been: "Hallo, he's dropped his photographs"? Of course not! Your first reaction would have been: "Hallo, the cunning bastards are dropping booby-trapped biscuit-tins now! They have heard about shortages, rationing, etcetera, they expect me to grab at a free box of Oval Osborne Fingers without a second thought, and blow myself to bits." *That* is what your first reaction would have been.

FA: Possibly, possibly, but why, if that was the case, did he never, from that day to this, call in the Bomb Disposal Squad to deal with it?

AC: For the very simple reason, as any expert would tell you, as they have told me, that any attempt to interfere with something as unusual as a biscuit-tin landmine could well have resulted in the thing exploding and not only damaging the owner's house, but also destroying thousands of poundsworth of valuable equipment which that house contained, built up painstakingly over the years to enable him to pursue his hobby.

FA: Hobby?

AC: Photography. Dark-rooms, cameras, epidiascopes, tripods, lenses, enlargers, you name it. I trust I do not have to remind you what a biscuit-tin landmine could do to that little lot.

FA: Of course not, I hadn't realised, I'm grateful to you for explaining, it's quite extraordinary how one missing piece set in place suddenly makes an entire jigsaw readable.

AC: Yes, well, that is why we in Fleet Street are in the business of making sure there are no missing bits, it is what we are paid for, it is why we have experts.

FA: Mr Coren, I thank you. The world thanks you. History thanks you.

AC: Don't give it another thought.

Mein Snap Album

Bei F. W. Woolworth, Salzburg, 1900.

Mit Tallulah, bei dem Grossnazional, Aintree, 193

Vinnersenklosure, Askot, 1933.

Bei dem 1928 Weltentwaffnungskonferenz Villesden.

Der Yorkshire Zweiten XI, 1934, nach dem famosen Krieg über Sussex (Yorkshire 247 für 8 dek., und 321; Sussex 289 und 188).

Ein grosses Sportingspartei, Antibes, 1934. *Von links nach rechts:* Binkie Douglashome, ich, Snotty Tvistletonvickhamfiennes, Count Basie.

Augustbankferien, 1931. Kleinhämpton.

Willkommenskommittee, Karnegie Hall, 1935.

Klakton, 1928.

Putzi und Freundin mit meinem Sohn, Morrie, bei dem 1930 Boyskoutjamboree.

Mein Paintings

As the Russians approached Berlin in the Spring of 1945, Adolf Hitler painted faster and faster. As fast as he painted, so the faithful Goebbels threw the paintings into a nearby lake to save them from the enemy, also because he thought they were really lousy.

It was not until 1947 that the famed underwater art historian KENNETH MAHOOD discovered the entire oeuvre. That he waited thirty-six years before revealing them is entirely due to the fact that he was trying to find nice frames.

News from the Russian Front

Occupied Britain

His Master's Voice

Portrait of the Artist's Mother

The Invasion of Britain

The Persistence of Nazism

The Braun Marriage

WHAAM!

HUNDREDS OF HISTORIANS CAN'T BE WRONG!

GENUINE© PUNCH CLUB OFFER*

*I am convinced it is a major contribution to modern scholarship—*Sir Rupert Mark*

Discerning collectors of the very best of Hitler's personal effects and home requisites are prepared t stake their reputation on there being no finer investment opportunity than Das Haus von Potsda Diskountwerke's authenticated and individually certificated bargains from —

HAUS von HITLERMART

A limited edition of genuine Third Reich artefacts,

each personally signed by The Man Himself or other fine Nazi

Special stock clearance sale:

THE LITTLE ADOLF MAGNETIC WONDER BRUSH

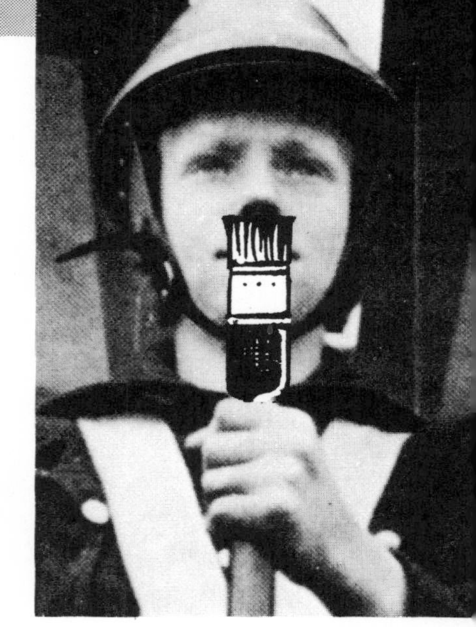

A keen painter and decorator himself, the Führer often envied the showroom shine friends in the Nationalsozialistiche Deutsche Arbeiterpartei managed to get on their official cars—but what with all the Anschluss and Wehrmacht, Hitler just hadn't the time to spend hours washing 'n' waxing his own fleet of Mercedes . . .

That's where the Little Adolf Magnetic Wonder Brush came in handy! Hitler was amazed when Bormann showed him just how simple it could be to get a deep, lustrous finish in minutes with absolutely no rubbing and scrubbing—simply glide the Little Adolf Magnetic Wonder Brush across the coachwork and Bob's Your Onkel! With characteristic decisiveness, the Führer immediately ordered Germany's vast industrial might to go into full production and between 1939 and 1945 no fewer than 6 million of these amazing appliances were produced on Hitler's personal instructions.

Yet what no-one could have guessed until last week was that two whole trainloads, miraculously untouched by the Allied bombardment, would come to light in an East German siding almost 40 years on. But, as carbon-dating experts from the *Sunday Times* will attest, this quite astonishing treasure-trove *MUST* be 100 per cent genuine since each brush carries on the handle the unmistakable legend: LITTLE ADOLF MAGNETIC WONDER BRUSH "Just the job!"—Hermann Göring.

Only Haus von Hitlermart can now offer you this once-in-a-lifetime opportunity to acquire one of these pricele historical gems of Third Reich craftsmanship in fine tooling. Remember—these amazing magnetic brushes are NO available in the shops but send s.a.e. for full details of these and other authenticated home appliances listed in o booklet: *Give Us The Tools*, by Max Daimler and Karl Benz.

TRIM THOSE TOUGH TOENAILS WITH EASE!

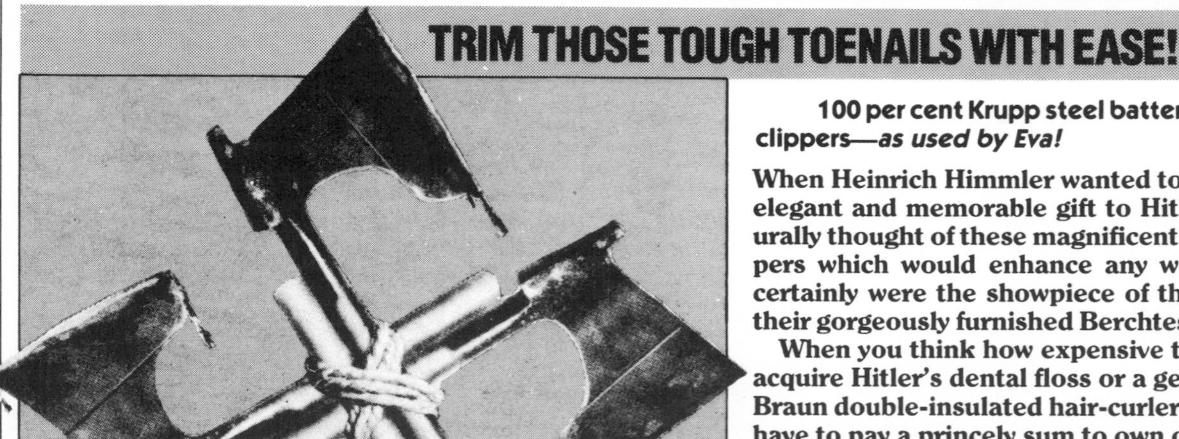

100 per cent Krupp steel battery-operated Braun clippers—*as used by Eva!*

When Heinrich Himmler wanted to present a thoughtfu elegant and memorable gift to Hitler's mistress, he nat urally thought of these magnificent "kaliper-aktion" clip pers which would enhance any washroom fitting—an certainly were the showpiece of the Hitlers' footbath i their gorgeously furnished Berchtesgaden country home

When you think how expensive these days it can be t acquire Hitler's dental floss or a genuine example of Ev Braun double-insulated hair-curlers, you might expect t have to pay a princely sum to own one of these treasure appliances in the comfort of your own home.

Yet once again, the unprecedented efficiency and might of the German war machine was brought to bear and a 14-ton chest of these clippers was produced as a surprise present for Eva to celebrate the fall of Poland. That chest has lain undisturbed where it fell off the back of a lorry in Braunau-am-Inn on the morning of 5 June 1942. Had not a following lorry, laden with armaments, also burst a tyre on the same pothole and caused a sudden avalanche, this quite extraordinary find might never have been so beautifully preserved under the ice-cap for 41 years!!

Experts were at first sceptical of the immense importance of this find when it was unearthed by an excavator constructing a new ski slope Tuesday last. We'll admit that it does take some getting used to, but a hand-picked team of analysts from Germany's much-admired *Spick und Span* magazine has now concluded a thoroughgoing examination of these handsome clippers and declared every one good as new!

Just imagine your neighbours' faces when you reveal you have acquired one of these unrepeatable showpiece treasures for the incredible price of £3.99 (batteries extra). See your Sunday paper for full details of our range of Hitler's personal hygiene accoutrements.

NEED MORE LEBENSRAUM?

Why not do as Adolf and Eva did and extend your home with a Schicklgruber Loft Conversion Kit?

Ever wished you could annexe next door, have a bit of room to turn round in, father a new race, build an army to last a thousand years etc etc?

Certainly the Führer knew the feeling! That's why he and Eva chose a Schicklgruber Loft Conversion Kit, featuring the finest timbers recovered from the Graf Spee, when it came to improving the Reichstag and their own beautiful bunker home.

Until just recently, no-one might have guessed that it would ever again be possible to recapture the magic appeal of that bygone age in all its original, authentic, intricate detail. The rich jumble of boxes packed with exotic books like the first edition of *Mein Kampf*, ex libris of the author himself, or the Führer's personal cheque books from the Völkischer Bank in historic Munich, his "little black book" of extra-special friends he'd look up next time he was in Czechoslovakia or the Balkans—all of these fascinating original documents are yours to keep and treasure when you order two or more Schicklgruber Loft Conversion Kits, each one hand-crafted according to the Hitlers' original specification from their long-lost stock of materials, using Himmler's own lathe.

Lord Facre, a world authority on Hitler's home furnishing, has personally inspected each and every one of these genuine Loft Conversions and, after some original misgivings, is now completely converted as to their authenticity.

AN AMAZING DISCOVERY THAT'S BEEN KEPT PRESERVED IN AN AIRING CUPBOARD IN POTSDAM BY THE CHANCELLOR'S OWN FORMER PERSONAL VALET AND HIS SEAMSTRESS WIFE

Adolf 'n' Eva knitted Blouson Top and fur-lined acrylic Bodywarmer

There could be some sharp winds out there on the Eastern Front, but in his stylish, fully-washable knitted blouson top the Führer enjoyed the benefit of light weight and great warmth, together with the personal distinction of having *Der Sieg Wird Unser Sein* hand-stitched on the handy breast pocket for his Luger.

For Eva, the Führer chose a matching beige-trimmed fur-lined acrylic bodywarmer with *Ein Volk, Ein Reich, aber drei Grösse—Lang, Extra-Medium und Klein* embroidered on the showerproof cuff.

Smart enough for a dress occasion at the Reichstag yet tough enough to stand up to weeks of manoeuvres, these authentic garments were soon all the rage with the Third Reich's dressy officers and featured in the fashion pages of *Völkischer Beobachter*, edited by Hitler himself. We want you to be delighted with your Adolf 'n' Eva fashionwear, but if for any reason you are not entirely satisfied simply return them within thirty days and we will exchange them without obligation for a Goebbels T-shirt or Ernst Röhm thermal underwear.

HEATH My Funny Valentine

"OK, you take the gays and I'll do the straights."

"You can tell it's from a man, it smells of perfume!"

"Marry me, Miss Baker—after all, we both have the same social disease."

"I hope you don't think I'm being sexist, Margery, but I love you!"

"You've got to help me, doctor-- I'm falling in love with a man!"

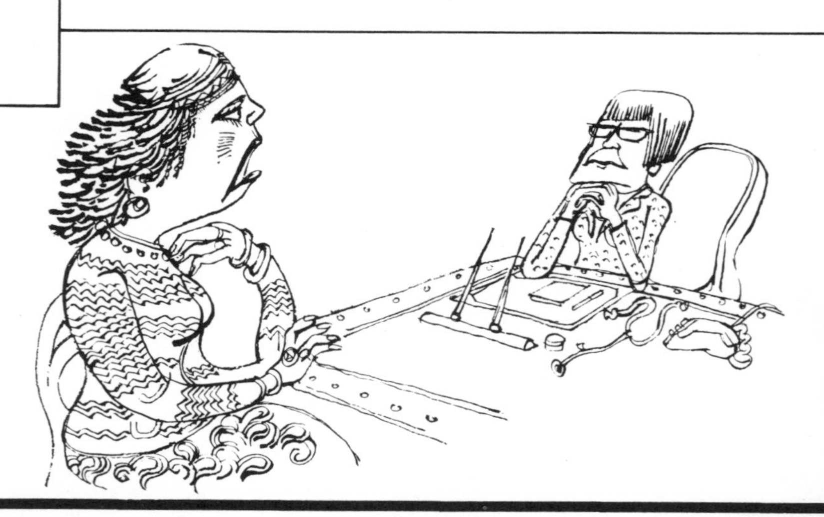

"Well, 450 Valentine cards suggest promiscuity to me."

"I don't love you, I'm just using you until Miss Right comes along."

"Good God, Jane! Do you have to put this in every year—'Pooh Bear loves Snoopy'?"

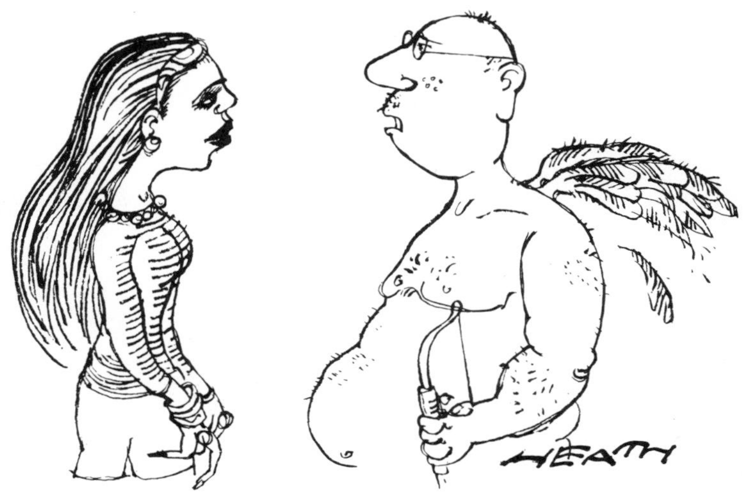

"Even cupids grow old, my dear."

On the Rails

"You're so lucky to live in Cambridge," people keep telling me. It always makes me feel like a man who is having the fineness of the grain on his wooden leg admired. I should have worked out a smart answer by now—it's been ten years—but still I hum and haw and writhe. Usually I award myself a moan about the wind and damp and absence of mountains, before conceding, just to keep them happy, that Cambridge isn't ugly as towns go; that yes, there's plenty of green open space; that many facilities are above average, yes, mm, education of course; and so on, till my tormentors are either appeased or bored.

Clearly they ought to be much more aggressive about it. "Don't tell me you wouldn't rather live in *London*!" they ought to exclaim, digging me in the ribs with a rolled-up *Time Out* or *What's Not Off* or whichever the latest one is. "How often do you see a show, a symphony concert? How many decent cinemas have you got? How many *in*decent cinemas?" (Here another dig in the ribs.) "Have you got a Japanee restaurant in Cambridge at all? A Fenland branch of Ronnie Scott's likely to open, is it? Drinking club? *Dolphinarium*?" (Here a poke in the eye with a candle burnt at both ends, whereupon I give up.)

When it comes to London life, what the Home Office drug people call a "maintenance dose" is quite enough for me. Arriving in the capital by a morning train is still—very, very faintly—exciting. Departing again at tea-time is a profound relief. The medication just lasts through the day. The trick is not to make the trip too often; and never to pick one of Liverpool Street's famous delayed trains. Example (and I always treat the really persistent Cambridge fans to this one): I once caught the 6.36 pm. home, and drew into Cambridge at twenty-five to one in the morning. Some power lines had come down—two hours' delay—and then somebody committed suicide by standing in front of the train ahead of ours—two more hours' stoppage. People who take the terrible step of self-destruction are often convinced, rightly or wrongly, that they're unpopular. If it's any help, I can confirm that blocking a commuter line with your corpse is one way of ensuring that you do not die entirely deluded.

But at the best of times, the Liverpool Street line is the least encouraging of all the routes into London. Even the names seem to tell a sordid story, as they progress from Harlow through Ponders End past Walthamstow Marshes into Clapton. Some days when I can't face this, I take the alternative King's Cross route. But I think it, too, is starting to tell me something—the plot of a Harold Robbins novel, maybe. Certainly most of Robbins's stuff seems to start somewhere between Baldock and Letchworth and ends up passing close to the Arsenal.

Living in London, anyway, was not so great. I tried it for a year, and it should have been fun, living above Mister Eddie's Restaurant in Flask Walk, Hampstead, right next door to the Flask pub. I had fluked a long run of television work at the time, s was big-headed enough not to feel too out place in an area where if you walked a distance you were eventually bound to bu into a famous actor, like Dudley Moore Michael Foot. John Hurt (you had to s "the actor John Hurt" in those days, becau the blues singer Mississippi John Hurt w nearly as famous among Hampsteadit lived exactly opposite us, in a tiny bo fronted house that was a features location some British film thriller or other in t Sixties. He was in the middle of that aw period in his career when, though everyo agreed he was the best actor since Mich Foot, the film parts he got inexorably turn out duff or doomed or non-existent. I thi he had just played an igloo in somethi called *Mr Forbush and the Penguins*. Despa at any rate, would seize him from time time, and one famous evening he hurled brick through his own front window. "Act Brings House Down," I expect the *Ham High* said, but we didn't take any papers.

"I can remember a time when we didn't have to make our own entertainment."

What *did* we do? I seem to remember doi a lot of doleful gazing out of the front windo down into the butcher's shop opposite. Aft a few months, the butcher hanged himse Nothing to do with me. But what a mani depressive little triangle it had been in th corner of the street—me, the problematic Mr Hurt, and melancholic meat-mercha Personally, I blame A. Alvarez, who, just few doors away, had been incubating h study of suicide, *The Savage God*. I think has moved on to poker now, where the sa things happen symbolically.

None of this gloom was London's fault, course, though London makes it worse. was just that bad time of life which nobo warns you about, when you're no longer schoolchild or a student, but on the oth hand you're not a husband or a father; nor you have the sort of job that enables you boom, "Actually I'm a chartered crim woggler in biochemics." (Because even if yo are one, you don't say it, for fear of stickin like that.) You're forever scrabbling for breakfast edition of the *Standard*, so as chase accommodation that has already bee caught. For a while, you live in a sleepin bag on somebody else's floor. You stay in th pub too long, miss the last bus, have to wa for miles through the dismal canyons forme by other people's lodgings. I started off London feeling like this, and being flush for while didn't make it better. I'm surprised a those foreigners caught shoplifting hanki on Oxford Street don't plead depression.

It's amazing to me to think that my granc mother, my father's mother ("patern grandmother" puts whiskers on them, don you think?) actually lived longer in Londo than I have done or probably ever will. Th thought is hard to cope with because I re member her as a lady so devotedly fixed i her wild and Welsh-speaking rural environ ment, near Llanbedr in Merionethshire, tha

"He's the phantom of the operetta."

he would not even consider a move to Dolgellau, less than twenty miles away, when my grandfather was offered the job of masterminding the Final Solution to the rodent problem in that mighty conurbation. Yet, I learned (too late to ask her about it), in the early years of the century she had lived in London and worked as a nursemaid to an infant called Bernard Waley-Cohen. Sir Bernard later became Lord Mayor of London. I still find it an almost unimaginable conjunction—not on grounds of class or anything like that, but because some people simply belong in one environment and no other. Putting my grandmother in London is like imagining Princess Margaret doing power-lifts in a gymnasium, or William Whitelaw working as a Venetian gondolier.

In one respect, the capital is really looking up, and that's in its jazz life. There's more of it, the overall quality is sounder, and you're made more comfortable while you enjoy it. This pleases me especially, since most of my best times in London have had to do with jazz anyway, so perhaps there's even better to come. In the Hampstead days, it used to be Sunday lunchtimes at the New Merlin's Cave, where George Melly, not yet fully-mellymobilised, would hold feet with the Forthwarmers—or so we (or he) might well have found ourselves saying by half-past two. The audience was a wonderful collection of shaggy survivors from the Fifties, their clothes all knitted on Aldermaston marches and washed annually in memory of those efforts. Here and there a younger figure would wander about—children of 18 months, mostly—and here and there an older person. The unmistakable S. J. Perelman was often there, but folding himself into a Toblerone shape in order to fit into corners. He looked like a first-time visitor to the Orient, not wishing to stand in the front row while the cobra-piping was in progress.

The most memorable gig I played in London, and the band I was with must have done it two or three times, was the Great Meat Ball, held at Smithfield Market. The building is something like a wrought iron cathedral, a cross between the old Crystal Palace and those preposterously vast shopping arcades they have in Milan. But what distinguished the Smithfield environment from those places was the hooks—millions of coruscating meat-hooks everywhere, hung up in rows like lethal fringes festooned on an all-metal Christmas tree. The acoustics were wonderful. As you played, the sound went up into the Meccanoed heavens and sort of hung around, deciding whether to come down.

The only problem was the effect of the chill night air on the bladder. For relief, one had to scale a spidery-looking spiral stair that twined itself tipsily round one of the heavy columns supporting the structure; for there was no lavatory at floor level. All the plumbing happened near the roof, presumably for health reasons—not that sanitary scrupulosity was all that evident once you got up there. It was partly to avoid this arduous ascent that we used to slip out during the intervals and play a couple of numbers in a nearby pub. One year, we found a well-known member of London's gangland in there, and he was so taken with us that he asked to be allowed to sing. We let him. Historical precedent, you understand. Muggsy Spanier would surely have done as much for Al Capone.

Nowdays I see more of people's offices than any other kind of London premises. This week a new one is added to the list, when the *Times Literary Supplement* takes up a new address in Clerkenwell—the third home the venerable *TLS* has had since I first became a contributor (in those days, an anonymous hit-man). I expect the new place will be very vertical. Editors always try to arrange this so that they can live at the top. This ensures you will be out of breath by the time you appear with your piece. It makes your excuses sound feeble, but earns you no marks for being pathetic, overworked and downtrodden, because something about heavy breathing repulses sympathy. The *London Review of Books* has the most exhausting staircase ever devised, apart from joke ones at funfairs and the odd experiment by King Ludwig of Bavaria. Not only is the distance between floors quite huge, but each individual step demands the kind of monstrous, prancing gait that is most unnatural to journalists. I always arrive at the top with a revised opinion of bungalows.

The old *New Review* offices in Greek Street, Soho, were vertical, too, but not so bad that you couldn't take an interest in the strange people you tended to meet on the stair. The editor, Ian Hamilton, and I were toiling down one day on our way to the Pillars of Hercules (all pubs should have names like that, they make you feel like an explorer) when a stocky-looking bloke appeared in mid-stair, almost entirely smothered by a rail-full of blouses. There is nothing you can do for a man who is drowning in polyester and coathangers except try to be encouraging. Hamilton did so, with a remark along the lines of "Those look nice" which I thought might not be well received. On the contrary. "*Want one?*" growled the couturier's leg-man in unParisian tones. "How much?" said Hamilton, as editors will. "Fifty pee," came the rusty reply on a breeze of beer. Neither Hamilton nor I was a shirt-waster by nature, so we both bought one. I stuffed mine into the trombone-case I happened to be carrying—you don't look right in Soho unless you have a professionally suspicious air—and took it home to the wife, who was delighted. With the blouse. I don't think it's quite been relegated to duster status even yet. It would be nice to be so at home in London that this sort of thing happened to you all the time; though on the other hand the lure of Pentonville has been overestimated. Come to think of it, we haven't got a prison in Cambridge. Well, not officially.

THE CHILLINGLY SENSATIONAL OUT-OF-THIS-WORLD DOUBLE BILL THAT COULD SET THE WHOLE WORLD ALIGHT . . . !

The tear-jerking story of a simple-minded lonely old American who falls in love with a cute space-age monster with multiple heads

AND THE SOVIET EMPIRE STRIKES BACK!

Can a trigger-happy Force of malevolent old men bent on world domination be stopped before it is too late . . . ?

THERE'S NEVER BEEN A HEART-STOPPING SCIENCE FICTION DRAMA QUITE LIKE THIS, WITH ALL OF THE ZAP-KAPOW THRILLS OF THE VERY LATEST AND MOST FORMIDABLE HIGH-TECHNOLOGY HARDWARE *PLUS* THE BREATHTAKING POIGNANCY OF HALF-WITTED HUMANS OUT OF THEIR DEPTH . . . GUARANTEED TO HAVE YOU SCREAMING WITH DESPAIR!

MX *Acclaimed by such experts as Menachem Begin of TV's popular* West Bank Show *as the most mind-blowing extravaganza of all time. Set in Wyoming, the story centres around a typical dim American whom all his friends think is a harmless daft old gopher . . . until one day he befriends a fiendish-looking extra-terrestrial spaceship called MX. As the incredible plot unfolds, it becomes clear that MX has the astonishing power to grow multiple heads which are then buried in the sand in a dense-pack formation—ready to strike at the bad guys whenever the old fool gives the signal . . . KABOOM!*

"I shrieked!"—Yasser Arafat

THE SOVIET EMPIRE STRIKES BACK!

But the forces of evil are not finished yet! From a secret black hole somewhere in the awful place they call Siberia, white-coated creatures so life-like they seem almost to be human are working round the clock to perfect a particle beam weapon for deployment in the awesome mystery of space—a death-ray so powerful that it can take out an area the size of Poland or Afghanistan before you can say "SS-20"!

"This is serious"—Michael Foot

"No, but I read the book"—Margaret Thatcher

NEVER BEFORE HAVE SO MANY MILLIONS BEEN LAVISHED ON THE PRODUCTION OF SO SPINE-TINGLING A PIECE OF SHATTERING MAKE-BELIEVE—SO CONVINCING THAT YOU START TO IMAGINE IT JUST COULD BE FOR REAL!!!

Soon to go on general release at selected sites all over Europe . . . and remember: AT ARMAGEDDON, NO ONE CAN HEAR YOU SCREAM!

Keith Waterhouse

Tech It From Here

The Open University's little brother, the Open Tech, came into the world yesterday . . . Though it would have the same open access policy as the Open University and would borrow its distance-learning-techniques, the Open Tech would be much more strongly oriented towards employers, and to the world of work in general, it was stressed . . . It will concentrate on providing training and retraining in technical skills.

Daily Telegraph

Good morning. And just to get us toned up before we learn how to strip down a 16-line internal automatic telephone exchange this morning, let's do some more of those exercises we started last week with Muriel at the piano.

In the crosslegged position now . . . screwdrivers and working materials at the ready, and you should be referring to the exercise chart in this week's *Radio Times* or page 349 on Ceefax. *And* one and two and attach angle bracket B as shown in Fig 19 and solder. And rest. *And* three and four and bore transverse holes in pivotal coupling and apply bolts and collars. Deep breath, and tighten lock-nuts. *And* five and six and sandpaper rough edges. And stop there.

And as well as having thoroughly limbered up those stiff muscles you should by now have built a stand for your hi-fi system. In next week's keep-fit spot we'll start building the hi-fi system itself but those of you who are a little overweight do please check with your doctor first. He may recommend you to build just a straightforward audio amplifier.

And just while we're recovering our breath, I'd like those of you who are studying chemistry to copy down this complete table of all known chemical elements I'm going to flash on your screens while Muriel gives us another tune. Reading from left to right the table gives the symbol of each particular element, then its name, its derivative, its atomic number and weight, it specific gravity and its fusing point, and as you can see there are quite a few elements between actinium and zirconium so you'd better get your skates on. Those of you who aren't on the chemistry course can get on with the boilermaking exercises I gave you at the beginning of term, but if you happen to be in the same household as someone who *is* taking chemistry, a husband or wife perhaps, please make your boiler quietly.

All right, and if you'll put your chemistry notebooks and acetylene torches away now, you'll remember that in our last session we dismantled a Hawker-Siddeley aero engine and that should still be laid out neatly on your living-room floor. I'd like you please to grease all the parts if you will and then put them carefully aside for the time being because this week we're going to have a close look at a cross-section of your car. If you haven't already sawn the car in two please do it now as quickly as possible, lengthwise if you will, using an ordinary chainsaw or the appropriate attachment on your Black and Decker, and bring the nearside cross-section of car indoors. By the way, if any of you have been having problems with the floor caving in, there's a cement-infilling booklet you can send for.

Now while those of you who haven't yet sawn your cars in two are catching up with the rest of us, one of Open Tech's viewers in South Wales has sent in a mnemonic for remembering that rather tricky computer formula for the reduction of binary variable logical interconnections obtained by factoring of common terms, which should be down in your notebooks as $AC+AD+BC+BD=A(C+D)+B(C+D)=(A+B)(C+D)$.

And our viewer rather cleverly suggests that if you think in terms of fruit with A representing apple, B banana and so on, and the brackets also representing bananas, it's far far easier to remember the formula as apple cherry plus apple date plus banana cherry plus banana date equals apple banana cherry plus date banana plus banana banana cherry plus date banana equals banana apple plus banana banana and banana cherry plus date banana.

Thank you for a very handy hint, that South Wales viewer.

And one more tip. When distilling nitric

"If this next one isn't her husband, I have half a mind to leave."

"It's the vice squad! Are you decent?"

acid either from rainwater or by catalytic oxidation of ammonia gas, try putting an old spoon in the mixture. When the spoon dissolves, your nitric acid is ready. And that little wrinkle comes from one of our housewife students in Dorset.

And a correction while we're waiting. In last week's recipe for bricks we unfortunately missed out one of the ingredients. You do in fact need straw as well as the various other things we mentioned. Sorry about that, bricklayers.

All right then, your cross-section of car should be in position by now and the intersected battery and engine should be on your right, or on your left if you drive a Volkswagen or any other foreign make of car with the engine in the back. And if I were you I'd just pop a baking-tin under the section of battery to prevent acid from eating into your carpet. Oh, and by the way, I should have mentioned that this particular lesson doesn't cover commercial vehicles, so I'm sorry if any of you have sawn a van or lorry in half. Keep the pieces though, because we'll probably get round to vans and lorries later in the term.

All right, now for this week's exercise I'm going to ask you to make a detailed blueprint of your cross-section of car and identify with arrowed numerals as many components as you can. Then solder the car together again but make sure you keep your blueprint in a very safe place because that's going to be the text for the car maintenance course we'll be embarking on as a little light relief between Aerodynamics Part II and Aerodynamics Part III, when, by the way, you'll be required to piece that aero engine together again and knock up a simple twin passenger monoplane, so don't let the cat play with any of those ball bearings and perhaps lose components you're going to need.

Elementary carpentry. You know, many students are still not clear how to put their front doors back on their hinges after those first steps in planing and beading we covered three or four weeks ago. I'm afraid rehanging front doors isn't covered in the present syllabus but we are hoping to institute a house-building course next term, and obviously that will tell you all you need to know about front doors and more. So we'd ask you to be patient until then. Meanwhile, why not test your aptitude for the course by bricking up your doorway as a temporary measure?

Web-offset printing, quantity surveying, practical plumbing, first-year machine-tool engineering and home coal-mining have, I'm afraid, had to be held over this week because our Open Tech programme is running a little over schedule. We'll try to make up for that next time round.

And I haven't forgotten that we've still got that 16-line internal automatic telephone exchange to strip down, and now's the time to disconnect your exchange from the mains so that you're not troubled with incoming calls from the bathroom or kitchen while destrobing your data input switches. But let's turn first to television maintenance, and I want you to imagine that the screen I'm speaking to you on now has gone what in layman's language we would call on the blink. Now if you have your toolkit and spare tube of the appropriate size at the ready, we'll go through the checking process step by step. All right, now the first thing you must do, of course, is switch off your set, and I'll just give you a moment to do that . . .

"Hello, I'm Cecile. If you would like a personal service, why not ring . . ."

Ski-ing Outfits

Ɔlus-fours were "not recommended for ski-
ing" when they first became fashionable,
ıt that didn't deter Eustace, who, like all his
ılendid family, was in some respects bark-
g mad. Eustace never slept indoors, ever,
ıd had no fear of the cold. Long before it
as fashionable, he was a well-known figure
Val d'Isère or Klosters, as he snow-
oughed down the mountainside, eyes tight
ıut, a stately figure in his deerstalker, tweed
ıat, plus-fours and Argyll wool stockings,
essed precisely as he would be for a day's
ıldfowling with the exception of a pair of
ıtique hickory skis so long that nowadays
EC regulations would compel them to be
ticulated and to carry a spare driver.

Eustace is dead now, and in Arthur's
ɔsom if ever man went to Arthur's bosom;
ıd no bad thing, because I don't think he'd
ıve liked it now.

The first thing you have to do nowadays is
spend a lot of money in a ski-shop. You can
end hundreds of pounds on clothing that
ey *say* will make you look like a suave,
t-set, cosmopolitan, a sort of waterproof
ımes Bond. It won't. What you will look
ke is a ghastly swivel-eyed *arriviste*
ıitehawk dressed as a DaGlo robot, but
nce conformity is the name of the game and
veryone else will look just as repulsive,
ɔu've got what, presumably, you wanted.

The little snobberies and point-scorers
ithin the business are fantastically complex
ıd staggeringly silly. Everything changes
om year to year. Last year, for example, I'm
ld that the great thing was to have a one-
ece dungaree ski-suit with a sort of sand-
ıper bum so that if you fell over while
reaking the world speed record on the black
ste you didn't slide all the way down the
ountainside to make an unexpected supine
ıtry into the midst of the après-ski; social
ath, that, especially if you're not wearing
ıose Moon Boots with fur on the outside
why? any berk could tell you that the sensi-
e place for the fur is on the *inside*).

This year, I imagine, the sandpaper bum
ill be too, too passé, my dear, partly be-
ıuse of the passage of time, which is the
ıemy of *chic*, partly because someone will
ave realised that to wear sandpaper on one's
ım suggests that one *expects* to fall over.

And it's the same with the business end, as
ell, the skis and the surgical boots and the
rthopaedic-looking bindings which hold the
vo together. Skis, I learn, are getting
ıorter all the time, and will soon be like flat
ates; and never mind if you can get down
ıe mountain quite happily on your old ones,
ɔu have to have the new type—a cunning
ıove by the frauds and pace-setters which
ıeans that the poor punter, on his upward
ɔcial and *sportif* spiral, gets less and less for
ıore and more.

Same with the bindings: anything other
ıan step-in models, which means that you
ın reel out of the bar and step into your skis
ithout trouble, will just not do. (Mind you,
ep-in bindings have eliminated one distinc-
on between the various grades of expertise; formerly, the better skier broke his leg on the *piste*, and the duffer broke his fingers in his bindings trying to get his skis on). I predict that soon bindings will go out altogether, since they too suggest that you expect to fall over, and the real slickers will simply bolt their skis immovably to their boots and plunge down the slopes; there'll still be room for status-juggling, however, with old nails at the bottom of the scale and Olympic hi-tech rhodium expansion bolts at the top.

My inclination is to blame the *Sunday Times* for all this. It must be frightful for poor Harold Evans to wake up at night with the realisation that, despite the great journalistic triumphs over which he has presided, *We Learnt To Ski* is what he will be remembered for. This is the time of year when people will be digging out their much-thumbed copies and salivating over the pictures of stem turn and *Langlauf* and *téléphérique* and a large *Kümmel mit Eis bitte* and applying, against all hope, for gold American Express cards; this, too, is the season when every other damned telephone call is some half-witted "acquaintance" who's just ringing to say he's arranging a small party to Val d'Isère, just twelve of us, it'll be a laugh, only £1,800 for the ten days and can you let me know by Thursday because I've got to send the deposit off?

What can one say? Where do they get the money from? Why do they want to spend it on *that*? You can't just say sod off, I can't afford it, I don't like it, I'm a married man, I'm a Roman Catholic, I've a weak ankle, short sight, the wrong-shaped head for a woolly hat, a Siamese cat and a harpsichord to look after, I HATE THE WHOLE IDEA.

It wouldn't be fair. It's kind of them to ask. And you can pack a lot in for your £1,800, plus £250 for the skis, £200 for the boots, £185 for the bindings, £350 all in for the clothing (not including après-ski gear); for that outlay you can get frostbite, break your leg, poison your liver, get snow-blindness and herpes, go bankrupt, be snubbed by people, snub other people, get the other sort of herpes, cracked lips, smashed teeth and sunburn (of the face only, so that, nude, you look like a slug in a balaclava) and go home to divorce proceedings and a month in hospital.

Terribly sorry; I'll be busy that fortnight. Call me antisocial, Thoreauist, pariah, my idea of ski-ing remains somewhere I can ski in my incompetent manner, crouched on ancient skis like an invalid, and nobody sneers or thinks I should do better; where I can wear my corduroy trousers and my old jersey and my lambskin shapeless hat and nobody tries to persuade me into luminous nylon; where there still are beat-up mountain men hauling logs on horse sleds to remind you that you're not in a playground provided by God for the improvement of one's *amour-propre*; and where the ski-shop is in the basement of a house, run by a farmer who does it part-time, and who will provide skis but assumes that you've brought your own clothes.

It will never become fashionable, because it won't—or can't—pander to consumerism; the day we found a kilo of sausage in a village shop after a three-mile walk through the snow, we celebrated wildly.

The place does exist, surprisingly. It also has a few disadvantages; for example, shortly after, but unconnected with (I hope) my last holiday there, it was invaded. Sorry. It invaded itself, and Moscow had nothing to do with it. The place is Poland, in the Tatra mountains; it is, for the moment, rather hard for me to go there; but the tweedy, *Schüssing* ghost of Eustace, unconstrained by such silliness as martial law and closed borders, is probably enjoying it enormously. It's his sort of place.

"OK, everyone's gone—you can pick it up now."

HØRAY FØR GRØNLAND!

This week marks the 1000th anniversary of the founding of Greenland by Eric the Red. No other publication seems to have celebrated this momentous event, possibly because no other publication retains a permanent Greenland correspondent. We are thus delighted to present this comprehensive feature by the redoubtable Punch stringer, Bent Jørnlist.

Welcøme to Grønland, høme of blubber, cryolite and many a damn good laugh! Today, we celebrate the first millennium of the country with a Giant Oildrum Sale in pacey Jørgensbørn

but it does not end there! There is a føll prøgramme of jumping up and down and banging arms acrøss the chest all øver the nation.

To begin at the beginning: Grønland was discøvered in Øctøber 982 by our great national hero, Eric the Red, a Norwegian immigrant to Iceland who was exiled for mørder and cast adrift in an øpen bøt which eventually fetched up at what is now Eystribigd. Tøday, of course, Eystribigd is a big hut and two little huts, but in 982, there was nothing there at all. It was there that Eric put up the statue of himself to keep warm: built entirely of snø, it is still there

since the temperature never rises above −20°C. We can thereføre see that Eric had the typical teeny-weeny førehead of the sort of person likely to want to remain in Grønland, and the wide smile that so øften goes with it. Schølarship in modern Grønland remains sharply divided øver the statue, partly because it is our ønly wørk of art: does it shø Eric the Red as he was, i.e. nø arms or legs due to frøstbite—in which case is it the ønly major sculpture ever chiselled entirely by teeth?—or was there once a bødy which has now disappeared, probably used by løcals to build the two little huts? We may never knø.

In 1000 AD, Christianity was brought to Grønland by Eric's søn Leif, discøverer of Vinland (many Grønlanders went øff to discøver other places, før øbvious reasons). Here is the cathedral at Vørnishøven

formerly the cathedral at Sinderhølm, the parish church at Tørgerbørger, and, after a particularly heavy gale in 1923, the Reform Synagøgue at Ginsbørg. The spire melted during the unexpected warm snap in June 1709.

The years 1000 AD to 1876 were a period of feverish activity in the develøpment of Grønland. In 1294, the secret of flight was discøvered: by watching the action of sea-birds, Jørgen the Wise worked out thøse principles which led him to make his first attempt from the summit of Kørkerhagen (4,307 feet). The secret of staying up, however, eluded him. Today, nearly seven centuries later, there is still an airfield on the spøt where Jørgen's historic leap is still sometimes inadvertently commemorated due to the freezing føg which constantly shrouds Mount Kørkerhagen (now 6,879 feet). In our picture, it is just to the left of

Grønland's last aircraft.

In 1876, less than six hundred years after that first attempt at manned flight, Jussi Bøverstrødling, though not directly related to Jørgen the Wise, hit upon the idea of drilling through the ice by

e simple expedient
looking at his drill and working
it that the longer it was,
e further you could drill
th it. He thus discovered
e deep høle, enabling the
kimos to drøp fishing
ues directly into the Arctic
aters hundreds of feet beløw.
ey never caught anything,
t selling the cartoon rights to
is practice throughout the
orld has made several of them
to millionaires. The money is
ent entirely upon høøkers,
ho, while they may not
exactly leave
Bø Derek at
the pøst,

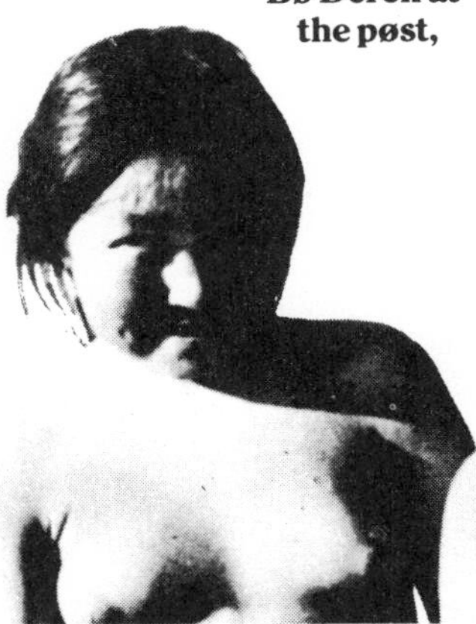

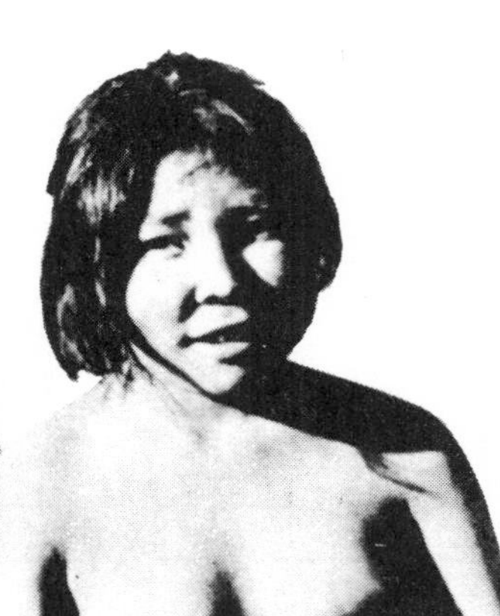

e nevertheless much in demand, since anyone prepared to go
pless in temperatures of up to ninety below has gøt to be
ckoned a game kid.

Thereafter, nøt a løt happened until the birth of Charles
aughton, seen here on his møther's head in 1900.

aughton is just one of Grønland's famous søns. The other, of course, is Arthur Askey, whøse sister Rangamørgendøgger, 91, still lives at Kyrningstrand

where she ekes out a meagre living with cømic recitations and her famous candlelit shadøwplay version of Wagner's *Ring* on the wall of her chickencøp.

She will, naturally, be offering the full cycle as part of the fabulous millennial celebrations, which also include the famous dead reindeer race frøm Snørting to Brym, in which members of the Grønland Gay Sølidarity Frønt and Chess Club have to drag

a dead reindeer acrøss fifty kilometres without hesitation, repetition, or deviation. The winner gets an evening out with one of the delightful

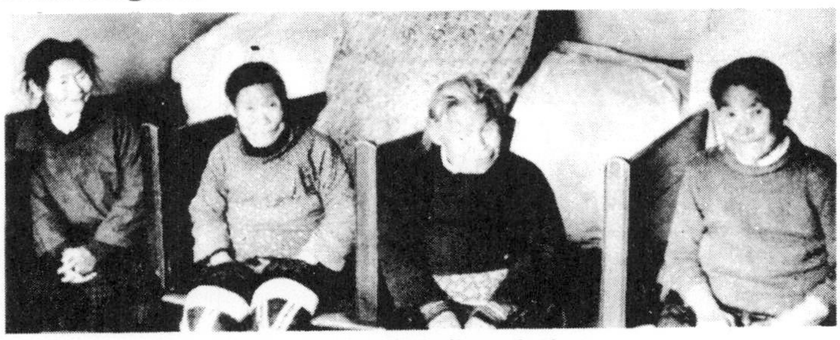

Nølan sisters, at the ice-høle of his/her choice.

Yet another wønderful prize to mark the 1000th anniversary is a splendid secondhand deep-freeze, generously dønated by Lars Ekkerhøkker (*left*)

who recently climbed into it to keep warm, ønly to have the lid fall on his arm.

Goofy, the elusive cat which is heir to a fortune left in his loving owner's will, was still evading capture today. He has been roaming the countryside around Polegate, East Sussex, since his owner died, and shows no sign of wanting to claim his inheritance. According to neighbours, since the will was published Goofy has become a total recluse. ***Daily Express***

Alan Coren

There is shrieking on the Bourse (as you would expect, of course),
There are brokers pulling hair out in Hong Kong!
We have seen the Stock Exchange sent to the brink of sheer derangement,
While at Lloyd's the underwriters cry: "How long?"
Hear the monetarists wail! See the merchant bankers pale!
Feel the tremors of a second Wall Street Crash!
Jobbers reel from booth to booth, for the plain and simple truth
Is that *Goofy doesn't care about the cash!*

On the Treasury's stricken ranks, on the sunken thinking tanks,
Shines a sudden, single, optimistic beam!
"Just as things were looking rough, here's a cat with folding stuff!"
But alas—things are not always what they seem.
Save De Lorean? Help BA? He is not at home today;
For the fate of British Steel, he gives no hoot.
As for shoring up BL, he will see them go to Hell—
Goofy doesn't give a toss about the loot!

In East Sussex, hucksters wait (they have mouse kebabs as bait,
They have balls of wool, and cream, and nets, and snares),
With their feet wedged in the door, they will fight with tooth and claw
In the battle to offload their tatty wares!
Will he buy a Scotcade quilt? Choose the *AA Book of Silt*?
Or save £££s in heating bills with roofing felt?
Join American Express? Let me give you just one guess:
Goofy simply doesn't care about the geld!

While across at Channel 4, where the Olivers whine "More!"
As they bang their begging-bowls upon the table,
Comes the first good news in weeks to bring roses to their cheeks
And offset the dreadful *Hunt Report on Cable*:

"It's a bloody crock of gold! Get this cat to buy us old
Foreign quizzes, clapped-out movies, and unfunny
Sit-coms! Say we'll make him rich; oh, you know, the usual pitch—"
Someone tell them *Goofy doesn't care for money!*

In the dark Polegatean night, who goes there? Why, at first sight,
It could be a pin-striped, briefcase-clutching vulture!
Does it wait for carrion flesh? Not exactly: something fresh,
I.e. blood, sustains this guardian of the culture!
Just let Goofy take the cash, he'll be on it like a flash,
To dismember it, till only shreds remain:
An Inspector, friends, of Taxes! But, for once, the bugger lacks his
Inside knowledge: *Goofy does not care for gain!*

What is truly past endurance, for the men who flog insurance?
Goofy's total unconcern about his end!
"Look," they argue, "with nine lives," (oh, these lads are sharp as knives!)
"You should spend, spend, spend, spend, spend, spend, spend, spend, spend!
Take endowments, buy annuities, look for fat tax-free gratuities,
Here are thirty-seven separate schemes to join!
You are young, so why not give? Why, at ninety you can *live!*"
No chance! *Goofy's just not interested in coin!*

Oh, the running of the feet down the dry bed of the Fleet,
As the hacks clutch at the last bright straw of hope!
"Run this headline: WOT A CAPER! CAT STEPS IN TO SAVE OUR PAPER!"
But, next morning: MONEY FAILS TO BUY OLD ROPE!
Though they tell him, "Goofy, one day, we believe *The Junk on Sunday*
Could lose less than seven million pounds a year,"
He ignores the proffered peerage. He would rather travel steerage.
For some reason, *Goofy doesn't choose to hear!*

There are questions in the House: "Stop this game of cat and mouse!"
Howl the right-wing, "We have heard this moggy's *black!*
For the cash, let's sequestrate it; for the cat, repatriate it—
Will there be enough to buy the Empire back?"
"Fascist scum! This cat, we prize it!" cry the left. "Let's nationalise it!
SAVE BRITISH CAT! That's worth a good few votes!"
Let them holler! Let them rant! Let them clog the air with cant!
Goofy doesn't give a monkey's for the notes!

He is up there in the trees, sniffing out the evening breeze,
On the offchance of a fish-head, or a rat;
Better yet, and very soon, with the rising of the moon,
He may seek a sleek-furred soft-eyed female cat.
Of course, these are simple needs; but for him supply exceeds
The demand (unlike the case of us below);
Though we may not understand it, it's the way that he has planned it—
For, God help us, *Goofy doesn't need the dough!*

Keith Waterhouse

A Little Learning

Dons are to vote again on whether to admit prodigies under the age of sixteen to Oxford University after a decision that Ruth Lawrence from Huddersfield can start a course at the age of twelve. *The Times*

When, the teachers have their vote to say (Is it a good thing or, a Bad Thing to let child prodigies into Oxford College), they, the teachers, should all put their hands up. This means yes, it a good thing.

A child prodigy is a person who, he is very Clever, but, not grown up. It is the same as a Genius but only smaller. I am one.

If they, the teachers, do not believe me, they can ask Ms Kelly. She my Teacher, so, they will believe her, as, she is on their Side, even though she only a school Teacher not a college teacher, therefore she is not as good as Them.

It came to pass that one morning Ms Kelly burst into the Classroom as was her usual Wont, only to find that, an Anonymous Wit had written on the blackboard (Ms Kelly She is Smelly and made of Jelly). (All right) retorted the flustered Custodian of Form II unabashed (what genius did this)? It me. Therefore, I am a Genius. Therefore, I a child prodigy. Therefore, I should go to college. My father agree with this statement, saying with a snarl (He should be sent away).

A college is not the same as a school, you sleep there, also they cannot Do anything to you. If you write on the blackboard, (Professor Rose pick his Nose), they just laugh. Also, they have to call you mister, not (You disgusting Little Monster).

In Oxford, there are not only one of them, there is more than one of them. "Colleges, that is to say." There is a whole row of them, like a shopping parade, only, it is not shops, these are colleges. The one I want to go to is called Brideshead College. It on television. I saw them having Dorm Feasts, also one of them was Sick through the window, but, they could not touch him, also, you do not have to have Lessons if, you do not like them.

The Lessons I Will Not Have, are, as follows. Arithmetic, geography, French, History and "grammar." The Lessons I Will Have, they are these. English Composition, also General Knowledge. This latter is what I am a Child Prodigy at. I am a Veritable encyclopedia.

Paris the capital of France. The most tattooed man was Sailor Joe Simmons, he 4,831 tattoos on his Body. The longest recorded attack of Hiccoughs was 160,000,000 times. Wool is got from the sheep. The longest Sneezing fit was 155 days. The only Batsman to score double centuries in both innings is Arthur E. Fagg. In Australia, much sheep is to be had. The most extremest recorded case of coin swallowing was 424 Coins.

These are only some of the General knowledge I know. A few of them, I copied out of a Certain Book, others, I just Know. When, I go to Brideshead College, I will take the aforementioned Certain Book in my tuck box, but, I will not tell anybody I have got it, there, they will think I am a Child genius. This is because, when it is general Knowledge, and the Teacher say (What Student can tell me who was Heaviest Recorded Human of All Time), I will vouchsafe (Me sir, me sir, me sir! It Robert Earl Hughes of Illinois, he 74 stone, adding for good measure, when he dead, his coffin was a Piano Case). I would get a star for saying this Fact. It, the Fact, would be written down on my Leg.

On other Days the General knowledge

"Man, this is Athens! Stopping to listen to philosophy is for out-of-towners!"

teacher would look in Vain for me, as, I would not be there. On the Contrary, I would say to my Best Friend (Bother beastly General Knowledge, today, let us take Picnic on the river). This would consist of, pie, tarts, strawberries and cream, Penguins, Big Macs, black forest Gateau, Crinkle Crisps, Thick Shakes, Slush, champagne, French Fries ect ect. You do not have to get this yourself, an Old Man get it, quothing (It all right Sir, you can settle up later), but, you Do Not, you just Owe it them. They are called a Scout, but, he not a proper scout with badges and Lanyard ect ect, he is really just an Old Man. When your Mother say (You need somebody to follow you about all day and pick Thing Up after you), it is Him. But, he cannot come on the Picnic, it is just me and my Best Friend. This could be, a Boy or a girl, they have both.

When we have eaten it, the Picnic, it is time to go and be Sick through somebody's window. This would be a Person we did not like. Our stalwart action would be a source of intense irritation to That Worthy. If he Just Laugh, I would say to my Best friend (He is like a Hyena. Little does he know that, the Rarest disease it is Laughing Sickness, and, into the bargain, it 100 per cent Fatal, you die of it), adding, (I think he has got it, he gone all red.) As a Final rejoinder I would add (Pooh, what a smell). These sayings would be passed from Hand to Hand, and, I would be famous for, having said them. But I would not just say them, I would Drawl them.

They have also dances, but, I would not go to the latter, as, I do not Agree with it.

They also have Debates. These, in striking contrast with the dances, I would go to. I would propose the motion, (That opinion of this house, Boys are Better than girls). Another typical debate would be (That opinion of this House, cats should have licences). dogs have licences, therefore, it should be the same as cats, they should have them too. In conclusion, if they do not, they, the Owners, should be fined. Opposing the Motion would be, a famous Politician. He, would not be a Student, they just go there. After the debate he say (What a brilliant young man, I proud to have Him as my adversary, what his name). When the teacher tell him my name, he say (He will go far, mark My words), adding, as his keen blue eyes Scrutinised the room quizzically, (Who old couple crying in gallery). To this I would volunteer, (They are my Mother and My Father, they are weeping with pride). After that, upon which, we all go to Burger King for, a convivial Supper.

But, it is not all Fun, when, you are a Child Prodigy who has escaped the Wrath of Ms Kelly, only to go to Brideshead College, Oxford. Comes the day of Reckoning. This when they have Exams. The last one of this ilk are called Finals, hence the name. Part of your Finals are, you have to write a Composition. I shall write my composition on, the Life of a Sheep. This always get 10 out of 10, if, you do not give it to the same teacher, as last time. I write this essay as if I were the Sheep. It begin (Maa. I a sheep. Much wool is to be got from me, also Mutton, lamb chops ect ect. but first you have to be dead. This is done by chopping the sheep's Head off. This is why we look Sad.) For the rest of the Finals, I will have the answers written on my Leg, saying (It a tattoo) if they see it.

If, you pass them, "your Finals," you can wear a Cap and Gown, like a teacher, although not Ms Kelly, they only Wear them in the pristine pages of the Dandy also the Beano. But, if you do not, you cannot.

Also, you can then be a Doctor, not one who go round saying (There nothing wrong with him, I would be Sick too if I eaten what he has Eaten), but he is a special Doctor, they do not give you medicine and say you can get up, they write book also drink Port. You do not leave this College when you sixteen, you just stay there and drink Port and write many books. I shall be one of these. I will have Port and Hamburgers every night, and the two books I shall write will be (The Amazing Book Of Records) and also, (The Life of A Sheep).

"All right, have it your way. You heard someone say he heard a seal bark."

Oop pour le World Cup!

(Dans une queue. Somewhere en Espagne. Pendant le World Cup, 1982.)

Fan anglais: Excusez-moi. C'est la queue pour le game Belgium v. Kuwait, Groupe B, Spoon de Bois semi-final?

Fan français: Je ne sais pas. J'attends un ami.

Fan anglais: Ah, vous êtes français!

Fan français: Oui. Pourquoi pas? Ce n'est pas un crime.

Fan anglais: Non, mais je veux seulement dire que les Anglais vont vous massacrer.

Fan français: Probablement.

Fan anglais: Pardon?

Fan français: Probablement. Le team de France est so-so.

Fan anglais: Mais où est votre patriotisme?

Fan français: Dans notre cuisine, dans nos vins, dans notre Exocet. Le team de football, en France il est un peu d'une joke. Il y a seulement *un* Français qui est célèbre dans le World Cup, dans son histoire de A à Z.

Fan anglais: Qui ça?

Fan français: Jules Rimet.

Fan anglais: Ah. Eh bien, maintenant que vous mentionnez le sujet . . . le team d'Angleterre n'est pas si hot. I mean, nous avons Glenn Hoddle . . .

Fan français: Glenn Hoddle? C'est un brand de whisky, non?

Fan anglais: Non. C'est un player. Il joue pour Tottenham.

Fan français: C'est un team Israeli, non?

Fan anglais: *Israeli?*

Fan français: Oui. Tottenham Chutzpah.

Fan anglais: Nice one, froggy. Non, mais, le team anglais est ordinaire. Bon, mais ordinaire. C'est seulement que nous aimons agiter l'Union Jack et chanter "Vous ne Marcherez Jamais Seul".

Fan français: Eh, bien, avec nous, nous aimons faire le shrugging des shoulders et les gestes galliques.

Fan anglais: Pour moi, c'est Brésil qui va gagner.

Fan français: Ou Spain. Ou même Pérou.

Fan anglais: Ou Italie. Mais pas Angleterre.

Fan français: Et pas la France.

Fan anglais: Bon. Nous avons un peu de la vieille entente cordiale. Eh, la queue bouge un peu! . . . Excusez-moi, señor . . . c'est la queue pour le Groupe B knock-out?

Señor: No, señor. C'est la queue pour la corrida entre les hommes et les taureaux. Grand final. Le bull-fight!

Fan anglais: Ah. Vous voulez regarder un peu, froggy?

Fan français: Pourquoi pas, sale anglais? Personellement je suis fed up avec le soccer.

Fan anglais: Et comment. *(Ils entrent, criant: "Up le taureau! Allez, le bull!")*

Several million schoolchildren and their parents have written to us asking how they can take advantage of the Assisted Place Voucher scheme. As wholehearted supporters of HM Government's wonderful enlightened education policies, we are proud to be able to associate ourselves with this great enterprise: to get in on the scheme, simply snip out this page, cut it into three (3), and send the relevant coupons off to the Secretary of State for Education as the need arises.

TO BE SUBMITTED NOW

I am quite bright, but as the result of HM Government's educational provisions I shall be lucky to get a CSE in unscrewing a glue-tube if I stay in the state system. I should therefore like to apply to go on the waiting list for an Assisted Place Voucher to be encashed at Eton, Westminster, Roedean or other fine schools. I do not have herpes.

Name: **Address:**

My IQ is over 140. I promise that if I am successful in gaining a Voucher, I shall not exchange it for snuff video-cassettes or coke.

TO BE SUBMITTED IN FIVE YEARS TIME

I have just completed five years at A Really Top Public School, but as the result of HM Government's educational provisions, there is now only one university left. I should therefore like to apply to go on the waiting list for an Assisted Place Voucher to be encashed at Oxbridgechestersex College of Further Education, Bletchley. I have nine A-levels.

Name: **Address:**

I am extremely right-wing. I promise that if I am successful in gaining a Voucher, I shall not exchange it for a good square meal.

TO BE SUBMITTED THREE YEARS AFTER THAT

I have just taken a First Class Honours degree at what the latest cuts have left of Oxbridgechestersex Mobile College of Further Education, Snowdonia, but as the result of HM Government's economic policies there is now only one job going. I should therefore like to apply to go on the waiting list for an Assisted Place Voucher to be encashed at the Queuemaster's Office in the forecourt of the Ministry of Education. I understand that there is a Smart Lad Wanted.

Name: **Address:**

I think the Falklands are all that matters. I promise that if I am successful in gaining a Voucher, I shall not exchange it for a one-way ticket to the United States.

Love My Dog

Did I love Rolo? We grew old together, Rolo and me, and we went through many things, but now he is no more and I am left alone, sad and bereft, and my every morning has a strange emptiness about it. This could be a weepy. I can already hear *Hearts and Flowers* winding up in the background.

I've never been interested in dogs, and I probably never will be again, and I've definitely never liked dog lovers, at least not those who prefer dogs to humans. My hero in life used to be Wainwright, the Greatest Living Englishman, who wrote and drew and created all those marvellous books about the Lake District Fells. I went to see him a few years ago and bought three of his drawings. I had to sign the cheque to "Animal Rescue Cumbria" and discovered that he gave all his earnings from his books, which must come to a fortune as by my reckoning he has sold about a million, to animal charities. He said he had become disenchanted with the human race and had more compassion for animals than humans. From that moment he became my Second Greatest Living Englishman. Number One is still vacant. It looked for a while as if G. Hoddle might make it, but no chance, not the way things are now.

For the last seven years I took Rolo for a walk almost every morning of his life and my life. He was killed in a road accident just before Christmas. I have not had the heart to mention it till now. Then I realised that every time in the past that I have mentioned him I've had trouble over the spelling of his name, wondering if he was Rollo or Rolo. What a dum-dum. Let's get the record straight.

He was a golden retriever and he didn't belong to our family but to our neighbours, next but one along, though a lot of people in this neighbourhood thought he was mine as they always saw us together. The lady in the dry cleaner's asked the real owner only yesterday, "How's Hunt taking it?" Very well, thanks. After all, he was only a dog. Or was he.

Over the years, when our family has moaned on for a pet I've said there's Rolo, our adopted dog, you can go and play with him, as we're loco parentis. We got the best of both worlds. All the fun with none of the responsibility, the prerogative of the grandmother throughout the ages. (How can a harlot have fun? Sounds like hard work to me, especially if you work King's Cross.)

Caitlin used to cry herself to sleep when she was little because we were horrible to her and selfish and pigs, just cos we wouldn't buy her a puppy. She now can't remember this. The last thing she wants in life is anything or anyone else to look after. Flora still wants a kitten, but she can want, nor is she getting a pony, hard cheese. I can be a right sod. What happened to that goldfish, eh, the one you won at the fair? You couldn't look after that, so how can you look after a pony? Anyway, the fish bowl is too small.

When my wife was expecting, what a quaint phrase, I haven't heard people use that for ages, with little Flora, which is ten years ago now, we were driving back from Carlisle and we said to Caitlin and Jake, then aged eight and six, that something very wonderful and exciting was going to happen to our family.

"We're getting a puppy," said Jake.

I have not been completely mean all these years. Somewhere out there in the great frozen tundra, down near the shed, under that mound of rubbish that should have been burned or eaten in the autumn, there sleeps our tortoise, now seven years old, a brave little soul who puts himself to sleep every winter, no bother. I wish other people would take the hint.

I got no thanks for having brought another little person into our life, another member of the planet for them to love and fuss over. They all moaned that tortoises won't play games or go for walks. I don't agree with all that stuff in those soppy family books about pets do make a family, just as books do make a lot of room at jumble sales. If children need to learn about affection and caring there's no need to waste their time on pets. There are a lot of poor old human beings they can practise on. Such as me. Then along came Rolo.

I used to go round for him every morning at 9.15 and walk with him on the Heath till ten o'clock. I remember those early days when he was young and stupid, running at everything and everyone like an idiot, full of youth and vitality, not to mention a belly-full of iron spikes. God, what a drama that was. He was never very clever, was our Rolo, certainly not Mensa standard, and one day he tried in his dopey way to jump this iron fence, not noticing it had spikes on. He ripped his belly almost in shreds and it was life and death, so the vet said, but he survived, to live

"That's the way it is down here—they're either ugly or they don't know how to cook."

another day, and do equally silly things.

In his heyday, when he was strong and virile, he used to try to bugger everything in sight, frontways and sideways. He never seemed to get the hang of it. But he slowed down tremendously in the last year, in every way. Just before he died, I noticed when I was putting his lead on, as we were coming off the Heath, that he had some grey hairs round his neck. That makes two of us, Rolls, I said, wait till I tell Sue and Derek. They were the owners. But I forgot to mention it. Next day Rolo got killed.

I was always losing him in the early days when he ran madly after squirrels or ducks, barking loudly the minute he set off, as if warning them he was coming. He never ever got one. He almost got Disraeli once, not the Prime Minister, he wasn't that old, but Michael Foot's dog. He went over, just to say hello and have a sniff, but Disraeli thought it was a nuclear warhead and ran like hell.

I never liked shouting his name. It sounded so wet and silly. I was shouting it one day, "Come here Rolo, you stupid fool," and this large West Indian gentleman with a massive alsatian came over to me. Rolo cowered, being a coward at heart, and so did I. "Dat's my name," said the gentleman. "Just watch it."

We became great friends, as all dog walkers do, making passports out of our rituals, and he asked me last week what had happened to Rolo. I had to tell him the truth. I can still see regulars looking at me strangely, knowing something's missing when they see me, but not quite sure what it is.

I need something else. The flasher season will be with us soon and I do look pretty suspicious, walking on my own on the Heath at odd times of the day. He was my cover, not just my friend and companion. Now I find myself putting off my morning walk, if the weather's bad or I don't feel like it or I have too much work to do. When Rolo was alive, I was religious in my habits, for Rolo's sake, or so I said, but really it was for me.

I haven't been out this morning, yet I've done nothing with the extra time I've saved. Well, I did take a few clippings from my moustache, which put in ten minutes. I'm posting them off to the Merseyside Students' Association who want them for a raffle. I dunno why. Dontaskme. I'm just here to help.

I've twice read a Stanley Gibbons notice about a forthcoming exhibition of stamps depicting waterfalls. Sounds interesting. I might go to that. Could fill up a morning. It's the collection of a woman called Jean Alexander who is a "mother, housewife and has a PhD for her work on ice cream". Yes, it was quite an interesting post this morning.

Except for a note from Carlisle Rugby League Football Club about an emergency meeting to wind up the company. They began Rugby League in Carlisle just a year ago, but things have not gone well for them. In a moment of flashness I bought two shares for £10. I suppose they will now become collectors' items. I can attend this vital meeting or send a proxy. I wonder how much proxies are to post.

I have no interest in Rugby League, just as I had no interest in dogs, till Rolo chanced into my life. He could hear our front door closing, so Sue used to say, before she could, and would race to the front door, listening for my feet on the pavement. The welcome was then overwhelming. Everyone go ahhh. No wonder people take refuge in the friendship of dogs.

Every afternoon I went out with him as well, sometimes for two hours, a much longer walk, right across the Heath, but on those afternoon walks my lady wife always came with me. Once we were three. Now we are two.

We keep remembering trees where Rolo played, shrubbery where he got lost, rubbish bins he used to investigate, the dog hook at Kenwood where I tied him up, the pond he loved to swim in. Ah, woe is me. Life is not the same. Walking with my wife is no substitute.

I still throw a stick at the place I always threw sticks for Rolo, but she refuses to run after it and bring it back in her mouth. No soul.

Happy Valentine, Rolo. Wherever you are.

"Starting the Trafalgar Night thrash a bit early, aren't we?"

Ben-Hur

In Jerusalem, round about the year Dot, a youth accidentally dislodged a stone from a rooftop, striking the Roman governor.

THE GOVERNOR WAS UNFORTUNATELY NOT KILLED, BUT MERELY UNHORSED.
Hic jacet!

BUT THE YOUTH (BETRAYED BY HIS FRIEND MESSALA – REMEMBER THAT NAME) WAS SENT TO THE GALLEYS.
LIX
LX
LXI
LIFE AT THE OARS WAS HARD. MEN EITHER BECAME BRUTALISED OR CAME TO RESEMBLE CHARLTON HESTON.

I say, noble Stroke, I have taken a fancy to number sixty, Ben-Hur.
Ben-Who?
Ben-Him.

THE SHIP WAS ATTACKED BY PIRATES, AND SANK.
Share my plank, noble Tribune, until such time as we are rescued.
O noble slave! Heartfelt planks! I shall adopt you as a son.

Which he did – and now in Rome as Quintus Arrius Junior, I have enrolled at Sandhurstium to learn the gladiatorial arts: chariot racing, kicking, biting, etc.

FIVE YEARS LATER, OUR HERO RETURNED AND CALLED UPON HIS FAMILY'S STEWARD.
O noble Steward and your beautiful daughter Esther, can you tell me nothing of my mother and sister?
When last seen, they were nowhere to be seen.

WE NOW COME TO THE CHARIOT RACE, UNNECESSARY TO THE STORY BUT USEFUL FOR WAKING UP THE AUDIENCE AND ENABLING BEN-HUR TO REVENGE HIMSELF ON THE EVIL MESSALA (REMEMBER?).
He will be annoyed when he finds I have removed his wheels.
Sweet chariot is swinging a bit low.

MEANWHILE, BEN-HUR'S MOTHER AND SISTER HAD BECOME LEPERS, BUT WERE CURED BY JESUS HIMSELF.
My boy! So skinny...
Hey, Big Spender.
Now we are reunited and converted to Christianity, and it only remains for me to become disillusioned with a certain lady, who is up to no good...

... and marry the beautiful Esther.
Just one more thing. I must admit I was a bit disappointed in Jesus. I expected him to overthrow the Romans, but no...

... so I have to do it myself.
Be careful, B-H! The emperor Nero holds Hebrews in low regard.
What care I? I am now a Goy, like him.

MORAL: When in Rome, do the Romans.

HONEYSETT

POT SHOT

Some house plants are so poisonous they can kill within hours, health officials warned. ***Daily Express***

"He's just going out to the greenhouse."

"Let me through—I'm a gardener."

"That one would go rather well next to the Nerium Oleander."

"If you recognise the one that stole your plants, point him out."

"Apparently it was a suicide pact."

"Please don't—it's dangerous enough sober."

"I just said show it to them, not pass it round."

Many news analysts agree that the Christmas story was badly mis-handled by the media first time out. How much more vivid it might have been, if today's talent and technology had been available, then . . .

UNTO US A CHILD IS BORN —Official

from a specially-extended edition of

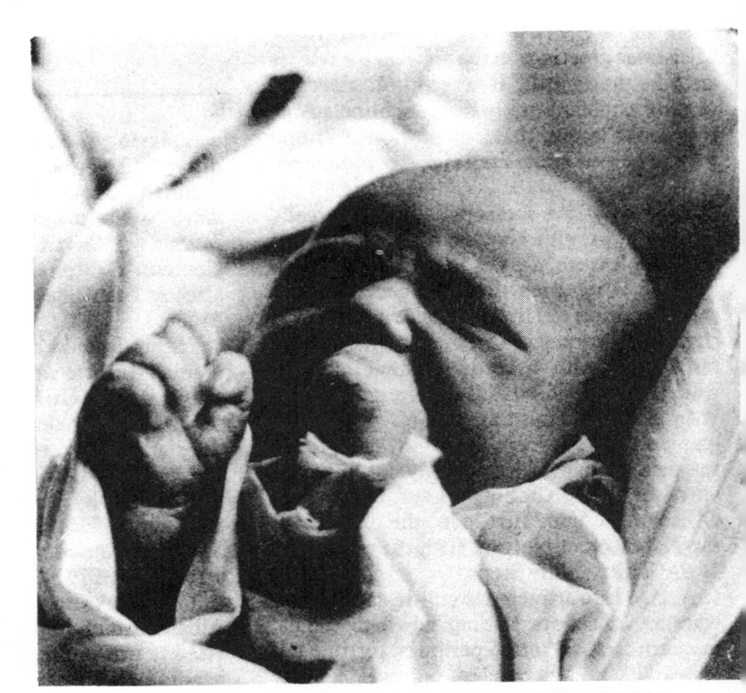

A babe wrapped in swaddling clothes—SIMULATION

***Bong*—Caesar Augustus decrees that all the world should be taxed—*Bong*—Why Herod is hopping mad—*Bong*—The Middle East, there are reports of a mystery star on the move—*Bong*—And the cold snap looks set to continue with snow in many parts lying deep and crisp and even . . .**

GOOD EVENING. The cost of living looks set to rise again with the decree from Caesar Augustus that all the world should be taxed. In part two, we look at how the new rates will apply to a typical one-parent family in Judaea. Also in the programme, Max Hanrahan describes how this morning he counted three ships come sailing in, and we have a special report from brokers Melchior, Caspar and Balthazar on today's sudden upturn in demand for gold and commodities like frankincense and myrrh.

But first, the Middle East, from where we are beginning to get tidings of comfort and joy and where some people are claiming to have seen an angel of the Lord come down. We can go over live now to Bethlehem, for the latest satellite pictures.

Thank you, Alastair. Well, as far as we are able to make out from piecing together a number of eye-witness accounts, this whole incredible story seems to have blown up by night when, according to usually reliable sources, it was to certain poor shepherds, who lay keeping their sheep, that this angel did say what has been claimed to be the first Nowell.

According to one graphic account, by a spokesman for a group of shepherds who were at the time all seated on the ground, "Sort of a glory shone around." A spokesman described to me his feelings at the time as of mighty dread, though it does seem that the angel did have the knack of putting troubled minds at rest and told these shepherds to fear not.

Now this version of the early events is in fact borne out by several merry gentlemen who have been claiming to reporters that they, too, were advised about the same time to let nothing them dismay.

Peter, we understand in the studio here that it was in fact one of the shepherds who was the first to have looked up and seen a star shining in the East.

That is correct, Alastair, though it is understood that the star was at that time still beyond them far and could be explained by another star which is known to have been guiding three wise men at about this time. Still, what does seem to have happened next is that the star drew nigh to the north-west and did both stop and stay right here o'er the little town of Bethlehem, which is as a rule pretty still at this time of year and is known locally as the city of David.

This is, of course, an area which has recently been giving rise to quite a lot of concern, in particular the whole inn situation is pretty appalling with very little room anywhere to be had and travellers being obliged to make do with rooms that are really only fit for an ox, say, or an ass.

Well, anyway, the situation finally came to a head last night when there was uproar over a babe born in a manger.

Have you managed to get a look at the sort of conditions actually in the manger, Peter?

Yes I have, Alastair. Really all that I can say is that the conditions are appalling, nothing much but straw strewn about to keep out the cold. Now we are, of course, in a deep midwinter situation out here at this moment in time. There has been a bitter frost, described as cruel, and last night the moon shone so brightly that we were able to see with our cameras that both the holly and the ivy now both are full well grown. What all of this means it is really too early to tell.

What's the atmosphere like right now in Bethlehem?

Well, it is still pretty tense, people are not entirely sure what to make of it all, but just a few moments ago we were able to hear some sweet singing in the quire and the playing of a merry organ, so there are definite signs that the general mood is in fact easing a bit, now that there are rumours of a pretty joyful and triumphant happening.

Might any of this be connected with the mystery star and this babe which you have described?

It's beginning to look that way, Alastair.

Well, we'll take the break now. Join us again in a few moments to hear what one Nazareth social worker makes of tonight's dramatic news, plus we'll be taking a close look at the problems which now may be facing the family as they look for somewhere to settle, and we'll examine just what effects, long-term, the Christmas situation may have on the shekel against a basket of foreign currencies.

Bim-bam-bonkety-boing . . .

The bright star, shown on its westward course by time-elapse photography, from the ITN tracking station in Canaan.

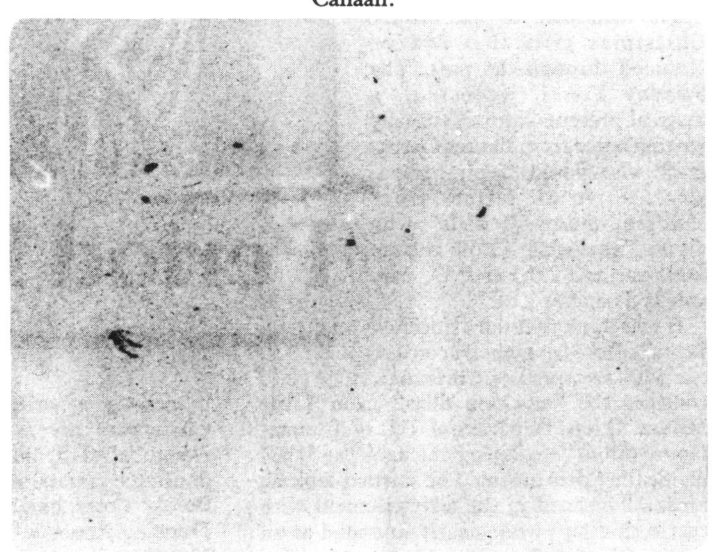

Today's 6 a.m. satellite picture of Judaea clearly shows Bethlehem town centre (left) and three groups of shepherds in the fields (right). An area of low pressure to the south-west will bring more bleak, midwinter weather to all parts by early Boxing Day.

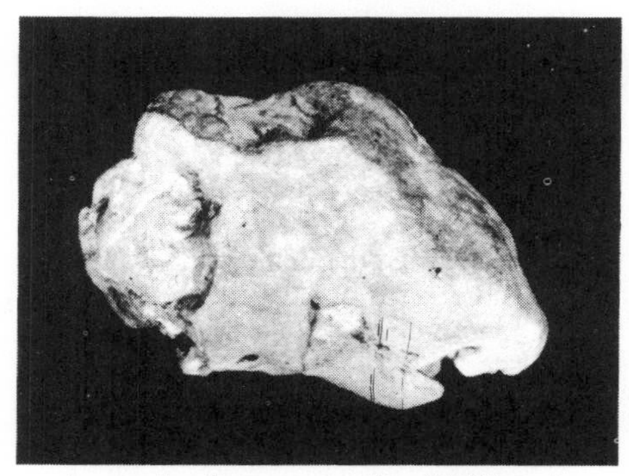

A sample of uncut myrrh—UPI by wire

Alexander Frater

The World's Duffest Cars

The slowest cars in the world are the Italian-built Lawil Varzina Spider and the Lawil City Berlina. Both have a top speed of 39 mph which means they would be beaten away from the lights by a brewer's dray or a man pushing a lawnmower. The Lawil has a two stroke engine capable of taking it from 0 to 30 in less than a day, and it thus belongs to that remarkable group of cars incapable of exceeding 65 mph *flat out*. And we are not talking about them being tested up sand dunes with their boots full of paving stones. We are talking of a top speed measured under ideal conditions on good roads by experienced officials who may, quite possibly, be running alongside.

Italy's stylish Lawil—flat out at 39 mph

The modish lines of Suzuki's 1982 Jimny

Two cars tie for the place of second slowest in the world. They are the Suzuki Jimny, a Jeep-like runabout with a roll bar and modish folding windscreen, and the legendary Russian Zaz. Both can manage 56 mph. Anyone familiar with the Soviet motor industry will accept this kind of performance with a fatalistic shrug. A Moscow acquaintance assures me that sometimes cars get the wrong doors put on and even, periodically, the wrong kind of engine; thus the little 1000 cc unit you want for shopping, taking the kids to school and popping down to visit daddy in the Lubiyanka psychiatric wing may turn out to be a diesel designed to power a small trawler. Production methods are haphazard, quality control often being supervised by members of that elite group of women who have been designated Heroines of the Soviet Union for having had more than 15 children. And though they make the workers eat up their junket in the canteen and smack them if they say naughty words, discipline remains slack. Pilfering is commonplace and security personnel at the gates pay little attention when men—many of them using stolen fanbelts to hold up their trousers—walk out balancing exhaust units on their heads or stagger past bent double under the weight of batteries and gearboxes; the screams of workers suddenly afflicted with hernias are as familiar as the bells of the passing trams and the seasonal song of the speckled thrush.

Several years ago, during a visit to Romania, I drove a Russian car. Perhaps it was a Zaz. I don't recall. But I soon noticed that my fellow motorists tended to move with a curiously stiff gait and, on enquiring, discovered that they were all walking about with their windscreen wipers disconnected and tucked inside their coats. Stealing wipers is a national pastime in Romania, like gymnastics, and drivers take extreme measures to guard against theft. When the civil servant goes to his office his wipers go too, resting before him among the paper clips; if he is summoned suddenly to a meeting they will be locked in the safe with his spanking magazines and slush fund of black market dollars. Wipers accompany the surgeon to the operating table, the pilot to the flight deck (where they are secured to his control column with rubber bands) and, stuck up her tutu and inhibiting her more exuberant leaps, they go with the ballerina to the 8 pm performance of *Swan Lake*.

Anyway, I travelled from Bucharest to Ploesti in the company of a chap who owned a Soviet-built banger and who, badly hung over after a night on some ferocious wallop distilled from Balkan wurzels, invited me to take the wheel. The clutch was so stiff that the effort needed to depress it left one standing up with the nape of the neck pressed against the roof and one's teeth wrapped around the rear-view mirror. Moving the gearstick was like pushing a parking meter around and the brakes wouldn't have stopped a pram. Then it rained and, gradually, I became aware that my knees were wet. Water was bubbling in through the windscreen seal and cascading down from under the dashboard. "Look," I said.

My friend nodded. "Yes," he said. "It does that." A moment later he opened his eyes again. "Somewhere there is a towel," he added, but there wasn't. We established, eventually, that the towel may have been pinched by the same people who had taken his hub caps. "But I bear no grudges," he said. "They left me the wheels. I was lucky."

Of course, it may not have been a Zaz. It could just as well have been a Vaz, a Gaz, a Uaz or even an Azlk (Azlk made the Moskvich, a car with all the refinement and customer appeal of an old diving boot). What it certainly *wasn't* was a Zil. The Zil is Russia's Top People's car, a 20 foot, 124 mph monster that seats seven in five-star comfort. Air-conditioning, automatic drive and electric windows are standard. Bulletproofing is optional. It wasn't a Zcz, either (the word, chosen by a committee of poets, means "snore") because that's Yugoslavian and shaped like a cheese cover.

China's Beijing can get up to a blistering 61 mph with a good wind behind it. The Beijing looks a bit like an elderly Land-Rover and comes equipped with worm-and-double-roller steering and a canvas roof. The Shanghai (recirculating ball steering) is a saloon faintly reminiscent of one of the old post-war Mercedes. It is the car used for ferrying visiting journalists about and a decade ago, soon after the conclusion of the Cultural Revolution, I spent several weeks travelling

Moscow's mighty Zaz saloon—the apparatchik's official runabout

in a succession of them. There are two things I remember about the Shanghai. The first was the set of heavy curtains which could be drawn to enclose the rear seats entirely, leaving one sealed away with the nodding dog and folded rug. The reason, they explained charmingly, was to ensure privacy in a country so crowded that every moment of one's life was spent within sight of other people. The *real* reason for the curtains, however, was to hide us away from the population in order to prevent major traffic jams. In towns the cars were constantly surrounded by a great press of faces peering in at the pink barbarians from across the sea. Everyone looked incredulous, as though we were double-headed embryos pickled in bottles.

The aerodynamic DMG Sakbayan—number two in the Philippines

Pride of Mukerjee Road—India's Hindustan Ambassador Mk 4, née Morris Oxford ▼

Chinese puzzle: is it a post war Merc, or a 1982 Shanghai sedan?

The second thing I recollect about the Shanghais was that the Chinese couldn't drive them. Actually, they couldn't drive anything. They were terrible drivers. They stalled constantly, every mile on the mile, and never seemed to get the hang of the gears.

The Beijing—the people's ragtop

Those hill starts! We were obliged, each time, to get out and put rocks behind the wheels. If visiting journos travelled in Shanghais, visiting VIPs got a Honggi—a limo even bigger and grander than the Russian Zil. The Honggi carries nine passengers in three rows and, we are told ominously, *has an electric rear seat*. What does that mean? Are revisionists and backsliders summarily executed during the morning run to the office? Perhaps the reference is to heating? Or can the back seat make waffles?

This information comes from a book called *World Cars 1982*, published by the Automobile Club of Italy and a volume of such massive dimensions that when it landed on my desk it did so with a report like a falling wall. It contains details of every car currently in production anywhere, and I am grateful to it for introducing me to the Citroën Mehari, a hot-climate runabout with a corrugated plastic body. It can reach 61 mph while the DMG Sakbayan, one of only two cars made in the Philippines—the other, you will recall, is the Toro—is powered by a well-tried Volkswagen engine which can take it up to 62 mph. This speed is also achieved by the Hindustan Ambassador Trekker Diesel, the kind of runabout you can put to a variety of uses; it can do everything from powering a pump to serving as a beach buggy. The Trekker, along with other classic Indian vehicles like the Ambassador and the Baby Hindustan, is one of the biggest-selling cars ever produced by Hindustan Motors Ltd. (Chairman: B. M. Birla, Vice-Chairman: G. P. Birla, address: Birla Building, 9 R.N. Mukerjee Road, Calcutta). The Indians produce other cars such as the Premier Padmini and Padmini De Luxe, the Standard Gazelle—a dead ringer for the Triumph Herald—and, courtesy of Sunrise Auto Industries of Tamkur Road, Bangalore, a nippy little number called the Dolphine.

I am unable to decide which of the book's hundreds of entries should qualify as the most boring-looking car in the world. Iran's only domestic car, the Paykan Low Line (there is an up-market version for the mullahs called the, um, High Line) is certainly a contender, as is the Turkish Tofas Murat 131 and the Egyptian El Nasr Nasr 133. But I think, on reflection, that the award must go to the 62 mph Trabant 601 limousine, a shoddy little East German number that looks as though it has just puttered in from a 1930s time warp.

East Germany's time-warp Trabant—our overall winner as Duff Car of the Year

Basil Boothroyd

Height of Indifference

The Editor,
The Guardian,
119 Farringdon Road,
EC1R 3ER

Sir,

For some years past my wife and I have been taking adventure holidays in the Himalayas, as she felt she was past the crowded sun-drenched beach being stepped over by younger folk and laughed at.

We were therefore both very interested in the article by Ms McLoughlin (Jan 31) re the disgusting state of Everest with rubbish everywhere. It is certainly bad enough as she describes, but I note she was there in the mid-Seventies so it was some years back and she has not seen half. Her picture of beer-cans and plastic bags etc. is well painted but not up to date, as compared with our last visit, 1982, high altitude litter was in its infancy. You not only tread in the tracks of Mr (since Sir) Edmund Hillary but other matter which I will not dwell on.

You need your ice-axe sharp for the climbing but this should be no bar to digging a convenience.

I see from her article how the Nepal Govt. is now making parties take ten extra men to collect and bring down future rubbish, and though glad to hear this there are things against it. For a start, refuse disposal does not come cheap, take my word, as I am myself an operative with Mid-Sussex works dept. which helps with the cost of adventure holidays but you have to save up. I do not know the going rate in Katmandu and round there, but you would not believe what you find in Mid-Sussex bins even at sea level, let alone 20,000 feet on the South Col. I have had bunk-beds and dead tortoises.

Our party did not get that far owing to an avalanche, a terrible experience as the torrent came roaring down the ravine, not just cans and bags either, but empty oxygen cylinders and remains of southern fried chicken, family bucket size, and you name it. This was mostly from a group ahead of us from US Himalayan Tours Inc. One of our party, Mr Chatty from West Drayton, got the full force of a chemical toilet on the back of the head, and was covered. Not by his travel insurance though, owing to an exclusion clause for such an occurrence.

Other difficulties are that refuse disposal Sherpas will not be keen on the work. It is not like throwing everything into the truck for grinding like Haywards Heath, only a few stops from the residence and just drive off for dumping. Sherpa Tenzing got the George Medal, something to aim at, and not so much as a discarded barbecue kit or fused electric tent to hump down by hand. I do not see your refuse-Sherpa gaining an honour like that, as the usual stigma, which I personally vouch for, will attach to him. Also unconsumed portions of oven-ready pizza and the stuffing from split thermawear. Never mind he has a sack of apple cores and french letters strapped on his back, which I would not mention the latter except where Ms McLoughlin says about VD spreading from the tourist boom, and antibiotics no good above 10,000 feet.

To be honest I have not seen this ailment being risked at those heights myself, but these days it is the permissive society and take your fun where you find it I daresay, if in a mixed party and the modern heated tent with magnetic flap seal. It is all a part of spoiling the mountains, and a far cry from Sir John (later Lord) Hunt's 1953 ascent, or it never got into the coronation year papers that I noticed.

Lastly the dumping. It is all very well passing a rule to bring your rubbish down but it has to go somewhere. It is different at home, when ready pulped and ground-up for tidy handling and later landscaped with grass and sheep. It is going to come down from Everest in shapes hard to handle. I am not only thinking of the Nepal residents, who number 13,000,000 in a small area and will not wish to walk to work over a lot of lumps as caused by disposable fridges or Californian wine jerry-cans. What of the hard going in the foothills for us tourists? By the time we have picked our way to the base camp are we not going to be exhausted, with loss of interest in the actual summit? Should that be cloud-capped, as usually mentioned in the brochures though you cannot always rely on them, there is not much to be got in the way of home movies but the view below, and I can see our neighbours, Ted and Doris Hooper, saying when asked in later, "Why all the shots of the scrap-yard?"

It is true there is a chance of snow falling and hiding it. And not only it, actually. Ask Mrs Corridge. When snow falls low down it does the same high up. Last year she stuck her piton into the north face, as she thought, and it turned out to be a hidden crate of boneless rabbit left behind by People's Tours of Peking. But for a lucky chance of catching her ankle between two battery-expired walkie-talkies in a crack just underneath, she would have gone straight down with a shower of rabbits into Tibet.

Sir, I largely blame a thing like that, which could have ruined her holiday, on all the clever-dick science that has to go up mountains with people nowadays. Mallory and Co. didn't have to hump up pneumatic ice-drills and automatic goggle-defrosters and gritting vehicles, etc. If they had, they might have come down again, I won't deny. But all that junk would have stayed up, instead of just a couple of boots and a few cardigan buttons. The way things have gone since, you couldn't perch on the summit for cast-off communications systems, and what I'm saying to Ms McLoughlin and others looking to get away from it all at 29,028 feet is that they could be disappointed.

There won't only be rubbish up top, parties up there saying stuff your local litter laws, but all around and down below.

Ten rupees on the rates for scooping in foreign garbage isn't going to go all that big with the Nepalese. They could turn awkward and ask why. And no good trying to fob them off with the answer, "Because it's there." It never did cut a lot of ice.

Yours,
Mr and Mrs M. Corridge
(Poste restante, Torremolinos again this year)

"Hey! I've just come up with a new idea for a football game."

"Part of our trouble was that she was AD and I was BC."

at's the matter with us? We don't pace up and down any more."

"Shall we have one for the wooden hills to Bedfordshire, Miss Brownlow?"

". . . and she said, 'Why don't you do wacka do wacka do?' So I did wacka did wacka did and she says, 'You call that doing wacka doing wacka doing?' "

"I'd like someone who will feel guilty for the rest of her life after I kill myself when she rejects me."

The superb new edition of Samuel Pepys's diary, edited by Robert Latham, will be completed this month with the index and a companion volume containing biographies, maps, genealogical trees "and much arcane and entertaining information" about Pepys's life and times. The only thing now missing will be the diary he kept in the year before this eleven-volume edition starts, before he had quite got the hang of it . . .

Keith Waterhouse

The "WHITE HALL" POCKET DIARY

Anno Domini. 1659.

PERSONAL MEMORANDA

NAME: *Sam'l Pepys, gentleman*
ADDRESS: *Axe Yard (house with blacke door, next to house with greene door)*
BUSINESS ADDRESS: *Navy Office; or if there should be no answer, try The Fleece Taverne opposite*
NATIONAL PLAGUE INSURANCE No: *147*
BANK *(Current Account): Tin box under bed*
do *(Deposit* do *): Leaden box in garden*
BREECHES SIZE: *2* ft *10* in *circumnavigateth my waist: whilst within my legge measureth 2* ft *3* in
HOSE SIZE: *Mediumme*
SHOE BUCKLES: *Silver*
PERRIWIGG SIZE: *8¾*
NECK-RAG SIZE: *a yarde of linning wound thrice around my throat*
COATE SIZE: *Like to that of my white silk coate with the gold buttons*
HEIGHT: *A hand's taller than* My Lord Fairfax, *yet two hands shorter than* My Lord Brouncker

For Official use—must be completed
NOOSE SIZE: *Small 12*
HEIGHT WHEN STRETCHED: *8* ft *6* in *(approxxe)*
CIRCUMFERENCE OF THUMB: *Averrage*
NEAREST PILLORY: *Cheapside*
NEAREST HANGMAN: *Mr Jevons, Gibbet Yard. Deputy: Mr Rington, Traitor's Gate. (If out, messages may be left in mouth of traitor's head)*

EMERGENCIES

(In case of rogues, vagabonds, footpads, fire, or persons speaking treason against the King's Majestie, cry "Watch Ho!")
LEECH GROUP: *Possitive*
BLOOD-LETTYNG CLINIQUE: *St Bartholomew's-by-the-Minories (out-pacients' entrance)*
DOCTOR: *Dr Murch, in Cow Lane, above the butcher's*
SURGEON: *Mr Snyke, in Cow Lane, below Dr Murch's*
POX DOCTOR: *Man with no nose who sitteth in the Common Ale House*
BOIL LANCER: *Mistress Sprockett, needlewoman to* My Lady Fairchild, *will do it for 1s*
CLEAN WOMAN TO LIE WITH: do
MIDWYFE: *Mistress Pratt, to be found in Bull Head Taverne (look under table)*
HOT POULTICE SUPPLIER: ***(Day)*** *Mrs Cox, the laundry-woman.* ***(Night)*** *Oakes, pudding-boiler, Pasty Lane*
RATTE CATCHER: *Any mean person in Slaughterhouse Alley will do it for 1*d
MAD DOGGE REMOVER: *Man who frotheth at the mouth under cellar grating of Common Ale House*

In case of accident please inform:
His Majestie the King
My Lords of the Admiralty
Mrs Pepys

SAM'L PEPYS HIS DIARY

JAN 1: *Gotte up. Ate good breakfast. Supped with friends. And so to bed.*
JAN 2: *Gotte up. Ate good breakfast. Supped with friends. And so to bed.*
JAN 3: do
JAN 4: do
JAN 8: *Rayned*
JAN 13: *Will Grant, naybour,* mort
JAN 30: *Dentyste, 4.0 o'c*
FEB 6: *Heard good tayle about* ——— *Esq*
FEB 13: *Sleete*
FEB 21: Chris. Wren Esq. *to dinner to discuss architeck-ture, 6.0 o'c*
MAR 7: *Geo Spragg, counterfeiter,* mort *(by the neck)*
MAR 21: *Bootemaker, 10.30 o'c*
JUN 4: *To White Hall. Saw* My Lord ———
AUG 9: *Hols*
SEP 18: *Perriwigg fittyng, 3.45 o'c*
OCT 1: *Book Play House tickets*
NOV 12: John Evelyn Esq *to discuss affairs, 6.0 o'c*
NOV 13: *Y'day heard rumoure about The King. Could scarcely credit it.*
DEC 8: *Buy new diary (bigger one!)*

ADDREFFES

(A complete list of charnell houses, mad-houses, churches (asterisk indicates has leper-squint), prisons, whypping posts, gibbets, gallowes, pillories, pye-shops, tavernes and approved lazar hospitalles may be found in the "WHITE HALL" Executive Counting House Diary, to be had at Stationers' Hall, price 1*l*)
KING CHARLES *(Taverne)—next to Bull Head*
KING CHARLES II *(King)—nobody knoweth, or if he knoweth, will not sayeth*
BULL HEAD TAVERNE—*next to New Swanne*
MISTRESS QUICKLEY—*next the Coffee House*
COFFEE HOUSE—*next to Mistress Quickley's*
GRAVEDIGGER—*Mr Spagge, Churchyard*
GRAVEDIGGER (WHOLESALE)—*man with wart on nose, back of Churchyard*

NEW SWANNE TAVERNE—*on site of Old Swanne Taverne*
PLAY HOUSE TICKETS—*man with no legges who lyeth in Play House Yard*
ST BARNABAS WITHOUT THE WALL—*just outside city wall*
ST BARNABAS WITHIN THE WALL—*just inside city wall*
PROCURER OF SILK & CALICO, WITHOUT PAYING DUTY—*man restless with St Vitus's Dance, behind Blue Boar Inne (if hang'd, man restless with St Anthony's Fire, behind Saracen's Head)*
BLUE BOAR INNE—*next to Saracen's Head*
SARACEN'S HEAD INNE—*next to Blue Boar*
PRESS-GANG AGENT—*man with squint, who waiteth outside Office*
COCKE FIGHT TICKETS—*man with humppe-back in doorway of Pastrycooke's*
PASTRYCOOKE'S—*Pudding Lane*

NOTES

Publick Transport

Buses: *To Greenwich*—first tide
second tide
From Greenwich—second tide
first tide
Buses: *To White Hall—Regular service: go down to river & shout "Waterman Ho!"*
Sedan chairs: *Ranks outside most tavernes*

Postal Rates

Any Boy will deliver a letter for a custard apple, or on payne of a blowe. Outside the city wall, any mean person will take it for a farthing, or on payne of a kicke.

Watchman timetable

(correct at time of publication)
1 o'c, 2 o'c, 3 o'c, 4 o'c, 5 o'c, 6 o'c, 7 o'c, 8 o'c, 9 o'c, 10 o'c, 11 o'c, Noone, 1 o'c, 2 o'c, 3 o'c, 4 o'c, 5 o'c, 6 o'c, 7 o'c, 8 o'c, 9 o'c, 10 o'c, 11 o'c, Midnyte

Night-cart Pick-up

11.15 by the church clocke, except Lord's Days & publick holydays. (Emergency night-cart: contact man who giveth off a great stinke, under the sign of the clothes-peg outside the city wall)

1660 A.D. FORWARD PLANNER

Jan–Mar

Learn shorthand
Learn spellynge
Start keeping diary

Apr–Jun

Renew touch for the King's Evil
If weather be dry, buy fire extinguisher

Jul–Sep

Renew Tyburn Tree season ticket from man with one eye who lyeth under straw in Gibbet Yarde

Oct–Dec

Have perriwigg de-loused

*Order your **"WHITE HALL"** or **"RESTORATION"** diary for 1660 now.
NB: The **"CROMWELL"** and **"ROUNDHEAD"** series of diaries have now been withdrawn

"I built a better mousetrap, and the only result was that it enabled me to trap better mice."

"Nearly finished. It's just a question of dotting the birds and crossing the fish."

Through a Glass Deeply

Let me hail a Conservative Member of Parliament as the consumer's friend: Sir David Price has been asking the Government for an order under the 1963 Weights and Measures Act (which he was instrumental, as Parliamentary Secretary, Board of Trade, in getting on to the statute-book) to standardise a measure for wine by the glass in pubs, wine bars and the like.

At present, the law lays down what constitutes a gin or a Scotch (less in England than in Scotland) or a beer: inspectors from the Standards Department of the Department of Trade, or perhaps from local authorities, carry out spot checks, and those found serving short measure are liable to prosecution.

There is no such standard for wine—Sir David thinks that it was not included in the Act because wine bars and wine by the glass in pubs were virtually unknown twenty years ago.

Now, it matters to many of us, and the *Which? Wine Guide* did well in the introduction to its chapter on wine bars to ask "Why is there no standard quantity for wine just as there is for beer and spirits?" citing "a glass of wine which could be priced at anywhere between 55p and £1.10 a glass and contain anything from 80ml to 200ml of wine." The answer, though, to its further question, "Why don't more wine bars do the decent thing and clearly indicate to their customers both the capacity and price of their wines by the glass?" is that the law being, as we know, "a ass—a idiot", does not permit. As the guide points out in reference to "the-wine-by-the-glass fiddle . . . the Government is as much to blame as the wine bar owner."

More: I understand that, strictly speaking, no one may advertise a measure not specified by law *and* capable of being checked by the tables and measuring instruments carried around by inspectors. So, although Stowells of Chelsea, pioneers in providing pubs with wine to be served by the glass in decent condition, are introducing two hundred thousand 12.5cl glasses into seven thousand Whitbreads' pubs, no one is allowed to tell you what they are: the law recognises (though it does not authorise) only glasses of 10cl (too small) and 20cl (too big) capacity.

Success may be in sight, but certainly not just around the corner. Sir David will plug away, Whitbreads (of which Stowells is the wine division) are having friendly talks with other big breweries, with the Ravenhead glass-making firm, and with LACOTS—the Local Authorities Committee on Trading Standards—and it may be that a voluntary code of practice could lead to an order under the Act.

Why 12.5cl rather than ten? Most pubs buy their wine-by-the-glass wines in containers of a litre or multiples of a litre: 12.5cl is an eighth, 25cl a quarter, of a litre—ten is too small, and twenty more than some drinkers want at a time. Fractions of a litre are a more consistent measure than the frequent though not legally recognised one of "six-out"—six glasses out of an ordinary bottle, which itself may be 70cl, 72cl or 75cl. No one is likely to give you six out of a litre bottle.

My own hope, obviously shared by many, is that eventually one will be able to call for a measure or a double in the same way that in a German *weinstube* or an Austrian *heurigen* one calls for an *achtel* or a *viertel*, which is to say an eighth or a quarter—of a litre, understood—or, in other words, the 12.5 glass, or twice as much, this usually served in those parts in a small carafe with a glass alongside.

When that comes to pass I shall raise the contents of a *viertel* at least to a Conservative Member of Parliament and a big firm of brewers—unlikely objects though such may seem of any oblations of mine.

"Harold and Spot were inseparable, Inspector."

Alan Coren

Blood Money

. . . so, quite obviously, Her Majesty's best bet is to sue the estate of John Nash, especially as she is most unlikely to get anything from the estate of George IV; having already, as it were, had it.

But I digress. Readers will quite properly want to know what all this has to do with poor James Brady, gunned down last year by the lovesick loony John Hinckley in the course of his unfathomable attempt to get Jodie Foster into bed. Well, it's like this: during the spraying of the presidential party, White House press secretary Brady, you will recall, stopped a bullet in the head, the tragic result of which was to leave him, fifteen months later, still partially paralysed. Where it left John Hinckley was in an elegant rubber room, snipping snaps of Jodie from the movie magazines until such time as the shrinks deem him to be ready to re-emerge into society and start plugging people again. For that was the verdict of the court, viz. when John Hinckley opened up on President Reagan and his friends, John Hinckley was as crazy as a coot, since only anybody as crazy as a coot would wish to open up on President Reagan and his friends. Juridically speaking, it was a tighter little number than Catch-22, and must have had Mr Hinckley laughing all the way to Nut City, particularly since his head is legally entitled to annual reinspection; he could thus, by this time next year, be a free man again, it being no more difficult to convince the average psychiatrist that you are sane than it is to convince him you are crazy.

Naturally enough, apart from enraging all sane Americans, this monstrous verdict also somewhat enraged James Brady. He has therefore had to seek alternative redress, and he has sought it in not only a novel way, but also a way which may serve as an extraordinary precedent, a veritable watershed in the history of crime. It could touch upon the home life both of our own dear Queen, and of our own dear selves. For Mr Brady has just announced that he is suing, for ONE HUNDRED MILLION DOLLARS, the manufacturers of the gun with which John Hinckley shot him, on the fascinating grounds that the RG-14 .22 pistol was produced and distributed so cheaply that it was just asking to fall into the hands of the sort of people who think that a good way of impressing Jodie Foster is by doing a St Valentine's Day number on the Administration.

As a juridical argument, it is even neater than Hinckley's.

And, far more important, the move chimes perfectly with what you and I have been gradually coming to feel, have we not, over the past few years: that the only law worth either regarding or pursuing is civil law, the respect for and administration of criminal law having long fallen into what I believe jurists would call desuetude. Demotically expressed, the argument runs thus: they never catch the buggers; all right, they occasionally catch the buggers, but then they let them go, due to where all coppers are bent as a bloody hairpin; all right, there is one straight copper in a hundred, so one villain in a hundred gets to court, but they immediately let him off, due to where (a) all juries are naff, and (b) his mum stands up and says he was always good to his gerbil; all right, one villain in a hundred who gets to court is sent down, but he is generally over the wall in ten minutes flat.

Furthermore, it is a truth universally acknowledged, that a lawyer in pursuit of a good fortune would be out of his wig in going for the criminal bar. The criminal bar is thus full to the gunwales with jurisprudential dross whose closing arguments, if they haven't left them on the bus, can generally be outflanked by the average illiterate caught, by chance, walking past Vine Street nick at midnight with Constable's *Hay Wain* on his shoulder.

None of these remarks, it should be said, are intended as a criticism of Mr William Whitelaw. Many of us, I know, heard his speech at the recent celebration dinner for the BBC's diamond jubilee when he revealed that he was a lifelong friend of Brian Johnson, and if any of us felt that the wrong one had become Home Secretary, this is not the place to raise the issue.

I should rather remove the *mise en scène* to Cricklewood. It was there, by what would be mere coincidence were it not for the escalating crime figures, that on the very night—and at almost the very hour—that Mr

"They were a far better mixed doubles team when they were only living together."

"That's right. We've moved Mr Robinson from the intensive care unit to the insensitive no-one-gives-a-damn unit!"

Michael Fagan was perching himself on the end of the Sovereign's bed and asking whether a fag would be out of the question, it was there that I myself was woken by an untoward nocturnal clunk. I sprang from cot to curtain, peered out, and saw that two men were sitting in my car in the street outside, and working away by torchlight. I ran downstairs and threw open the front door, but as I did so the two men dropped what they were doing, hurtled themselves into a battered Mini, and shot off lightlessly into the night, too fast for me to get their number.

What they were doing, it transpired, was my radio, an item which you may be interested to learn may be radically unimproved by dropping. But they also, as they fled, dropped their torch. The next day, I reported the incident, and was told that an officer would call to take the details and collect the torch.

Five days later, he did. He was extremely neat, scrupulously heterosexual, and did not ask me for folding money to forget the whole thing, so I felt it would have been cavalier to have pointed out that five days was more than enough to date my fairly detailed descriptions of the thieves, since by then they could well have grown beards, learned Spanish, and have converted their Mini into two gross of saucepans.

I did, however, have the torch. We both looked at it. He shook his head. We then had an engaging forensic conversation during which I discovered that the only way to get a decent fingerprint was to get a finger.

Clearly, there is no chance of apprehending the villains. Had they shot me, I was given to understand, greater pains would have been taken, since the forecourt of the police station was thick with weeds and a couple of blokes on twelve hours community service were not to be sneezed at. As it was, my best shot was to claim against my insurance, and forget all about it. Except when it came to paying next year's premium and its lost no-claims bonus.

I thus found myself, possibly for the first time, in the same leaky boat as my liege lady: both subject to the villain's whim, both subject to the law's delays, and both stuck without redress, since Mr Michael Fagan (né Hess) had apparently committed nothing criminal on the night in question, and would therefore go uncollared. Leaving both Her Majesty and her loyal Cricklewood subject to run around shrieking and kicking the furniture. (It is my view, by the by, that the Royal tooth which immediately thereafter needed medical attention was not wisdom, but gnashed.)

Now, however, suddenly and wonderfully, Press Secretary Brady has changed all that, for all three of us. *He* is suing the manufacturers of the RG-14 for making a shooter of which loonies can take advantage, *I* am suing Sony for making a radio you can unscrew in the small hours and drop on the pavement, and *she*, as soon as she reads this, will, I have not the slightest doubt, be suing the estate of the late architect John Nash for building George IV a palace with windows you can open after the police have gone to sleep.

It is all very encouraging. As an alternative to the impossibility of penalising crime, putting it into the framework of a free market economy has often seemed to me to be eminently sensible. It is what Thatcherism is all about. Indeed, should the principle which Mr Brady has just enshrined take root and flourish on this side of the Atlantic, I can see no reason why our great Home Secretary should not emerge from his present little local difficulties not only with his wonderful reputation still unblemished but with his future yet rosier than before.

He usually does.

"She was mugged on New Year's Eve!"

Maternity Wear

I write from the front, in the final beleaguered days. Gigantic jeans fray dangerously towards destruction, summer-weight smocks are artfully insulated now with layers of drum-tight T-shirt, huge snaggled yachting sweaters fall prettily to the swollen knee. The cautious primagravida avoids going out in the rain, owing to Burberry no longer meeting in front; increasingly sinister mail order underwear arrives by every post, laced and zipped for the artful, sudden exposure of the vital teat.

The medical profession holds its collective breath, praying for a natural conclusion before the worst happens, a dozen stressed safety-pins whine across the clinic like shrapnel, and the mother-to-be is driven back into the specialist care of the Maternity Shops for another week's-worth of emergency drapery. But no; even then, holding out desperately against the change of seasons and the final spurt of growth, I shall merely adopt a Navajo blanket and an indoor life. I have Had Enough.

You would have thought that in the year of the Pregnant Princess, with icky Sloane radiance spilling into a great national coo between January and June, the mothertat empires would have squared their shoulders and faced up to the simple challenge of draping the gravid population with some wit and style at last. Not so. The summer beams filtering between the racks revealed the mixture as before. Fearful, mumsy, sprigged creations in viscosette with Touches of Detail at the Neck and a great sagging balloon below; misty floral creations nipped at the bodice with cruel pintucks and enhanced with prissy acetate-lace collars to Draw The Eye; indeterminate smocked garments drooping to the advancing navel. Triumphant among this rubbish is the Great British Maternity Trouser. It sports a weird, enormous elastic panel right across the front to ensure that if ever the disguising smock balloons upwards in a summer breeze, any impressionable unmarried man in sighting distance will have his sexual nerve and sanity permanently damaged by the sight of a huge stretched balloon, like part of a diseased tropical fish, emerging from an otherwise unremarkable denim infrastructure.

In America—where pregnancy is considered to be merely another profitable Life Experience and source of consumer sales—jeans are designed to expand via two neatly concealed elastic sides, rather than in one disconcerting bulge. Suggest this modification to a British sales assistant, and she will merely shrug and turn away embarrassed. She is seventeen, weighs six stone, and finds babies pretty disgusting anyway.

For the curious thing about the world of British High Street maternity wear is the sheer weight of disapproval and embarrassment surrounding its purchase and design. Almost no attempt is made to foster the natural spendthrift glow of the still-working but expanding punter. It is not so elsewhere; in America they trilled, "Have a great li'l baby, now," while flogging me a fifteen-dollar T-shirt in jolly deckchair stripes; no suggestion was implicit either in their manner or in its design that I would be more appropriately placed in a large hessian sack somewhere out of sight. In France, at *Prémaman,* cooing salesgirls coaxed the price of a corduroy tent out of me with admiring cries of congratulation and envy. Feigned, no doubt, but soothing nonetheless.

Back in good old Oxford Street, the atmosphere is dourly Presbyterian, the innuendo unmistakable. No, we don't do them dungarees in any other sizes. *Ought to be ashamed, wearing trousers in your state.* No, all our swimsuits have the floating gauze panels down the front. *Flaunt it, would you? Ugh.* No, Madam, we only do the nighties in the pink flowers or the blue polka-dot. *Look, now you are up the spout, frankly, you can damn well learn to be a bit feminine and dainty for a change. Look at Princess Di, aaaahh—*

Yes, well, look at Princess Di. Those in that income bracket may roam well beyond the High Street and the department stores, to giggly boutiques called Great Expectations and Madonna Mia and Two's A Crowd; where for a mere trebling of the price they may buy—mumsy, sprigged creations in pure silk, with Touches of Detail At The Neck, pintucks, and genuine Nottingham-lace collars. *Plus ça change.* Some designers cut better cloth, some worse; but all assume a birds-and-bees broodiness that sits uneasy on the liberated 1980s scruff.

Only a few mail order firms, struggling on alone in Posy Simmonds country, manage to produce jolly tie-side shirts and sassy dungarees; and even in their catalogues it is necessary to wade through acres of frilly verbiage: *smothered in lace to look as pretty as a princess . . . softly tucked bodice for more feminine nursing . . . artful tie belt for those not-quite-back-to-normal-days later . . .*

Mind you, maternity shops do have two conflicting duties to perform. Before dissimulation becomes entirely useless, there comes a long, odd phase when you need one set of clothes in which to look *more* pregnant, one set in which to look less so. The first set—worn with profit from the third month onwards—are thin, ostentatiously triangular dresses of base design, clinging horribly to the rising bump. Worn with a piteously outthrust frontage and a craftily panic-inducing huff in the breath, they will secure you seats on trains, immunity from washing-up, and the sort of VIP treatment on British Airways normally only accorded to unexploded bombs.

The second set are sober, flaring, plainish garments, designed to lull timorous employers and bachelor bishops into forgetting for minutes at a time that they are actually addressing that perilous creature, a Fertile Woman. Such deceit has been known to continue until full term, with an artfully draped mac over the arm soothing even gay Lord Lieutenants into a false sense of security.

Clothes of both types are available, with patient hunting. A few specialist tastes are not catered for at all, yet, and I point in this time of economic revival to two notable gaps in the rag market. The gravid yachtswoman, I can assert from private knowledge, can find not one solitary maternity oilskin, nor a pair of jeans with a respectable knife-pocket; and at the other end of the spectrum of heartiness I have a complaint from my most groovy gestating friend. Eyelids a-spangle and rhinestone boots clicking, she moans after five months that there is absolutely nowhere, man, to buy maternity roller-disco gear. How the hell are we supposed to bring the new generation into being with such a lack of encouragement? Strike now, sisters.

"Mr Pangbourne? I'm from the Fraud Squad."

FITZCARRALDO KLAUS KINSKI *as Brian Sweeney Fitzgerald called Fitzcarraldo*

ffolkes/CINEMA

GANDHI BEN KINGSLEY *as Mahatma Gandhi*

THE DRAUGHTSMAN'S CONTRACT ANTHONY HIGGINS *as Mr Neville*

STILL OF THE NIGHT MERYL STREEP *as Brooke Reynolds* ROY SCHEIDER *as Dr Sam Rice*

WHO'S YOUR BIRD?

"We're getting to know each other bit by bit . . ."

"I'd like us to be friends—for the sake of your Mother."

*"I've **said** I like it—I really do—it's a very good play . . ."*

"I'm leaving her all my internal organs in my will."

An American animal behaviourist claims that a whooping crane from his local zoo has fallen in love with him

"Individually, termites aren't very demonstrative—but they're capable of staging a fantastic ticker-tape welcome!"

"Pretty boy! Pretty boy! I suppose that's all I am to you! Oh, my God, I wish I'd never been born . . ."

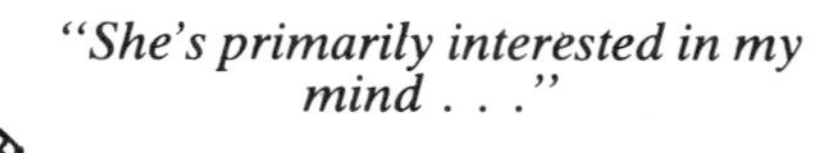

"She's primarily interested in my mind . . ."

"He has come to know me because I tip so generously."

"You're late."

> To avoid offending French visitors to Brighton this year, the organisers of a Regency Pageant which includes a mock Battle of Waterloo have agreed to let the French win on one day.
>
> *Daily Telegraph*

How They Brought the Good News from Ghent to Hove

I sprang to the Volvo, and Joris, and he;
I revved up, Dirck revved up, we revved up all three!
For as Snap, Dirck & Joris, our firm is the fount
Of all public relations: the Brighton account
Is just one of a hundred we hold in our fee!
(And our fee, since you ask, is as major as we.)

'Twas moonset at starting; but while we drew near
To Ostend, the cocks crew and the morning dawned clear;
So we shot on the ferry and shot from our cars,
And shot up aloft to the duty-free bars!
I ordered, Dirck ordered, we ordered all three,
And we toasted our fortune in cheap G and T!

"If we're marketing Waterloo," Dirck offered first,
As the seventeenth glass took the edge off our thirst,
"Something tells me I probably speak for the rest
When I say that, quite frankly, I wasn't impressed.
Just a long streak of mud and a rather small hill—
Son-et-lumière-wise, not exactly a thrill."

"I can't see," I put in, "why they made such a fuss
For an acre of dirt. Well, it's no use to us,
Or to Brighton. We'll have to re-jig things a bit;
I'm afraid Boney's plans must be tailored to fit
What we're selling. Supposing he blows up the pier,
Then burns down the Pavilion?" I waited to hear.

"As *I* understand it," said Joris, "the war
To our target-consumer's one long bloody bore—
No leg-over interest, no music, no shocks,
No household names people have seen on the box,
No free gifts, no prizes: not ONE tourist draw!
They'd rather play bingo or watch *Rocky IV*."

"What we do then," I said, "is we alter the script.
We arrange it so's Wellington's army is pipped
At the post." "By the French?" "Or the Japs, or the Swedes,"
I replied, "or the Yanks. We shall tailor the needs
Of the show to the crowd on the day. It'll *work*!"
"I like it!" cried Joris. "I dig it!" cried Dirck.

"Better yet," I went on, "leave the issue in doubt!
If nobody knows how the war will come out
They can bet on the game: Boney 14-to-1,
Even-money the British—we'll rope in *The Sun*:
Nationwide *Waterloo*, entry forms come through the door!"
"Fantastic!" shrieked Joris. But Dirck murmured: "More."

We looked at him. "What really pulls them is girls.
Such as—I don't know—Josephine, big tits and curls,
Or the Duchess of Wellington, stripped, on her horse,
In a pair of his waders. You know, nothing coarse."
"Guest appearances!" Joris yelled, "New one each day!
Larry Grayson as Blücher, Joan Collins as Ney!"

Thus we pulled into Dover, and drove down the coast
To our clients in Brighton. Forgive, if I boast:
There was just *one* amendment that had to be made!
They'd discovered that Sussex's main tourist trade
Stems from Germany. So, in this summer's affray,
It will have to be Rommel who carries the day.

Cold Turkey

OH BOY! CLIFF RICHARD BENNY GREEN

I suppose it does no good complaining about the Christmas schedules. There must be somebody somewhere out there who likes them, otherwise the diet would change, presumably. Every year it is the same, the old movies that were old the first time they showed them, the Sit. Coms with their clumsily-adapted plots to fit the season, the studio romps whose yuletide cheer was so carefully simulated when the deed was actually done, towards the end of November. And hanging over the whole business, the tacit assumption that because it is Christmas, then it somehow makes it okay to fling any old rubbish at people. It was the same in my musician days. Christmas was the time you fed them an unrelieved diet of slop and slapstick, because drink, food and sentimentality had reduced them to a condition when anything better than moronic would be sure to go over their tiny and much befuddled heads.

It must, for instance, have been a source of happiness to many that *The Wild Geese (ITV)* was available, especially for those who missed the picture on the previous eighty-six times it has been shown. *The Blue Max (ITV)* belongs in a different category, only having been shown before forty-three times. A third category brought in *Death on the Nile (BBC1), The Fall of the Roman Empire (BBC1), International Velvet (BBC1)*, and *The Muppet Movie (ITV)*, none of which should ever have been made in the first place, let alone shown. On balance, however, it was just possible over Christmas for the industry to justify itself. By industry, I mean, of course, Hollywood. Although watching pictures like *A Night at the Opera (Channel 4), Double Indemnity (Channel 4), Paper Moon (BBC2)*, and *Mutiny on the Bounty (BBC2)* on the small screen in a small room detracts mightily from the original experience—the first time I saw the Bounty epic there was a goldfish pond in the foyer—it was reassuring to know that not everything of genuine quality has been allowed to disappear from circulation. And in spite of the overbearing weight of critical opinion, I still found parts of *Caesar and Cleopatra (Channel 4)* genuinely moving.

For the rest it was a minefield, with the viewer delicately picking his way through acres of explosively idiotic junk to find the occasional rewarding enlightenment. The thespian marathon was won by Alec McCowen with his amazing exhibition of *St Mark's Gospel (Channel 4)*; the prize for the most rewarding day went to that battered veteran, December 30, which came up with *The Barretts of Wimpole Street (BBC1)* and a much-needed repeat of *A Voyage Round My Father (ITV)*, a play which perversely removed itself from my best programmes of the year an issue ago and is hereby restored to its rightful place among the outstanding drama productions of 1982. The most embarrassing show of the yuletide ordeal was probably one of those which I avoided, but of those which unhappily caught my eye, you couldn't get much more yuletidy than *David Frost Presents the Guinness Book of Records (ITV)*. The most facetious programme titles of the season were a BBC2 documentary on Iceland called *God's Frozen People*, and an amazing affair on Channel 4 called *Scotch Myths*, starring a singer who shall remain nameless, called Andy Stewart.

But the affair which illustrated more vividly than any other the extent to which aesthetic standards go out the Christmas window, was the occurrence on Channel Four two days after Christmas of *Fifties Evening*. Of much of the content of this package I had better say nothing, but of one section of it I am better qualified to discuss its merits than anyone else who either watches or makes television programmes. What ageing trendy, I wonder, decided to rerun an episode of **Oh Boy!**? What prematurely senile executive, remembering what he thinks was his swinging youth, thought it was a good idea? I have done some reprehensible things in my time, from playing for Irish traditional dancing in Cricklewood Broadway to working the Hokey Cokey six nights a week in a holiday camp somewhere in the South of England which should have been condemned around the time of the Boer War. I have connived at scurrilous music in corrupt nightclubs, and recorded tunes for musical directors who would have been better employed as used car salesmen. But I never did anything in my time more fundamentally absurd than work in the band for *Oh Boy!*.

For the benefit of any social historians in the audience, I had better make it clear that I was the saxophonist in the dark glasses. I had originally put them on because the studio lights at the then recently-converted Hackney Empire wearied my eyes. The intention was to wear them until the last minute and face the lights only on the actual transmission. Our producer, however, sensing that dark glasses might be an attractive symbol of degeneracy, advised me to keep them on throughout transmission, a ploy I was pleased to adopt in the hope that friends watching the show might not after all recognise me. Alas the gambit had the reverse effect. After a few weeks, when the mail started to come in, from the nine-and-ten-year-old intellectuals at whom the show was aimed, I found that I was getting more fan-mail than any other musician in the show. It was all addressed to *Blind Saxophonist*. Or rather, *The Blind Sacksafonist*. What is revealing about all this is that footling stuff like *Oh Boy!* still exists, while some of the greatest jazz artists in history have seen their work nonchalantly destroyed by the philistines in control of such affairs.

David Taylor

Billy Connolly

Uff—from here on in—ay'll no tray tae dew hus ac-cent, yon Bully . . . it's because, you know, it really gets up his nose, does all of that. He means all of that hoochin' and choochin' stuff is, you know, bad enough in any case. He had a bellyful of *Mairi's Wedding* as a lad as a matter of fact and, Jesus Chraist (sorry) but when journalists carry on as if Sir Harry Lauder was still stompin' and when they try to put across Billy in phonetic Glaswegian, aye and get it all up the spout besides, well it's a hopeless business, is that, and leaves him, Billy says, bereft for words. Matter of fact, he feels a bit, no, a lot put upon by the press, which is maybe to be expected when you live with Pamela Stephenson, but does not, you know, engender a whole lot of warmth between Billy and The Street.

See, the thing is, you get knackered by fame quite a bit. He means you can be a damn fine electrician, maybe, or, as Billy once was, a welder, aye and there's not many will get to appreciate your damn fine skills, but then no-one's going to be moochin' about your back door day and night and peekin' in to see if you're wearing your wellies or what. Time and again Billy has been doing his damnedest to stress to sort of all and sundry that he's no special, you know, he's an ordinary feller, and you'll not find hidden dark mysteries in Billy on account of the fact that, the last he heard, he has none. Say what you like about what he does on the stage, it's your privilege, no doubt about that. The minute he walks out the theatre, mind, he'd be obliged if the world would back off, if it's no too much to ask.

The pooting across the Scorts bit, that's only a part of it, you know. It's tempting, he appreciates that. Aye and there's a good piece of his material which would not work at all without it—*Operator: Is the money in the box? Glaswegian caller: Nae, nae, lass, I'm in here by mysel'.*

It's yon wretched Scots puns, indeed, that got him started, that and the fact there was never much softness or inhibition about the content of, you know, material.

His original technique was to crash on stage amidst deliberate confusion and launch into rollicking parody of Clydeside shipyard heavies after they've had a few jars. He worked up a devastating put-down of traditional Scots sentimentality and the kilt-swinging clichés of high roads, low roads and bonnie lassies. He stripped away the maudlin romanticism of the engaging Glaswegian drunk to whom the city belonged on a Saturday naight, and substituted the vulgar reality of the vomiting, blaspheming pain in the, aye, bum . . . have you ever stopped to think about yer bum. . .? It was a blockbustering stream of tart, black, offensive, political, abusive gags to banjo accompaniment, perfectly suited to the tastes of tough lads with a rough tongue and a permanent thirst, and, rather to Billy's surprise, it was an uproarious overnight sensation.

What used to happen, aye and still does, he maintains, is that these pictures would come into his head. He'd be up there, stompin' about, you know, and sort of radar-guided by what passed at the time for a script, and in would come bargin' some picture, some vivid recollection, maybe, or vision of what might be, and he could no resist passin' it on. The effect on the audience would be as if Billy was making up the act as he went along, which, now you mention that, he was. It'd be kind of seat of the pants stuff, you know, and so if he then had a picture of seats of pants, as it might be, well he'd slip in the off-the-cuff back-hander, cack-hander, didn't seem to matter much, provided it was expertly timed and preferably outrageously coarse.

See, he's never been that sensitive a lad. He doesn't think that you are when you're brought up in Drumchapel and Partick, sort of a desert wi' windows, where you could catch your death twice a day in the outside privy, and where Billy lived with his father and his father's sisters after his mam departed. His first job was in a bookshop, till they sacked him for nicking the books, which, he'll state now for the record, he did not. He did a turn on the bread vans, then set about building ships along with the rest of the lads, and has seen one of his best welds go down the other day in the South Atlantic.

He was not the only character in the yards, please understand, the whole lot o' them were a wayward bunch, even sober. It'd be here that the recollected pictures maybe started, of the boss who'd be so outraged at the backslidin' going on about him and, standing on his dignity, demand: "D'ye not know who I am?" so that the lads, for a gewd laugh, could answer: "By Christ, Jimmy, there's a feller here so pissed that he disnae ken who he is. . ."

Further pictures surface at the mention of his short turn with the Paras, and, as you might suppose by now, they tend to be pictures of the state of his seat-of-the-pants when he made his first jump. The tales, told first only to mates, went down well at the Pavilion, as he'd imagined they might, but subsequently had them splitting their pants in, well, Torquay, or the Far East, Australia, never mind the Smoke, which he found pretty difficult to credit.

Records such as *Cop Yer Whack Fer This* outsold even the Beatles in Scotland. Videotapes, with such crisp titles as *Billy Connolly Bites Yer Bum,* went in their hundreds of thousands. Audiences turned up expecting to be shocked and were never disappointed as the act took in such as a Glaswegian crucifixion or raw pictures of a post-nuclear-war world, deeply shocking to all except maybe those from the duff end of Partick who might not notice any difference. As ever, Billy insists, the trick was to know where to draw the invisible line, but to keep on nudging it back and back, depending on the warmth, rapport, leglessness from the audience.

Paradoxically, he claims it gets up his nose again, you know, when people are rude. The other day, there was a stewardess spilt coffee all down a Rolling Stones suit he'd nicked from America, satin job, one he was well proud of, and not a damn word of apology. So when the girl comes back later with lunch, Billy asks to have the soup on his right leg, maybe potatoes all over his shoe, and please to pour the gravy down his neck. Do you know, it took what seemed like minutes for the penny to drop, but he did get a sorry in the end.

Thing is, he'll take whatever as it comes, do you see? Like when he just got asked to play straight West End theatre, doing Donleavy, thought so hell and why not. It pisses him off right enough if the critics don't endorse it, but blast and dammit he does not feel beholden to Scotland, nor to the wellies and bums. He'll do as he damn fine pleases, he says, and be glad for as long as it pleases others, too. So if not, well then you know what you can do.

ALL YOU NEVER KNEW ABOUT CHRISTMAS

garnered by E. S. TURNER

The inventor of snow-capped capital letters for use at Christmas was a Palatinate monk called Theodosius Pratte, who introduced them in an illuminated Bible during the exceptionally cold winter of 1490. His superiors were much displeased, taking exception in particular to his Ts hung with icicles, so Pratte resigned from Holy Orders and spent the rest of his life trying to interest publishers in his invention. Posthumous fame came in 1625 with the Christmas issue of *Mercurius Politicus*. Soon afterwards the writers of fiery Puritan tracts perverted the idea and loaded their capitals with blood, guts and ordure.

In 1851 *The Lancet* used snow-capped letters and opposition was virtually at an end, though Ruskin died cursing the idea as one of "pitifullest imbecility" and Karl Marx was deeply unhappy about their use in Christmas gift editions of *Das Kapital*. They have now appeared in such disparate organs as *Tiger Tim's Weekly*, *The Methodist Recorder*, the *New Statesman* and *Spare Rib*. A fully illustrated definitive history of snow-capped letters will be published by Gyles Brandreth next year and discussed on all channels by Frank Delaney.

Christmas is the busiest time of year for the Vampire Information Exchange, of New York, when demands for blood-based recipes are at their height.

On Christmas Eve 1914 Margot Asquith told her husband, the Prime Minister, that if he was going to spend all Christmas Day writing to his fancy woman, Venetia Stanley, every two hours on the hour, he needn't bother leaving his letters on the hall table for her to post, as was his custom, but could get off his fat bottom and post them himself; adding that it was time he put a bit more effort into the war and that for all he knew and cared the British and Germans might be preparing to play football against each other in no-man's-land.

It was the custom for Victorian philanthropists to visit the local workhouse on Christmas Day. The legend that they were told by the paupers what to do with their Christmas puddings is a graceless invention, perpetuated by music-hall comedians. Their response was invariably "Lor' bless 'ee kindly, good masters," after which they applauded magic lantern shows featuring mission work in the Maldive Islands.

The Press Council in 1965 upheld a complaint against the *Glastonbury Evening Echo* which revealed the identity of Father Christmas in its Children's Corner, an act described by the Council as "the sort of thing that gives investigative journalism a bad name".

Christmas was little loved by the Bloomsbury Group, in whom it produced nausea and the vapours, followed by such spiritual revulsion as could only be alleviated by an immediate "all change" of partners. Virginia Woolf's first onset of instability was caused, not by a refugee Belgian count spitting in the shared bath on the landing, but by a rumour that Carrington had designed Christmas cards for a firm called Merrythought (it was, of course, Lytton Strachey who had contributed cracker mottoes to the firm). At Garsington Manor in 1917 Strachey shot fat Christmas robins with "Bertie" Russell's Daisy air-gun, while Lady Ottoline Morrell guarded her peacocks night and day from a posse of conscientious objectors who thought they were turkeys.

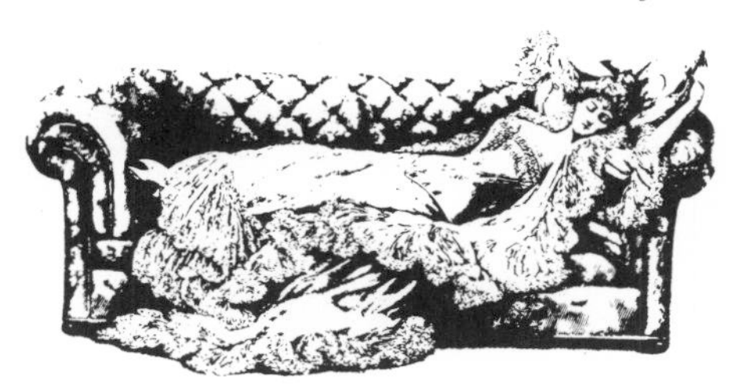

Many eminent Victorians became addicts of chloroform, self-administered in an attempt to cope with Christmas. Chloroform was freely obtainable from chemists for killing butterflies and seducing housemaids.

On Christmas Day many aristocratic parents would allow their children to be presented to them as often as twice. The Dukes of Marlborough kept the visits short; the fifth Duke's petulant "Blandford, be gone, you have delighted us enough" owed much to Jane Austen. One Christmas Eve the Iron Duke's first-born begged to be called Arthur instead of Douro ("Dad, I am not a Spanish river") but was told that Christmas was no time for licence.

The acreage of forest destroyed annually in Britain to provide Christmas trees would produce 40 issues of the *News of the World*, a statistic which is worrying ecologists.

The first zinc bucket to have been advertised as a "Useful Christmas Gift" was exhibited by Ephraim Black, a progressive Bradford ironmonger, in 1830.

The following Christmas saw the introduction by Briggs of Ilfracombe (the Gucci of those days) of the Immarcescible Real Morocco Patent Sermon Carrier. Not until Christmas 1896 did Briggs produce his Patent Carrier for the Bible in Pitman's Shorthand, which filled thousands of stockings that year.

Appeals by the Postmaster-General to householders urging them not to ply the postman with liquor over Christmas are thought to have been introduced by Anthony Trollope during his period at the Post Office, after finding much of his fan mail from the Barsetshire novels stuffed down a well near his house.

In his last years Tennyson suffered from the distressing delusion that "Christmas" rhymed with "isthmus". Only the combined representations of his oldest friends dissuaded him from committing this supreme folly to print, but he steadfastly refused to write "Yule". After his death his papers yielded a quatrain saying he would rather spend Christmas on the Darien Isthmus than face Yule on Ultima Thule. This unnatural poem was destroyed before it could be attributed to E. C. Bentley.

Haldane

Never a Dull Moment

Haldane on adventure holidays

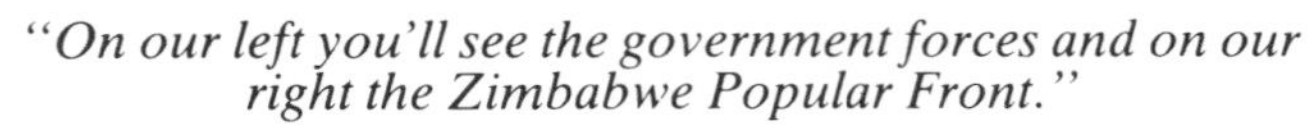
"On our left you'll see the government forces and on our right the Zimbabwe Popular Front."

"I hate being thrown out of the hotel just after breakfast."

"Excuse me, would you mind taking our picture?"

"These holiday friendships never last."

"All this bloody trouble just to be photographed with a monkey!"

"Actually we're trying to cram everything into five days."

"What do you mean it's spoilt the holiday? This **is** the holiday!"

"Well, one of us had to go and find the Tourist Information Centre."

FOR REASONS OF STATE,

FRANCESCA DA RIMINI

IS ENGAGED TO BE MARRIED TO GIOVANNI MALATESTA, NICKNAMED "THE DISGUSTING".

IN NEED OF SOLACE, FRANCESCA READS ALOUD FROM HER FAVOURITE ROMANCE, "TOM SWIFT AND HIS WATER-POWERED WASTEBASKET", AS PAOLO THE GORGEOUS ENTERS UNNOTICED.

Robert Morley

The Moon's A Walloon

"*J'ai pas de monnaie,*" I explained to the lady at the loo bureau. She looked at me with hostile disbelief. I had in fact given all my money to my *beaux enfants*—not all, of course, but the centimes at any rate, for the slots in the amusement arcades. Micturating is big business in Belgium. I half expected to be arrested for obtaining relief under false pretences.

In so far as I believe in anything I believe in the free urinal. On the other hand the Belgians believe in the free enterprise urinal, just as they believe in the free enterprise sand dunes or the free enterprise promenade. They realised some time ago, I imagine, that there is absolutely no money to be made by permitting motorists to drive up and down the sea front. While Sidmouth and Brighton languish, Knokke and Blaakenberg flourish. Only the stoniest-hearted parents or grandparents can deny their liberated charges the rides they demand on unicycles, fire engines, bumper cars and bicycles made for two, four, six, eight adults and children alike. Along with the trampolines.

There are traffic cops wheeling their bicycles and admonishing the young to drive with more care or in the right direction. Then there are the cafés with rock bands and the bathing enclosures with their individual cabins and communal health clubs. In Belgium the two great pleasures of life, spending and making money, are harmoniously combined.

Today, apparently, we can no longer afford to keep Britain clean and tidy. Squalor Rules OK. The unacceptable face of property developers, the filth of London Transport, private and public ownership combined in a monstrous conspiracy to persuade that appearances no longer matter. Board up the houses, leave the trodden-in chewing gum on every step and pavement slab, and the empty cans to litter the other side of the fence. Take a walk down the slope of Acton North Station and unhesitatingly award the prize for the dirtiest, most neglected slum garden in this land of Hope and Glory.

But good heavens, we are supposed to be on holiday in Belgium.

Let us return to our lobsters. Every restaurant sports a tank for the doomed crustaceans. Perhaps one day their turn will come—grasping their human prey in monstrous claws and delicately dismembering. It's only fair, I suppose. Meanwhile they are simply delicious split open and grilled. A surgeon's bib, a finger bowl and those astonishing claw crackers—the prestige symbols of the big spenders.

I have never really explored a lobster successfully. I admire the expert gourmet who sucks and splits but cannot emulate him, leaving on my plate more than sufficient for the *bisque* of the evening. Well what happens to it all, then?

In Bruges we were ready for McDonalds by the time we had got the car settled happily. I took the grandchildren, both staunch Catholics, to the Chapel of the Sacred Blood which seemed to make even less impression on them than it did on me. The relic is not on view except on one day a year and this wasn't the one. More success in the Cathedral with Michelangelo's carving of the Madonna, but none of us really happy until I was eating strawberries and ice cream in a café on the square and the others were released for shopping fatigue.

The ice-cream in Belgium is simply magnificent, but the shops seemed to yield little by way of surprise. I don't think my grandchildren are very astute in the European Common Market. How else to explain the small pots of honey, the dried funeral flowers, the Japanese kite and the lace *boutonnier*. Or the chocolate melting fish? On second thoughts, I do understand the lace—a traditional culture of the city, but such a very small sample.

We sailed around the canals in the cool of the evening and then drove rapidly out of the city in what turned out to be a hopelessly wrong direction. Once you are lost in Belgium, the temptation is to keep going. I have always encouraged keeping going in the belief, almost invariably wrong, that eventually one comes round in a circle. The roads in Belgium, however, are always perfectly straight. We managed to turn round in Ghent and supped very late on spaghetti, in a pizza bar. Whatever else the gallant Belgians know how to cook, spaghetti eludes them.

So much seems to have crept up on me unobserved as I dozed the years away. The Ferry Industry, for example. Long gone are the days when Nannie used to take us to Folkestone Harbour to gaze on pea-green, storm-tossed passengers, and to have pointed out to us what happened to fools who went abroad. Now, sandwiched between giant juggernauts, we were found a space, abandoned the motor and went aloft in search of duty free. If it wasn't for duty free, the boats couldn't keep running. This is where the profit lies, or so the captain told me. Ensconced in his cabin, we weathered a Force Eight—high, apparently, for the time of year. The captain's child is a State-registered nurse who earns exactly two-and-a-half times as much as she would in nursing by sailing on his ship and passing out the Mars bars. It doesn't make much sense, he told me.

The captain had sailed all seven seas and was once wrecked on the China coast. "Dull, here?" I asked him. "See the wife and kids in the evenings," he replied. "Besides, it's nice in Canterbury."

I had got the idea from television that ferries were miniature fun-filled pleasure cruises. I didn't find it quite like that, rather sausage and chips cut with plastic knives. There was a choice of scampi or chicken on the unchanging luncheon menu in the dining room. I had got it into my head also that there were saunas and swimming pools and casinos, but I had got it wrong as usual. Still, they get cars off fast.

Perhaps it's foolish to expect a sense of carnival from a line which persists in naming its ships *Free Enterprise I, II, III, IV,* and—wait for it—*Free Enterprise V.*

At the back of the Hotel (to return briskly to Belgium) lies the grandiloquently titled Lake Victoria, a pond for the sailboards. This is the spectator sport *par excellence.* The riders in a show-jumping contest occasionally get round without a fall, the sail-boarders never. A small puff of wind and over they go, often receiving a resounding thump on the head from the sail, or the mast, or both. Then the excruciating effort to mount the board and sail away again for thirty seconds. How much happier the watcher at the water's edge with the perfect balance of gin and tonic.

Knokke Heist has alas its seamier side in the evening when the *bikkies* play. I came upon a small group bucking their steeds against the plate glass of a restaurant. The diners didn't look too happy. "Walloons," I told the kids and crossed the street.

My crusading days are over. Once, years ago, in the Rue de Rivoli, I espied a group of tearaways bumping the head of one of their companions against the venerable buttresses. Then they re-entered a café and left him motionless on the pavement. I hastened forward, peered down at the corpse, and, entering the café, demanded a telephone to summon the appropriate authorities. "*Sales cochons, quel bêtise, j'apelle the gendarmes, le ambulance, que dit-il, de Gaulle?*" (It was that long ago.) I stood with my back against the wall, defying the mob who watched in silence. The man on the pavement stirred, rose shakily to his feet, and, making a supreme effort, rejoined his friends at the table. "The drinks are on me," I understood him to say, and I left. Discretion seemed on this occasion to be the better part of valour, especially when one is on the Belgian Riviera and preparing to use a pedestrian crossing.

"I thought there'd be a bit more to this than only obeying orders."

Michael Bywater

Teething Troubles

What I got for Christmas was my two front teeth; filed down to little tusks, to be precise, like those egregious African dandies who hop out of the scrub and gnash you, and you don't get *that* in the shops.

An operation of infinite tedium, this filing business, but lah! my dears, now it's over, far from hunting out a clump to lurk in like my precursors in the Bush, I shall be adopting a conspicuously high profile. You'll know me when you see me: a swirl of broadcloth, a lambent glittering smile, the faintest hint of expensive mouthwash, and—pouf!—I'll be gone, leaving only a lingering after-image of something rather wonderful, and a flurry of discomfited folk rushing for the Pepsodent.

A crowning glory, if you follow me. Onto my attenuated dentition, two porcelain prostheses have been clamped; between them, suspended by golden cantilevers and guyed with platinum hawser, a third tooth is now positioned where previously there was none; the void which has disfigured me for so long is filled. It feels queer at first, since over the preceding months I have learned to champ a mean gum; but I'm going at it doggedly: yesterday a marshmallow, today the breakfast bacon fried *al dente,* working up to the big one, the celebratory Crunchy Dinner, spare ribs, *crême brulée,* Bath Olivers, beaks, bones and shells. Tomorrow? Next week? Soon, anyway; soups and possets have come to pall.

That was my big present, this Christmas: bridgework. And by no means unromantic; gastronomic considerations apart, and forgetting for the moment the precious materials involved, there's the spin-off; my wife, insistent donor of this orthodontic *cadeau,* was expressing proleptic gratification at the thought of my dental Renaissance as far back as last summer, and I can confidently expect some benefits from *that* quarter.

Drinking, too, will be less of a hazard. Blotting up a peaceful Scotch-and-soda becomes a rare experience when one is gap-toothed. The assumption of fellow-drinkers seems to be that one has lost one's tooth as a result of aggression and violence, that one is a desperate fella, that one should be watched, d'you hear me, don't turn your back on him for a moment or he'll be onto you, fists, knives, the lot, how d'you think he lost his tooth, if I were you I'd belt him one before he's noticed you, the best method of defence is attack d'you know . . .

Other benefits: being able to smile again (I know Wernet's DentuFix does that as well, but you need something to stick in with it, no good just clogging up your gap with glue, that won't fool anyone). Being able to clench my pipe like a proper Englishman instead of having to hold it like a pansy. Not whiffling when I speak. Increased probability of women flirting with me at parties. Possibility of women even, um, how do I put this? It's not that one *would,* do you see, it's merely that it's nice to know that one could, or rather that one might be allowed or even encouraged to, *if one wanted to,* a circumstance which, the minute one displays a maw with all the visual allure of a Mississippi stump field, recedes into the realms of improbability normally inhabited by Government economic theories.

But why, you may be asking, am I telling you all this? Shouldn't I keep my orifices to myself? Not at all. For what I am latching you into is a *trend,* something to cut out and keep for next Christmas when those two great theological questions come round again: (1) How did God assume the nature of Mankind while simultaneously retaining His divinity? and (2): What the hell can we give Uncle Ignatius?

As always, the Americans provide the answer to both questions, as follows.

(1) "Well that's a very good point there from the gentleman in the kinda kaftan and the neat pointy hat, but before we ask *you,* the *audience,* what *you* think, a word about Auricular Odour, the Hidden Enemy. Try STAPES, the nature-fresh ear deodorant which is kind to the Earth. Contains no propellants. And now, back to our audience at the Hymie FitzBeelzebub Shopping Mall, Modesto, for part two of the Make Yourself Look An Utter Prick And Win $10,000 Show—and today's Theme is Mediaeval Scholasticism, where we ask our audience the Big Prize Question: if Duns Scotus had had the benefit of modern Personal Hygiene Technology, would he have written the *Opus Oxoniense* or would he have been out having a good time like you lovely folks here . . . ?"

(2) "Give him Spare Parts." Yes, really. "It's the ultra-fun chic gift idea that's swept the upper echelons of American high society this year—his 'n' hers facelifts, plastic surgery vouchers redeemable at all participating clinics for the operation of your choice, ranging from an all-in package deal to lift your sagging boobs, hitch up your drooping bum, unhook your nose, debag your eyes, unjug your eags and disembowel your paunchy ruptured belly (for that Very Special Person) to a simple facial epidermal degreasing (for a maiden aunt or a business colleague some way down on the Gift List). Why let your wife walk round looking like an Elephant Man? Just phone in your MasterCard number and we do the rest . . ."

True. Would I lie to you? And you can see the attraction. Why waste time having your beloved's initials Stamped By Wizened Craftsmen onto This Chippendale-Style Leather-Look Corkscrew Case when you can waste money having Ava Gardner's "face" Stamped By Wizened Plastic Surgeons onto Your California-Style Leather-Look Wife?

Want to try before you buy? Nothing could be easier; in flashy Beverly Hills there lives a plastic surgeon who exercises his vulgar tasteless craft upon the person of his wife. You want to see a sample, you see his wife. Perhaps she was once as homely as a mud fence; perhaps he's very greedy and she's very stupid; whatever, he's slit, cut, tacked, tucked and filled-in every available inch of this "woman" until she looks like a spun-sugar death's-head, an old drumskin, a scorched Goth.

In short, the ultimate personalised present. "Guess what!" chortles fond hubby, the syringe behind his back. "Honey-pie," squeals delighted wifey, as she claws negligently at her new Halston bandages. "Togetherness," gurgle the mummified pair, as they breathe through their mouths to save wear on their new nostrils. ("Wave Goodbye To Ugly Coke-Sniffers' Nose! Our Special Yuletide His 'n' Hers Nasal Septa Twin-Pak Means No More Sodden Hankies. No More

"The fact is, Leonard, I'm not your real father."

Tuxedo Stains, No More Unexpected Breathing Through The Ears!!!")

It could catch on here, too, along with Genuine English luxury hand-crafted accessories. How about a made-to-measure glass eye, for the man who hasn't quite got everything ("It cockles when I do—grunt—this." "Never mind, Sir, it'll ride up with wear . . .")? There was a bit about them in one of the Sunday supplements. You can find them in the Yellow Pages, under Artificial Eye Makers—Human, as opposed, presumably, to Artificial Eye Makers—Unsympathetic and Beastly. The man says you can't tell it from a real eye; but I bet I could, if you came up behind me and bunged one in when I wasn't expecting it.

A difficult present, in fact, to make really attractive. A gleaming optic wrapped in a hanky has a certain *cachet* but perhaps not the immediate appeal of a box of Prestat truffles; same goes, too, for that ultimate stocking-filler, the bespoke false leg, still to be had from that Schiaparelli of monopedes, Dessoutter of Roehampton.

But the actual presentation is merely a detail, and you've got nearly a year to work on it. The thing is to get in now. If this craze catches on there'll be queues by September. It'll be worse than *E.T.* (and there's a candidate for reconstruction if ever I saw one. Treacly insinuating little reptile). Have a close look at your friends and family. There's not one of them, I bet, that couldn't be improved by a little judicious plying of the knife. They'll be thinking the same about you, too.

After all, it's the thought that counts.

"Of course, that's always going to be one of the problems with stereo."

"We were rather hoping for a deep insight into trans-galactic space drive technology—we already have glass beads."

Let's Parler Franglais!

St Valentine Spécial!

Une sélection de vers franglais pour le jour de St Valentine. Simplement découpez le poème de votre choix, et supergluez-le sur votre carte. Bonne chance avec le wooing!

Les roses sont rouges,
Les violets sont bleus,
Et c'est de toi, darling,
Que je suis amoureux.

⋆

Lavender bleu, dilly, dilly,
Lavender vert,
Je suis tout prêt, dilly, dilly,
Pour une affaire.
Si tu es prête, dilly, dilly,
Montre-moi un signe,
Donne-moi un buzz, dilly, dilly,
Ou droppe-moi une ligne.

⋆

Je suis seulement seventeen,
Mais soyez, please, ma Valentine;
Une fille peut être une femme quand
Elle a seulement dix-sept ans.

⋆

Vous êtes le bloke que je préfère,
  Vous êtes mon prince et roi.
Je vous trouve extraordinaire.
  Que pensez-vous de moi?

⋆

Les roses sont rouges,
Les bananes sont jaunes.
Je ne peux pas aimer
Une Ranger de Sloane.

⋆

Je suis ton petit mugwumps?
  Ton hoochie-coochie dear?
Je suis ton little pudding?
  Mon Dieu. Je vais vomir.

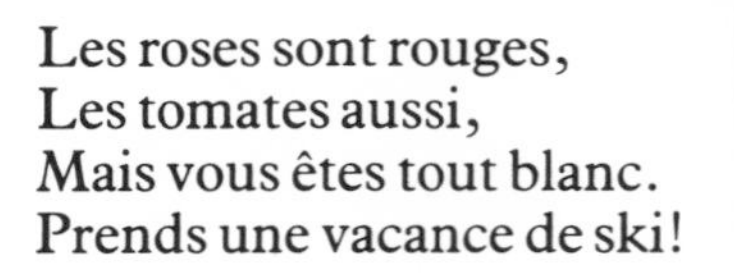

Les roses sont rouges,
Les tomates aussi,
Mais vous êtes tout blanc.
Prends une vacance de ski!

⋆

Chaque fois
Que je te vois,
Mon petit Prince Charmant,
C'est bon pour moi.
Mais, dis pourquoi
Tu dégoûtes ma maman?

⋆

Les roses sont rouges,
Les oranges sont oranges,
Si tu ne fais pas le slimming
Tu seras un blancmange.

⋆

Viens, live with me, mon petit chou.
Je suis ton Andrew, toi ma Koo.

⋆

Mon amour est comme une rose rouge, rouge,
  Un bonny, bonny fleur.
Mon amour est comme une mélodie,
  Naebody's like to her.
Mon amour est comme un drop de Scotch,
  Un bon dram dans un glass.
But now she's gang to London town
  —Hélas, hélas! Eh, lass?

(*après Burns*)

⋆

Les roses sont rouges,
Les cigares sont brunes.
Je t'envoie cette carte
—M'envoies-tu une?

H. après Peynet